WALKS & CLIMBS
IN THE
PICOS DE EUROPA

PICOS DE EUROPA   3 Massifs and surroundir

Hibeo ▲

Cangas de Onis   C. 6312

Pedroso ○

Río Güeña   Benia ○

Avín ○   Ortiguero ○

Gamoneda ○   Demués ○   La Molina ○

Covadonga ○

Río Dobra   Cabezo Llorosos ▲   P

Río Sella   WESTERN MASSIF   Río Cares   CE

Amieva ○   Torre de Sta María ▲   Caín ○

C. 637   Peña Santa ▲   Torre de ▲

Soto de Sajambre ○   Torre Bermeja ▲   Cordiñanes ○

Soto ○   Posada ○

Jario ▲   Sta Marí

Oseja ○

Gildar ▲

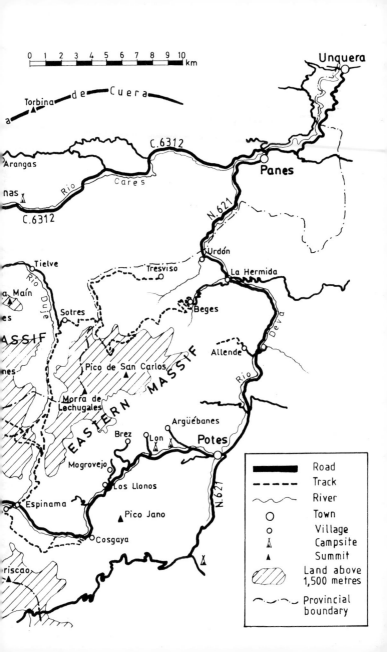

PICOS DE EUROPA Eastern Massif

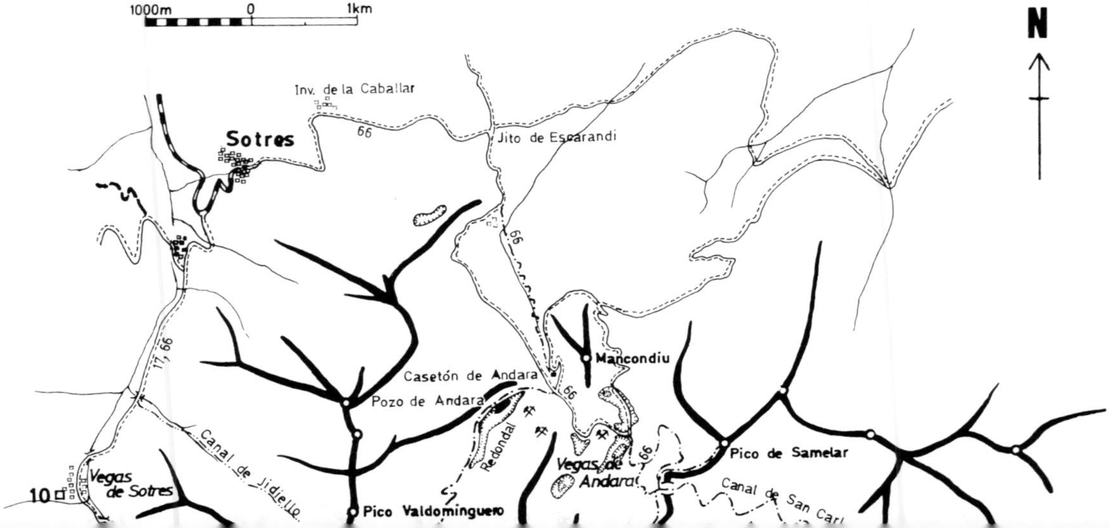

N

1000m 0 1km

Inv. de la Caballar

Jito de Escarandi

Sotres

66

66

Mancondiu

Pico de Samelar

Canal de San Carl

Casetón de Andara

Vegas de Andara

99

Redondal

Pozo de Andara

66

Pico Valdominguero

Canal de Jidiella

Vegas de Sotres

99 71

10

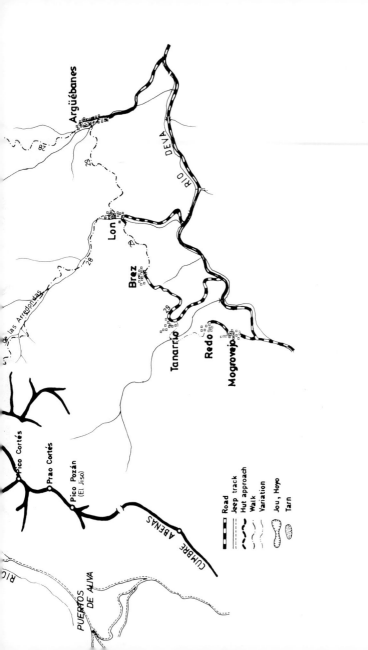

The West face of El Naranjo from Urriellu.

WALKS AND CLIMBS
IN THE
PICOS
DE EUROPA

ROBIN WALKER

CICERONE PRESS
MILNTHORPE, CUMBRIA, UK

© Robin Walker 1989
First edition 1989
Reprinted 1993, 1997, 2003, 2007, 2010 and 2015
ISBN-13: 978 1 85284 033 4
ISBN-10: 1 85284 033 1

A catalogue record for this book is available from the British Library.

Printed by KHL Printing, Singapore

All photographs and diagrams are by the author.

Front cover: Gaining the summit of the third Torre de los Tres Poyones
(Western Massif)

CONTENTS

ABBREVIATIONS

cdo(a)	collado(a) – col (see Appendix A)
diag.	diagonally
FA	first ascent
h	hour(s)
hdo(a)	horcado(a) – col (see Appendix A)
L	left
m	metre(s)
mda	majada – upland pasture (see Appendix A)
min	minute(s)
N (E, S, etc)	compass directions
p	page
PB	peg belay
PR	peg runner
R	right (the terms L and R are given facing the rock or in the direction of travel unless otherwise indicated)
Sta	Santa

FOREWORD AND ACKNOWLEDGEMENTS

Spain, despite its recent incorporation into the Common Market, continues to be the great unknown of European mountaineering. Most people's knowledge is limited to occasional sorties into the Pyrenees, and yet within the Iberian peninsula there are a surprising number of important ranges, foremost among which are the Picos de Europa, the subject of this guide.

Though relatively modest in terms of altitude and extent, the Picos are, in fact, unique amongst Europe's mountains in a number of ways: geologically, for being the largest single mass of mountain limestone in the continent, a mass radically affected by the process of karstification; geographically, for being the only true maritime range Europe possesses, some of the implications of which are clearly and precisely conveyed in Teresa Farino's authoritative article; and sociologically, for retaining even to this day a large part of the culture that has for centuries been the basis of life in the towns and villages dotted about the area.

The uniqueness of the Picos became apparent to me, as indeed it does to most people, almost as soon as I had set foot in them. A first, fleeting visit in 1979 took me down the Cares gorge and up to El Naranjo, leaving me convinced of the need to return. This I have done on countless occasions, in both summer and winter, since coming to Spain to live in 1981. Walking, scrambling, climbing, or simply sitting watching the wildlife, no one activity proved, or proves today, more satisfying to me than another. This plurality, itself an attraction of the range, is reflected in the content of the guide.

The first section of the book deals with such background information as geology, flora and fauna and history. These sections are, perhaps, longer than is normal by current standards, but I feel that it is only through knowledge of such areas that a full appreciation of any range can be achieved. Chapters 4 and 5 deal with the routes themselves, whilst the last two chapters cover the more specialised activities of multi-day tours and winter mountaineering.

The classic division of the walks and climbs into three main chapters, one on each massif, was not felt to be an effective way of organising the guide. Thus, the routes have been divided into two main groups, those in Chapter 4 being essentially valley-based walks, whilst scrambles and climbs approached from a mountain base make up the bulk of Chapter 5. This division is not 'water-tight', of course, and some climbs will be found in Chapter 4 and vice versa. Within each of these two main chapters, the activities are organised working around the range or massif in question in a clockwise direction, starting from the most popular entry point for each area.

The choice of routes is principally the result of my own experience, together with recommendations by friends. In the few cases where I have not been able to do a route personally, I have used local sources to compile the description. This does not mean, of course, that the guide is free from errors, and, with a view to a second edition, I would be grateful to receive any corrections, comments or suggestions felt to be of interest, at:

a) Oxígeno
   Manuel Pedregal, 4
   33001, Oviedo
   Asturias, Spain

or b) 7 Eshott Close
   Gosforth
   Newcastle upon Tyne
   NE3 3PD

ACKNOWLEDGEMENTS

As is almost always the case with works of this type, the guide would not have been possible without the help and encouragement of many friends and companions. My thanks then to *Alberto Cabrero, Terry Hudson, Steve Jones, Eduardo Martinez, Kike Oltra, Isidoro Rodriguez, Mick Vasey* and, in particular, *Jorge Malgor*, for sharing the climbs with me, and to *Saturnino Fresno* and *Javier Fidalgo* for their splendid company on the walks. My thanks also to *Teresa Farino* for finding time to put together the piece on flora and fauna, and to *Jerónimo López*, lecturer in geology at the 'Universidad Autónoma' in Madrid, for checking the geology notes. Finally, a special thanks to *Miguel Adrados*, co-author with Jerónimo of the definitive Spanish guides, and author of three excellent Picos maps, for sharing his vast knowledge and experience with me.

Robin Walker
Oviedo, 1989

BACKGROUND

TOPOGRAPHY

Running along the length of the Atlantic shore, the Cordillera Cantábrica form an immense physical barrier between Spain's northern coastal provinces and its great central plains. To the north of the central section of this mountain chain, though in every sense independent, lie the Picos de Europa, a limestone range straddling the autonomous regions of Asturias, Cantábria and Castilla-León. The limits of the range are marked out to the east and west by the rivers Deva and Sella, whilst an approximately east-west line connecting the course of the rivers Cares and Casaño to that of the Güeña, can be taken as defining the northern boundary. No simple division exists to the south, but without doubt there is a significant change in both vegetation and rock type once the imaginary line 'Potes – Fuente Dé – Valdeón – Sajambre' is crossed. Within these boundaries, the range is clearly divided into three independent massifs by the south-north course of the rivers Duje and Cares. The three massifs are known quite simply as the **Macizo Oriental**, the **Macizo Central** and the **Macizo Occidental** though each has, in addition, an historical name, these being **De Andara, De Urrieles** and **De Cornión**, respectively. Whilst in general local names will not be translated, the names **Eastern Massif, Central Massif** and **Western Massif** will be used throughout.

The Eastern Massif

Of the three massifs, the Eastern is the smallest and least impressive, except perhaps when viewed from the Liebana area, from where the huge SE walls are seen to best effect. Rising comfortably from the wooded slopes between Pembes and Espinama, the Cumbres Avenas are the only things of significance before the Collado de Cámara, an important pass between the puertos de Aliva and the Camaleño district of Liebana. From this col a long ridge climbs northwards over the summits of the Pico de Pozán (2170m), the Prao Cortés (2287m) and the Pico Cortés (2370m), reaching its maxium height of 2,441m, with the summit of the Morra de Lechugales. The ridge continues to the three minor summits of the Picos del Jierro, a subsidiary ridge going off east from the first of these to the Silla Caballo Cimero (2433m). Next on the main ridge comes the Pica del Jierru (2426m) which, like so many of the summits in the range, has seen its name changed by the mining activity in the area during the last century, or by the visits of royal hunting parties in the same period.

The Pica del Jierru is also known as the Pico del Evangelista, after a mine owner, and the Tiro de la Infanta, after the daughter of King Alfonso II who came hunting here in 1881. Other peaks which have

9

suffered notable name changes are the Pico Pozán, often called El Jisu, which is actually the name of the area at the base of the famous South Ridge (see Route 68), and the Pico San Carlos, now most commonly called the Pico del Sagrado Corazón after a bronze statue of Christ placed on the summit in 1900. Attempts are being made by local mountaineers to return to the original names, though with this last summit their efforts have been to no avail so far.

Of special interest with regards toponymy is the case of the Picos de los Llambriales Amarillos, as it is known in Potes and Camaleño, or the Pico del Diablo of those from Sotres, which is the Cuetu de Janciana to anyone from Tresviso. Here, then, the name changes according to the area from which the mountain is viewed, a practice far more acceptable than that of the arbitrary imposition of names by passing industrialists and royalty, though nonetheless more than a little confusing to first time visitors.

At the Pica del Jierru the ridge splits, and one part continues north over the Cdo de Valdominguero, the Pico Valdominguero (2268m), the Cuetu Tejau (2158m) and the Picu Boru (2128m), before petering out above the village of Sotres. The other part runs off slightly north of east, crossing La Rasa (2285m) and the Pico de los Llambriales Amarillos (2261m) to swing north at the Pico del Sagrado Corazón (2212m) and so reach the Pico de Samelar (2227m). Together these two ridges form a huge cirque known as Andara (the accent is on the first 'a'), which in the last century was the base of extensive mining operations directed by an English company, operations which, as has already been seen, have left their mark on the area.

The Central Massif

The Central Massif, the most abrupt of the three, is the place where the provinces of Asturias, Cantabria and León meet, the triple junction on the summit of the Pico Tesorero (2570m) being an easy walk from El Cable, the upper cable car station (see Route 82). Moreover, this attractve summit provides a magnificent viewpoint from which it is possible to begin to decipher the complexities of the whole range, particularly those of the Central Massif.

To the north-west of the Tesorero lies the Torre de Cerredo, which at 2,648m is not only the highest point in the Picos de Europa, but in the whole of northern Spain. Still from the Tesorero, but looking north-east, the view is dominated by the unmistakable profile of El Naranjo de Bulnes (2519m), Spain's most famous mountain. Between these two stands the Neverón de Urriellu (2559m), a summit which is unjustly ignored considering the excellent views it offers of its illustrious neighbours. A chain of little-visited peaks runs south from El Naranjo, culminating in Peña Vieja (2613m), a popular activity with day-trippers from the télépherique because of the unrestricted views it offers of the Cordilera Cantábrica to the south.

Looking south-west from the Tesorero, the view is filled by the enormous ridge which runs north-west from the Pico de Madejuno (2513m) to the Torre de Llambrión (2642m), the second highest summit in the range. To the south-west of this ridge, and parallel to it, lies the Cifuentes group, the only major group in the Central Massif which cannot be seen from the vantage point of the Pico Tesorero.

Finally, coming full circle and looking west, the awesome Jou Grande dominates the view. Long and barren, it is one of the wildest places in the Central Massif, if not in the whole range. Beyond it lies the Cares gorge, a mere 4km west of the Torre de Cerredo, but a full 2,200m below it. Above the gorge stands the knife-edge form of Peña Santa de Castilla (2596m), the finest summit of the Western Massif – for some the finest of the whole area.

The Western Massif

The largest and most varied of the three, the Western Massif can be usefully divided into three sectors: the first lies to the north of the line Amieva – Vegarredonda – Ario; the second, which includes most of the highest summits, revolves around the Jou Santu, an enormous glacial cirque in the centre of the massif; the third, which is known as the Bermeja sector, marks the southern limit of the massif.

The first sector cannot be reduced to a simple description of chains and individual summits. The highest summits are those in the Peña Jascal – Cabezo Llorosos chain due east of the Lagos de Enol, the latter providing excellent views of the Cares gorge. However, it would be unjust to give the impression that these were the only worthwhile peaks in the sector, which in practice is a complex area of minor summits dispersed among a multitude of genuinely beautiful *vegas* and *majadas*. Mapping and navigation in this area are both difficult, but for walkers it has to be one of the most rewarding parts of the massif.

The main sector of the Western Massif is that dominated by the two Peña Santas, that of Castilla (2596m), and the smaller Peña Santa de Enol (2478m) which is more correctly known as the Torre de Santa María. The 2km crest of Peña Santa de Castilla marks out the southern limit of this sector, running east-west between Vega Huerta and the Jou Santu. From its west end a continuation ridge goes north over the summit of the Torre del Torco (2459m) to that of Torre de la Horcada (2456m), a very good viewpoint for the whole of this area.

A number of satellite summits such as the Torrezuela (2302m) lie to the west of this group, whilst the main chain rises again to the summit of the Torre de Santa María. An important subsidiary ridge breaks off north-west here, takes in the Torres de Cebolleda (2438m), then continues west via the Requexón (2170m) to Ordiales, the resting place of the Pedro Pidal, the Marqués de Villaviciosa. Apart from being the first man to climb El Naranjo, the Marqués was also the founder of the Covadonga National Park which covers almost all of the Western Massif.

11

To the east of the Torre de Santa María, and enclosing the north-east side of the Jou Santu, is a somewhat broken chain of peaks which, beginning with the Torre de la Canal Parda (2369m), runs roughly north-east to the Jultayu (1935m), a summit offering outstanding views of Caín.

The Bermeja sector, which is little-visited and, in general, under-valued, forms a sub-massif which dominates the view north-west from Posada de Valdeón. The Torre de Beremeja (2393m) is the highest of the sector's main summits, and gives first-class views of Valdeón and the Cordillera Cantábrica, as well as of the South Face of Peña Santa de Castilla. The absence of routes on the huge south-east walls of the Torre Ciega (2261m) and the Torre de Aristas (2136m) reflects, more than anything, the neglect which this sector currently suffers.

Whilst the majority of the routes in the guide lie within the three massifs just described, there are a number of walks to summits outside the strict limits of the range. These have been included because of the views they offer of one or other of the massifs, views which, quite apart from their own natural beauty, will help newcomers to complete their vision of the Picos de Europa mountains.

GEOLOGY

The mountain was in its beginning; slender pinnacles, tapering needles and graceful towers had still not risen from its surface. These refinements of its architecture were hidden in its depths, like a work of art trapped in the heart of a block of marble. And the Supreme Artist would have to work for thousands of years before revealing the great marvel of his enormous sculpture.

Thus begins the first-ever guide to the Picos, published in Madrid in 1918 under the title *Picos de Europa. Contribución al estudio de las montañas españolas.* Written by the Marquis of Villaviciosa and José F. Zabala, it provides a unique insight into what is actually a very complex subject: the geology of the Picos de Europa. What follows is a far more conventional, though necessarily simplified, treatment of the same topic, the other quotes given being from the same source as above, and offering a further glimpse of Pidal's very original description of events over the last few hundred million years.

Some 600 million years ago the region now known as the Cordillera Cantabrica witnessed the beginning of a sedimantation process that was to last about 300 million years, the last 50 million years of which saw the laying down of large quantities of Carboniferous, or Mountain, limestone in the area presently occupied by the Picos. Despite the vast timespan involved, the sedimentation was fairly continuous, giving rise to layers of rock over 1,000 metres thick in places. The compact nature of the resulting strata is apparent even today, particularly on some of the harder rock climbs, where protection from natural features is, at times, uncomfortably hard to find.

Collado Jermoso with Peña Santa de Castilla in the background across the Cares gorge. The predominance of abrupt S faces over gentler N slopes is clearly seen.

Two periods of major mountain building activity, the first of which began 250 million years ago, then folded and faulted the limestone mass. The second period, some 200 million years later, was also broadly responsible for the formation of the Alps and the Pyrenees. The direction of these movements, from south to north, folded the rock strata concertina fashion, one result of which is an unexpected predominance of steep south faces over relatively gentle northern slopes, an effect clearly visible in the deep valleys (Amieva, Valdeón and Liébana) that characterise the southern edge of the range. Huge south facing walls dominate these valleys, and even in the high mountains south faces often provide the best climbing, as is the case with Peña Santa de Castilla, the Torre de los Horcados Rojos and Peña Vieja.

A second result of this folding was the superimposition of one layer of limestone on another, such that today the total rock thickness exceeds 2,000 metres in many parts of the range. All of this can be clearly seen in the view west from Collado Jermoso, or, alternatively, when looking east from the Ario area of the Western Massif.

Rivers of ice tumbled to the base of the colossal hills, carving out valleys, and leaving their mark on the high rock walls . . . They reached level ground and there abandoned their load, forming with it other smaller mountains that still stand like the first steps in this enormous stairway, from whose summit man marvels at and becomes entranced by the work of Nature.

13

Despite the predominance of south faces, steep north faces are also to be found in the Picos, but they are the product of a much more recent geological phenomenon, that of glaciation. During the Quaternary period glacial ice covered the area completely, reaching down to as low as 600m above sea-level in some places (e.g. Bulnes). The main glaciers, taking advantage of fractures produced in the limestone by the earlier earth movements, formed long tongues which carved out embryo valleys that would later become the gorges of the Sella, the Cares, the Duje and the Deva. This same glacial activity was responsible for the north walls we cherish in winter (Peña Santa de Castilla, Torre de Santa María, Torrecerredo, etc), and the east and west walls that offer so much sport in summer, none more so than those of El Naranjo de Bulnes.

The last of the glaciers disappeared at the end of the last ice age, some 10,000 years ago. Nowadays the only reminders of the Picos' frozen past are the permanent snowfields such as that below the north face of the Torre de Santa María (Western Massif) which is known as the Cemba Vieya (= old snow). A second permanent snowfield lies below the north wall of the Torre de Llambrión (Central Massif), sometimes complicating the approach to the mountain from Collada Blanca.

And the monument went on perfecting the filigree of its dome with the chisels of ice, snow, rain and sun. And Time, that great painter, continued to colour the great work with a misterious patina, which changed colour with the changing sunlight.

The eventual retreat of the glaciers left the chaotic landscape so typical of glaciation with its U-shaped valleys, circular hollows and polished walls. Yet for most people visiting the area, there is little that could be called 'typical' about what they see, for a third phenomenon, karstification, has been at work throughout the range. A physico-chemical process through which basic limestone rock is dissolved away by slightly acidic rain water, karstification has been acting upon the range since long before the arrival of the glaciers, and, moreover, is still in action today. Its effects are spectacular and wide ranging.

Water, collecting in the hollows has dissolved away the lake beds, then drained away to create the deep and complex subterranean maze that currently delights the caving fraternity. At a surface level, drainage, first from rainfall then from glacier melt, has cut into the U-shaped valleys, creating a deep V-shaped groove in the floor of each. These cuts form the lower sections of the dramatic *gargantas* and *desfiladeros* for which the region is so rightly famous. Similarly, though on a far smaller scale, surface water has run down the polished slabs etching out the organ-pipe grooves so characteristic of the area, and which are known locally as *canalizos*. Not always easy to climb, and always difficult to protect, the canalizos are the key to a number of classic climbs. Finally, but on the steeper rock, water has eeked out the tiny finger pockets or *hueveras* which provide vital holds on the harder rock routes.

The dry and lifeless hollows left by this karstification process are called *hoyos* (*jous* in the local dialect), and can be major features of the landscape as is the case with the Jou Santu, the Jou Sin Tierri and the Jou de los Boches, to name but three. Clustering together one upon another, in a wilderness of ups and downs, they can make navigation a desperate affair in thick mist. Indeed, even in good weather it is hard to move swiftly across such terrain. Abandon Naismith here, and dig deep down for the resolve you will need to keep going on a hot day.

With water playing such an important role in the formation of the range, it may come as a shock to some people to find that anywhere above 1500m it is noticeable principally for its absence. Whilst lower down layers of impermeable slates cause underground rivers to resurge in impressive fashion (the *Farfao* near Puente Sabugo in the Cares Gorge), the only water to be had in the high mountains is from tiny springs. Here, clays and other erosion products force the water to the surface, though it very quickly finds its way back underground. Springs then, must be correctly located (a task complicated by many older, inaccurate maps – see Technical Notes) and sufficient water carried to see you through the day.

CLIMATE AND WEATHER

Despite standing at approximately the same latitude as Rome, the Picos de Europa enjoy an essentially temperate climate which is not unlike that of Britain. The Atlantic depressions which are the cause of most British weather, are also responsible for the frontal troughs which sweep across the whole of the Cantabrian coast. On colliding with the mountains, particularly with the Cordillera Cantábrica and the Picos de Europa, these fronts discharge, producing the abundant rainfall that makes Northern Spain so green. It is not without reason that the Bay of Biscay coast is known to the Spanish as The 'Costa Verde' or Green Coast.

Fortunately for the visiting mountaineer, most of this rainfall occurs in the winter and spring, the period from mid-June to late-September being reasonably dry. Mid-June to mid-July often produce fine hot spells, whilst the hottest weather generally occurs, as is to be expected, in August. It should be borne in mind, however, that hot, humid weather does tend to give rise to thundery, late-afternoon storms. These can sometimes be violent, though are seldom as bad as in the Pyrenees or the Central European Alps, for example. In such weather, which can occur at any time from July to September, an early start is obviously advisable, most storms beginning after 4pm. September is widely recognised as a month of stable, good weather, with the result that visibility is often very good, though it should be borne in mind that the shortened day can be a handicap.

The first snow normally arrives around the end of October, snowfall continuing in a fairly constant fashion throughout the winter, though late January and early April can give periods of stable, dry winter

Arriving at Vega Urriellu from Sotres. The sea of cloud is a sign of stable, good weather, though the northern valleys will be suffering overcast days with occasional drizzle.

weather. Recent years, however, have seen the traditional patterns of winter weather seriously altered. 1987-8, for example, saw very heavy snow in mid-November, followed by an almost total lack of significant fresh falls until late April.

The distribution of the rainfall throughout the range is a factor of particular interest when choosing a valley base, or looking for a possible poor-weather activity. As the frontal systems arrive mainly from the NW sector, the weather, is cooler and wetter on average, than in those areas to the S and SE of the range. The latter benefit from a marked rain-shadow effect, and thus the Liebana, Valdeón and Sajambre valleys enjoy noticeably better weather than the valleys on the Asturian side of the range.

In general bad weather comes from the NW. However, with the barometer low or falling, all weather associated with winds from the SW to the N should be treated with respect as it will most probably produce rain and storms. All such weather creates a lot of cloud at all levels and, whilst often highly photogenic, it makes navigation very difficult because of the featureless nature of the terrain. Moreover, low pressure weather is generally unpredictable, and though the change from sunshine to storm may span a matter of hours, the onset of thick cloud over a whole area can occur in the space of a few minutes.

One of the most spectacular cloud effects common to the Picos, that of an immense sea of cloud filling the valleys to heights of up to 1,800m, is, surprisingly, not the result of poor weather, but rather a sign of good. With anticyclones over the Azores creating a light, northerly airstream, warm, moist air drifts in from the Bay of Biscay, filling the northern valleys with a wetting mist (*orbayu* in the local dialect) capable of completely obscuring the sun. It is not uncommon to walk up from the valleys in cloud and suddenly come out into bright sunshine at around 1,500m, or to do the first half of a climb shrouded in mist and the second half baking in strong sunlight. This enviable situation lasts as long as the anticyclone, and so it is very important to take into account the origin of cloud masses when interpreting their significance, especially if doing so from a base to the north of the range. Too many visiting climbers abandon climbs early, or never even leave their base, because of their failure to distinguish between low and high pressure weather.

The weather is inextricably linked to the great beauty of the Picos de Europa and, whilst not ignoring the added problems bad weather involves, it is fair to say that a number of outings, particularly certain approaches, are made a good deal more dramatic by the subtle play of light and cloud that 'poor' weather often generates.

FLORA AND FAUNA

Despite their relatively small extent, the Picos de Europa are surprisingly rich in both plant and animal life, which, unlike in many other wilderness areas, can be experienced with little effort. Indeed, even the most hardened tourist can scarcely fail to be awed by the colourful arrays of wildflowers and the frequent encounters with the birds and other animals of these mountains.

A stroll around the older buildings of the villages and small towns, will reveal black redstarts, swallows and house martins nesting under the eaves or inside the roof itself. The ash trees planted about the village, whose branches provide fodder and bedding for livestock in the autumn, are filled in spring with goldfinches and yellowhammers. Nearby, on the level land immediately surrounding the village, potatoes, maize and cabbages are grown, and, since pesticides and artificial fertilisers are almost unheard of here, corn-cockles, blue pimpernel and other arable weeds thrive among these crops.

Leading into the hills from the villages is an extensive network of tracks and paths once only trodden by shepherds and woodcutters. These ancient pathways are lined by crumbling stone walls festooned with ferns and the beautiful, shining cranesbill. On sunny days wall lizards bask in the warmth, darting back into the safety of the crevices when disturbed by passers-by.

Soon the paths are winding through meadows, cut each summer for hay to sustain the livestock through the long winter months. Although no two meadows are alike, most contain masses of yellow rattle and kidney vetch beneath clumps of white asphodels. Other haymeadow

17

plants, however, are more sensitive to variations in climate, geology and altitude. Thus, the lowest meadows of the warm, dry Liébana valley are filled with early purple orchids in spring, together with other such Mediterranean species as wild clary and tassel hyacinths. Meadows in the wetter valleys of Asturias, on the other hand, contain plants more typical of marshlands: ragged robin, louseworts, globe-flowers, marsh helleborines and early marsh orchids.

The higher meadows are populated by species more tolerant of a cooler, later summer, including spring gentians, alpine pasque flowers and sheets of white and golden daffodils. Naturally, with such an abundance of wild flowers even the most fleeting sunny spell brings out a wealth of butterflies; tiny, bejewelled blues and coppers and exotic swallowtails are especially common.

Above the meadows, and separated from them by walls to protect the growing hay, lies a zone of *monte* or scrub. This is usually dominated by woody plants of the heather family, joined by Spanish and Cantabrian broom and several species of the closely related greenweeds and gorses. In Liébana, sheltered as it is from Atlantic weather conditions, the *monte* also contains a number of shrub species more typical of the rest of Spain, including Mediterranean buckthorn and wild jasmine.

Although there is a relatively sharp division between meadows and *monte*, there is no distinct line between these essentially man-made habitats and the native woodlands of the Picos de Europa. Before man began to carve himself an agricultural niche in northern Spain these mountains were thickly wooded. In some places, such as the extensive beech and oak forest that stretches between the passes of Pandetrave and Panderruedas, the original woodland remains more or less as it was thousands of years ago. For the most part, however, it is now highly fragmented, forming an intricate mosaic with the meadows and *monte* on the valley slopes.

Most of this woodland is of the type already mentioned – beech and deciduous oaks – but other types occur where conditions are slightly different. As you drive through the gorge of La Hermida, for example, it is impossible to miss the evergreen oaks clinging to the sheer cliff faces. Further on, where the gorge widens into the Liébana valley, these stunted individual trees, mostly holm oaks, mass together to form small pockets of Mediterranean woodland, their tough, dark leaves well-adapted to withstand the prolonged absence of summer rain so typical of this corner of the range.

Elsewhere in the Picos the woodlands are more mixed, with ash, field maple, wych elm, hazel and small-leaved lime contributing to the canopy. The road from Cordiñanes to Cain passes through some particularly fine examples of mixed woodland around Corona. Yet another woodland type is that dominated by the Pyrenean oak, an easy species to distinguish due to its hairy leaves, which sometimes appear white. Such woodland is found mainly on the acid soils of Liébana and southern parts of the Picos.

The Angón meadows in the Western Massif. The transition trom meadow to 'monte' and woodland is apparent, as is the abruptness of the southern side of the range.

The quite large areas of ancient forests which still exist in the Picos, often undisturbed except for the sporadic wood-cutting activities of the local people, are an ideal refuge for many species of birds and small mammals. Great and lesser spotted woodpeckers are a common sight and you might also be lucky enough to catch a glimpse of the magnificent, though increasingly rare, black woodpecker. In the valley of Sajambre the extensive beechwoods are alive with crested tits and short-toed creepers in winter, whilst in the Pyrenean oakwoods around the villages of Pembes and Llaves in Liébana you can observe the spring courtship of pied flycatchers and tree pipits.

Most mammals, in contrast, are rather secretive, although it is not uncommon to see a pair of red squirrels chasing through the branches overhead, or the white rump of a roe deer as it bounds away through the trees. Wildcats and wild boar are less common, though not impossible to see, but the chances of seeing wolves or a brown bear are a great deal smaller than the less scrupulous tourist brochures would have us believe.

Continuing up through the woodlands you eventually arrive at the tree-line. Again this boundary is not well-defined, with stunted trees extending stubbornly into a thick scrub zone rather similar to *monte*. The component shrubs are different here, however, with species tolerant of higher altitudes replacing those which thrive in the comparatively warm valley environment. Dwarf juniper, bearberry and ling form a dense mat of vegetation, their dark greens relieved in the spring by buttercups and oxlips, and later in the year by the elegant fringed pink.

In some places, as at Asotín in Valdeón, this upland scrub is absent, and you pass directly from the high altitude beechwoods into the vast expanse of limestone which forms the peaks and pinnacles of these mountains. These rocky uplands may appear at first sight to be devoid of plant and animal life, but closer examination will reveal that this is not the case. The numerous cracks and crevices are home to all manner of secretive, low-growing plants: stonecrops and saxifrages, and such stunted shrubs as mezereon and alpine currant. Some denizens of these 'rock gardens' are found nowhere else in the world, including the columbine *Aquilegia discolor* and the delicate toadflax *Linaria faucicola*.

Dotted about the high mountains, oasis of green in the desert of limestone, are the *vegas*, or upland pastures. Small streams are often present, along the edges of which grow a variety of wet-loving plants, whilst black alpine newts secrete themselves under the shady banks, out of the heat of the sun. In the late summer the drier grasslands are studded with crimson- and pink-flowered rosettes of rock storksbill and the single, star-like blooms of merendera.

The wild uplands of the area are home to many of the larger birds, and anyone travelling through the peaks is almost certain to see griffon vultures, or to hear the croak of the ravens as it circles on a warm updraft.

Among the birds of prey, you are most likely to come across short-toed eagles and buzzards, though the latter are more abundant in the valleys. Smaller birds which nest in the rocky uplands include the alpine accentor, rock thrushes, wheatears and snow finches, all of which are easily spotted in the breeding season when they are most active.

It is also here in the high peaks that you are most likely to come across the elusive wallcreeper, a shy bird resembling a large crimson and grey butterfly as it hovers on cliff faces searching the cracks and fissures for insects. This bird, the sight of which is so coveted by ornithologists, was once fairly common in all the major gorges of the Picos, but it is now retreating to the safety of their highest peaks as increasing road traffic and tourist disturbance make life unacceptable in the valleys.

While the vultures rule the skies with their effortless flight, the undisputed king on the ground is the *rebeco*. This small, deer-like animal almost disappeared from the mountains of the Cordillera Cantabrica, but following a strict hunting ban it has recovered to the point where nowadays it is almost impossible to visit the higher regions of the Picos without seeing small groups of this graceful and agile animal. With its black eye-stripe, chestnut summer coat and tiny curved horns, the *rebeco* is easy to recognise as it travels with ease across even the most rugged terrain.

The Picos de Europa, then, are home to a significant variety of both plants and animals, with the exact species to be found in any one area depending not only on the altitude, as is the case in all mountain ranges, but also on the area's location with respect to the prevailing Atlantic fronts. An ascent starting in the sheltered valleys of Liébana and Valdeón, for example, will reveal important differences to a similar outing in the north and north-western quarters of the Picos. The walks in this guide, especially those which venture into the mountains from the valley floors, offer visitors a valuable opportunity to explore this important facet of the range.

GENERAL HISTORY OF THE AREA

It is no exaggeration to say that the history of man in the Picos de Europa reads like a history of Europe. Cavemen, Celts, Romans, Gothic hoards, Arab armies and Christian kings have all left their mark on the area. More recently shepherding and mining have had a lasting effect, whilst stepping firmly into the last quarter of the 20th century we find that tourism is making its presence felt, though in a regrettably negative way at the present time (see Appendix B).

The Cantabrian coast of Spain is, of course, famous for its palaeolithic cave art, the caves of Altamira near Santander being of great renown. Less well known, though equally worthwhile, are the caves in the vicinity of the Picos, those of **El Buxu** near Cangas de Onis, and **Tito Bustillo** in Ribadesella being particularly interesting. The latter has a wealth of paintings, mainly of animals, and a visit is easily combined with an afternoon on the beach, thus providing a varied and satisfying rest day.

Celtic tribes were, of course, present in Northern Spain, and suffered, here as elsewhere, at the hands of an intolerant Roman Empire. Each defeat drove them higher and higher into the mountains, a campaign led by the Emperor Augustus finally forcing them into the area known as **Mons Vindium** to the Roman historians, and now generally felt to correspond to the Picos. In order to defeat the few remaining tribesmen, the Roman legions constructed a network of roads and forts throughout the area. One such road, the **Calzado de Caoru**, runs from Arenas de Cabrales to Sotres. Certain sections are still in very good repair (See Route 55).

Despite the importance of the above, it is probably fair to say that the most significant historical event the Picos were to witness was the defeat of a contingent of Arab soldiers in 722 AD, in the vicinity of Covadonga. Time and national pride have done much to embellish whatever really occurred, but most would agree that the Gothic nobleman, Pelayo, after several defeats by the ruling Arabs, took refuge in the hills around Covadonga. So small was his band at this stage, that the Arabs were happy to ignore it. Pelayo, however, made use of his time, gathering together a new army, until eventually the Arab leaders decided to try to buy him off, or, failing this, destroy him in battle. The defeat they suffered in Covadonga was their first in Spain, and marked the beginning of the Christian Reconquest of the Spanish peninsula. The defeated Moors attempted to escape south, over the Picos, to the safety of Castilla. There is some discussion as to the exact route they took, but available evidence suggests that they crossed the Western Massif, the Cares Gorge, and the Central Massif before being engulfed by a landslide near Espinama in the Liebana valley – a remarkable traverse even today (See Route 170).

The Arabs vanquished, peace descended on the area and, in time, shepherds became the sole inhabitants of the mountains, living in close harmony with their world for centuries until a new invader broke their solitude. Mining, as has already been suggested, has left a permanent scar on the face of the Picos, and though some work was carried out by the Romans, most of what can be seen today dates from the middle of the last century. The main areas to be worked were Andara and Beges in the Eastern Massif, Aliva and Liordes in the Central Massif, and Bufarrera in the Western Massif. Of the above only the mine at Aliva is still being worked, though it also is said to be close to exhaustion.

Whilst the extraction of the zinc and lead ores hidden in the rock have undoubtedly been detrimental to the Picos, it is only fair to point out that mining is responsible for most of the tracks in the region. They abound in the Andara area, the track descending 2,000m via Beges to La Hermida on the River Deva being a remarkable statement of the skill of the engineers of the time. Equally impressive, and of greater use to the modern explorer, is the track which climbs in 29 tortuous hairpins from

Fuente Dé to Vega Liordes, whilst the mining around Peña Vieja left tracks going well into the Central Massif (La Vueltona). Tracks and access aside, however, mining is not really compatible with the conservation of a landscape such as that of the Picos, and the inevitable closure of the Las Manforas mine at the foot of Peña Vieja will bring a welcome end to the industry.

Considerably less agressive environmentally than mining, and with a much longer and richer history, shepherding has probably been the most significant human activity in the modelling of the present image of the Picos de Europa. The shepherds, in going back and forth to their summer pastures, have left us with a detailed toponymy of the area, as well as a comprehensive network of footpaths. The many small cabins and shelters that decorate the hillside from the valley bottoms up to the highest pastures, give the whole range a special beauty. Moreover, apart from providing shelter to both man and beast, they served as huts to some early explorers, a function they still readily fulfil today in an emergency. Stone-built and red-roofed, these simple dwellings offer an architectural style totally at one with the surroundings, a style that any new constructions would do well to imitate.

Both mining and shepherding have provided work to the local population of the Picos de Europa, whilst at the same time changing the physiognomy of the range. It was only natural, then, that the two should have been responsible for the first steps taken in the then unheard of sport of mountaineering. The shepherds in particular, in an attempt to reach new pastures, or simply to gain a better view of their flock, must have crossed many cols and topped many summits. As a result of their presence, names like *porru*, *seu* and *playa*, (See Appendix I for meaning), figure today on maps of the area. In a similar way, when the gentry of the last century hired local shepherds to guide their hunting expeditions, the toponymy of the area was enrichened by terms such as *tiro* (Tiros del Rey, Tiro de la Infanta, etc), and by names like *brecha* (Brecha de los Cazadores).

Mountaineering became fashionable with time, and a few shepherds were able to gain additional employment guiding those who wished to climb the more sought-after summits, especially that of El Naranjo de Bulnes. Pilgrims had been visiting the holy shrines of the Picos for centuries, of course, but now a new type of pilgrim was seeking their own particular Mecca. Tourism, already an important part of the Central European alpine scene, had arrived in the Picos de Europa. However, despite the obvious attractions of the area, remarkably little effort was made to develop the new industry, the first definite step being taken with the inauguration of the télèpherique at Fuente Dé in 1966.

The next two decades saw tourism grow in a piecemeal fashion, but never on the same scale as in the Alps, a factor which has been crucial in keeping the area as intact, and consequently as attractive, as it is at this moment in time. Whether the simplicity which characterises the Picos is to be left inviolate, or whether the range is to be exploited through tourism, only time can tell. Ecology groups are currently locked in battle with local governments, who are keen to turn the area into a major tourist attraction, with all that that entails (see Appendix B for details). It would seem that Spain, in its hurry to become fully integrated in the European Community, is travelling rapidly in the opposite direction to the other member states, at least in matters of mountain conservation. It can only be hoped that this lamentable situation is remedied before too much damage is done to the country's precious heritage of wild, mountain areas.

CLIMBING HISTORY

The Early Exploration – 1850 to 1904

Whilst the early climbing in the Picos, as has been noted above, was done by shepherds and hunters going about their business, the beginning of climbing as such is generally accredited to the Spanish geologist and mining engineer, Casiano de Prado. Working in the Cordillera Cantábrica between Palencia and León, he spotted the Picos in 1845 from the summit of Peña Corada. His first actual visit to the range, in 1851, was to no avail as bad weather prevented him reaching any summits. Two years later he returned and, in the company of two French colleagues, made the first ascent of the Torre de Salinas. He had thought this to be the highest summit in the Picos, but the view from the summit immediately revealed his mistake, the Mayor of Prada in Valdeón assuring him later (also mistakenly) that the Torre de Llambrión claimed that honour.

Prado resolved to climb the Torre de Llambrión and, after an unsuccessful attempt in 1855, was able to do so on August 12th, 1856. Little was written about the ascent, but it would seem that after a night in Vega Liordes, Prado and his party crossed to the north side of the Madejuno – Llambrión chain, ascending by what is considered today to be the normal route.

From 1855 to 1872 various teams of military surveyors were active in Northern Spain, carrying out mapping work and setting up primitive geodetic positions. In doing so they were responsible for the first ascents of a number of major summits, including the Pica del Jierro and the Pico Cortés in the Eastern Massif, and Peña Castil in the Central. Whilst not strictly ascents in the sporting sense the work of these teams was important as it represented a first approach to the mapping of the area. However, the figure largely responsible for the first systematic topographic survey of the three massifs was not to appear on the scene until some years later.

The Comte de Saint-Saud, an expert on the Pyrenees, arrived in the Picos almost by accident. Whist holidaying with a friend from nearby Ribadesella, he paid a brief visit to the sanctuary at Covadonga. Such was his surprise on seeing the abruptness of the range, however, that he resolved to return to the area, doing so for the first time in 1890, when he made the first ascents of the Morra de Lechugales and Peña Vieja.

A year later Saint-Saud was back, this time in the company of a friend and fellow mountaineer, Paul Labrouche. An attempt to climb the Torre de Llambrión failed due to bad mists, and the party ended up with the first ascent of Tiro Llago, after an unorthodox and, to judge by Saint-Saud's own account, exciting day[1]. Not content with this first, the two descended to Caín before climbing up into the Western Massif and making the first ascent of the Torre Bermeja. To the north, the imposing mass of Peña Santa de Castilla commanded their attention, so after resting in Cangas de Onis they attempted the mountain from the north. The attempt 'failed', landing Saint-Saud, Labrouche and their guide on the summit of the Torre de Santa María, which Saint-Saud immediately renamed as Peña Santa de Enol!

Between 1890 and 1908 Saint-Saud visited the Picos on eight occasions, but perhaps the most significant was that of 1892. After climbing the Pico Cortés, the Comte and Labrouche moved across to the Central Massif and were successful in their attempt to climb the Torre de Cerredo, the highest point not only in the triple massif of the Picos, but also in the whole of the Cordillera Cantábrica. A little later Labrouche rounded off the trip by making the first ascent of Peña Santa de Castilla. Three major summits, one in each massif – an outing that anyone wishing to get to know the range would do well to emulate.

This first phase of exploration in the Picos consisted of making first ascents of all the major peaks and, without a doubt, it came to a close on August 5th, 1904 when the Marqués de Villaviciosa, Pedro Pidal, reached the summit of El Naranjo de Bulnes for the first time. He was assisted in his venture by Gregorio Pérez, a shepherd from the village of Caín who was also known as 'El Cainejo'. Their ascent was a remarkable affair, especially if their complete outing is taken into account.

On August 2nd word was sent to El Cainejo asking him to join the Marquis in Ario in the Western Massif. This he did, leaving Caín after supper and making the approach to Ario by moonlight. Arriving at dawn the following day, he and the Marqués set off immediately for Peña Santa de Enol, which they climbed before going on to Peña Santa de Castilla. That evening they slept in Ario, and the next day descended and crossed the Cares gorge. From the Collado de Cerredo they traversed above Amuesa and Bulnes to the Canal de Cambureru, where they spent the night of August 4th. The following morning they finished their approach and made their ascent. The descent was not without its problems but at 7pm they were down off the climb after over three days' intense activity[2].

---

(1) Conde de Saint-Saud, *Por los Picos de Europa*, Salinas, Asturias, Ayalga Ediciones, 1985. pp. 43 & 45.

(2) Pedro Pidal and José Zabala, *Picos de Europa*, Asturias, Ediciones Noega, 1983 (re-edition of 1918 issue).

In search of the great walls – 1920s to 1970s

With all the major summits climbed, the focus of interest shifted to exploring the possibilities offered by the more difficult faces. In 1924, Victor Martínez, a local shepherd, put up the South Face Original Route on El Naranjo, and two years later another member of the Martínez family made the first ascent of the Paso Horizontal on the same face. But the real driving force behind this second phase came from groups from further afield.

During the 30s and 40s a number of Madrid-based climbers made the Picos their own. In an early sortie in 1944 Odriozola and Alonso put up the Original Route on the South-East Face of Peña Vieja. The group's main interest, though, centred on the magnificent, 600m South Face of Peña Santa de Castilla. Several climbs resulted from these early explorations of the wall, though the most significant product of this era was undoubtedly the South Face Direct route, climbed in 1947 by José González, Florencio Fuentes and Antonio Jojas. One of the classic climbs of the range, it provides a long, but excellent outing for middle-grade climbers.

On the same face, some distance to the right, a deep gully runs the height of the wall. A first attempt in 1945 was defeated at one third height, though the name – Canal del Pájaro Negro – dates from this attempt, being in memory of a black bird found dead at the foot of the wall. A second attempt in 1956, by the Basque climbers Pedro Udaondo and Angel Landa, failed in the upper chimney-cracks, but success was theirs two years later when one of 'last' of the Picos' plums was picked. During the 50s, Udaondo and Landa, along with the Régil brothers, were responsible for a number of important climbs, including the 1955 Cepeda Route on El Naranjo, and the 1958 Original Route on the South Face of Horcados Rojos.

Little commented on, though remarkable for its time, was the first winter ascent of El Naranjo, whaich Landa and Udaondo made in 1956 via the North-West Ridge and the chimneys of the North Face. The route was not repeated in winter until the mid-80s and was reported to be hard and poorly protected.

If the first ascent of El Naranjo de Bulnes in 1904 signalled the end of the first phase of exploration in the Picos, the second would be brought to a close by the ascent, in 1962, of the mountain's superb West Wall. A number of ridges and face climbs were put up after this date, such as the Espolón de los Franceses (1967) and the South-East Ridge of El Jiso (1969), but none were of the calibre of the Alberto Rabadá and Ernesto Navarro's daring climb. Put up in two attacks lasting a total of 5 days, the route is a classic not only of the Picos, but of the whole of Spanish climbing, and, as with all great climbs, it has been the centre of much attention, having been climbed in winter, soloed, soloed in winter, freed, and 'done' in as little as 4½ hours.

The coming of age – 1974 to 1988
After the ascent of the Rabadá-Navarro the pace dropped and it was not until 1974 that a third phase of climbing began. Two routes mark its start: Miguel Angel Gallego's somewhat anachronistic 'Directísima' up the centre of the West Face of El Naranjo; and the very bold Martínez-Somoano also put up in 1974. Both climbs deliberately looked for difficulties on faces already climbed, though it was the less sensational Martínez-Somoano that really broke new ground, with what was then hard free climbing over unprotected slabs.

In what remained of the 70s a huge number of climbs were put up, no stone being left unturned, and no face unclimbed. Particularly active during this period were Jesús Mª San Cristóbal and Javier Alonso, but their futuristic use of loose rock meant that their creations were seldom repeated. Of note among the more conventional offerings they left us are the South-West Face of the Torre de Coello and the Casiopea Route on the Torre de Salinas, but it is safe to assume that wherever loose rock is found approaching the vertical, this intrepid pair will have already made their presence felt.

Despite this increasingly intense activity throughout the range, however, attention was being drawn inexorably towards El Naranjo. Moreover, whereas routes here had previously indicated the culmination of developments, the mountain was now to become the centre and source of change. First, the West Face became the property of climbers from Murcia who, returning summer after summer, put up a total of six climbs beginning in 1978 with the now classic 'Murcaina 78', and finishing five years later with Excalibur. The winter of 1983 also bore fruit in the form of Sueño de Invierno, an attempt by José Luis García Gallego and Miguel Angle Díaz Vives to put up a new route through the overhangs on the left of the face. The attempt lasted 69 days and, as with other routes by the Murcia climbers, created a certain amount of controversy. In general, it was felt that on all their routes the Murcia group were guilty of using seige tactics, tactics deemed inappropriate on a 500m wall. Be this the case or not, when their hegemony finally ended in the mid-80s, no major change was noted in the style of the new first ascentionists.

Away from the West Wall other groups had begun to move into action, particularly on the blank East Face. The summer of 1980 produced three routes, of which 'Amistad con el Diablo' is the most direct, the easiest and the most popular, whilst 'El Cainejo' produced hard, unprotected friction climbing as a fitting tribute to the skill of the mountain's first ascentionist. 1980 also yielded the 'Sabadell', a solitary climb up the cold and lonely Northwest Wall, whilst across the vega, on the East Face of the Neverón de Urrielu two climbs were put up. The best of these is the 'Vía de los Celtas', which tackles the dominant crack system that splits the face.

Suddenly, anything and everything was possible as a crag mentality imposed itself in the high mountain arena permitting the liberal use of bolt protection, as in the 1983 'Esto no es Hawaii', a short, hard route up the Northwest buttress of El Naranjo. The Vega de Urriellu became the scene of frantic activity as everyone rushed to put up routes before the rock ran out. At the beginning of 1978 there were 14 routes on El Naranjo de Bulnes, two of which climbed the West Face and two the East. At the time of writing 14 routes make their way up the West Face alone, along with 8 up the East, and over 40 up the mountain itself.

Perhaps because of the publicity it always attracts, El Naranjo gave the impression of being the only point of interest in the 80s. In practice, however, things were happening everywhere. Climbers from Cantabria, for example, worked away at the crags around El Cable, the upper cable car station, in the same modest way they had done throughout the 70s. As yet, their routes on Peña Vieja and Peña Olvidada have received little attention, but it is only a question of time before people rationalise their present obsession with El Naranjo and begin to look elsewhere.

Asturian climbers, on the other hand, chose Peña Santa de Castilla, making their mark with three climbs takling the huge walls between the South Face Direct and the 'Pájaro Negro' routes. Of the three 'Rescate Emocional' (1981) and 'Manatial de la Noche' (1982) are the best, the former providing hard, sometimes unprotected climbing on superb rock. Another two climbs in 1983 pointed out the scope of the buttresses that make up the right wing of the south wall – a suggestion of future trends on this strangely under-rated mountain.

Where the future of climbing lies in the Picos is hard to say. New routes on and immediately around El Naranjo are not really part of any new trend, but a reflection of the mountain's fame, and, to some extent, of the incurable desire to 'get into print'. If anything, it would seem that at the end of the 80s two quite different groups of activists are developing, each with its own vision of tomorrow.

For the die-hard alpinists atmosphere is as important as the technicalities of the route. For them, Vega Urriellu, with its summer swarms, has all the charm of Stanage on a warm Bank Holiday. Their sights are set on other walls in hidden corners, the attraction increasing with the diffiulties of access. A recent route above the stark Jou Grande is indicative, perhaps, of this school of thought, and it would not be that surprising to see fresh efforts being made on the almost unclimbed walls of the Bermeja group.

For the other group, the sport rock climbers, access should be easy. As a result, they are turning to roadside crags in the surrounding valleys for new routes. The walls of the Cueto Agero in the 'La Hermida' gorge are a case in point, as is the attention that has been paid to Peña Fresnidiello since early 1983. In both places the emphasis is very much on rock climbing, the summit itself being of secondary importance.

The opening up, in the autumn of 1988, of a new, low-lying crag on the north bank of the River Casaño just beyond La Molina, is further evidence that the 'new wave' are here in force; bolts, battery-powered drills and all. However, there is no immediate reason for alarm on behalf

28   *Hut at Collado Jermoso, Torre del Friero in the background.*
(Central Massif)

of members of the first, currently less fashionable group. From a climbing point of view at least, the beauty (and perhaps the future) of the Picos de Europa is that it is able to offer something to both these factions, the one complementing the other. There is no reason not to suppose that with a little care and mutual respect, both sides will be able to find ample room to continue carrying forward their respective sports, and the range will come out enhanced, and not degraded, by the process.

2: GENERAL INFORMATION

ACCESS FROM THE UK

Access to the Picos de Europa from the UK is not difficult, a variety of approaches being possible. The most common of these are by sea from Plymouth, by air from London, and by road through France.

Sea – Brittany Ferries currently run a twice-weekly service from Plymouth to Santander, some 2h. from the Picos by car. A car is an undoubted advantage when moving around the range (local transport is infrequent), so the service bears consideration by car owners, though it is not cheap.

For those arriving on foot by ferry, a good bus service (Turytrans) covers the ground from Santander to Unquera or Arriondas.

Air – Both British Airways and Iberia run daily flights to Bilbao. With advance booking (APEX), the flights do not work out a great deal more expensive than the ferry. Turytrans are again responsible for the coach to the Picos, tickets and the coach being picked up at the Plaza Arriaga in the centre of Bilbao. There is also an overnight service which is run by the 'Intercar' company, and which leaves from the ANSA coach station (Autonomía, 17). Taxis prove the simplest way of reaching the city from the airport. For those who have hired a car with their flight (both BA and Iberia offer very good rates as part of an overall deal) crossing Bilbao will prove a little trying, though the new motorway helps. Leave the airport and turn R. At the first main junction, a very disorganised affair, go straight on and up a rise. After about 1km, swing L onto the motorway system and pick up the Santander signs, thus avoiding Bilbao centre.

Road – For three or four people in a car this is the cheapest route to the Picos. Moreover, it does not require a great deal more time than the 24h ferry crossing to Santander. On reaching Bayonne in SW France, join the motorway (toll) to cross the border near Irun. The motorway ends just W of Bilbao, from where the N-634 is followed to Unquera or Arriondas.

In recent years there has been a coach service from London (Victoria Coach Station) to Oviedo. This is the cheapest way of reaching the area, though it is slow (30h.) and comparatively uncomfortable. It does not, however, require such advance booking as does travelling by sea or air, whilst at the same time providing the cheapest form of one-way only travel to or from Northern Spain.

Whichever mode of transport is chosen, the town of Unquera will eventually be reached. Here the N-621 leads S to Panes where it is possible to travel S via Potes for the Central (S side) and Eastern

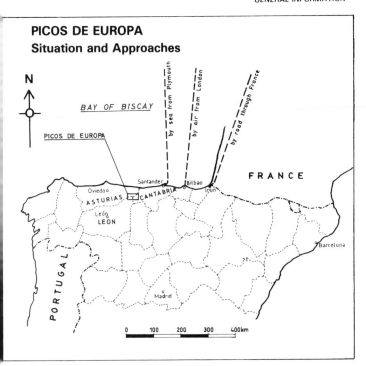

PICOS DE EUROPA
Situation and Approaches

N

BAY OF BISCAY

PICOS DE EUROPA

by sea from Plymouth

by air from London

by road through France

FRANCE

Santander   Bilbao   Irún

Oviedo   ASTURIAS   CANTABRIA

León
LEON

Barcelona

PORTUGAL

Madrid

0   100   200   300   400km

Massifs. For the Central Massif (N side) bear W at Panes, and so reach Arenas de Cabrales, whilst for the Western Massif, stay on the N-634 at Unquera, and hence arrive at Cangas de Onis via Arriondas. Buses cover all of the above routes for those on foot, though as suggested above, services are limited and connections poor between valleys. Local taxis provide a reasonable alternative, costing around 50ptas/km, the final price being calculated to allow for the taxis' return journey.

VALLEY BASES

For a variety of reasons most people will wish to make use of one or more of the following valley bases. Those selected provide, as a minimum, shops and accommodation, whilst also giving relatively easy access to at least one major area of interest. Moreover, anyone visiting the Picos with a family could comfortably use these bases throughout their stay, making their route approach on the first day, then completing the activity and returning to family or friends the next.

31

Accommodation in the centres given is in hotels, *hostals, fondas* or campsites. Hotels, as might be expected, are much the same as their British counterparts, though almost always less expensive. The 'paradores' are state-owned hotels of a high standard, often located in buildings of great historic interest. The one at Fuente Dé is relatively recent, however, having been built in 1966, at the same time as the télèpherique. Hostals generally offer cheaper, but more personal, 'Bed-and-Breakfast'-style accommodation, frequently with good restaurant facilities in the same building. Many modern hostals also have private bathrooms in the majority of the rooms, yet the overall cost for a double room seldom exceeds £20 per night in 1988.

For the impecunious there are the fondas. These provide simple 'pension-style' accommodation which can sometimes be good value for money, though they do tend to be older, and consequently simpler, establishments than the previous two. Finally, those who enjoy camping will want to take advantage of the growing number of very good sites in the valleys around the range. As is usually the case with continental sites, they offer a range of facilities, from the essential showers and washing facilities, through shops and bars, to Land Rover hire and guiding services.

Personal experience in all of the above types of accommodation has shown me that those in charge are invariably both friendly and helpful, especially to foreign visitors. Moreover, any attempt to speak in Spanish, no matter how faltering, inevitably serves to dispel any initial coolness, the basically hospitable nature of the local people coming to the fore. In the unlikely event, however, that the need to make a formal complaint should arise, the official government complaint sheet (Hojas de Reclamación) should be requested and completed, then sent to the relevant authorities. These sheets are available by law in all public establishments, as well as in all tourist information offices.

Potes

A bustling, attractive town, the capital of the Liebana valley and an important tourist centre. Follow the N-621 S from Unquera, through Panès and the impressive Desfiladero de La Hermida. Lying in the rain shadow of the range. Potes enjoys a relatively dry climate and can make a good base for certain activities in the Liebana Valley and the Eastern massif. It is connected with Valdeón via the Puerto San Glorio (N-621), Portilla de la Reina and the Pandetrave col. Buses to Panes and Unquera, as well as up the valley to Espinama and Fuente Dé (3 times a day in summer).

Accommodation: 3 hotels and many hostals. Campsite at Turieno ("La Isla": 2km from Potes on the Espinama road; pony-trekking); a second in San Pelayo ('San Pelayo": 5km from Potes on the Espinama road; swimming pool).

Services:	Many restaurants, cafeterías and bars. Banks, Post Office, shops, petrol. Tourist Information Office. Mountain Rescue Post (Guardia Civil – Phone: 46 06 98).

Espinama

An increasingly busy hamlet in a delightful setting, Espinama is well-situated for activities in the Eastern and Southern Central massifs. 3km from Fuente Dé on the main Potes-Fuente Dé road. Bus service from Potes.

Accommodation:	Hostal and 2 fondas. 3 restaurants. No campsite.
Services:	Shop and small but modern supermarket. Land Rover hire at 'Casa Máximo', 'Casa Vicente Campo', and the bar 'Peña Vieja'.

Fuente Dé

Once an alpine meadow of great beauty, now a major tourist attraction. Though the first views never fail to impress, the summer's coach-borne crowds can detract from the feel of the place. Strategically situated, Fuente Dé is a good base for activities in the southern half of the Central Massif, and is the start of an important track connecting the Liebana Valley to Valdeón via the Collado de Valdeón.

Accommodation:	Parador and a small hostal. Good campsite attractively located in the woods 200 metres beyond the télèpherique car park (guide service).
Services:	None – see Espinama.
Télèpherique:	The cable car, which is very popular during July and August, facilitates access to routes in the El Cable/Aliva sector, although the lateness of the first cabin (9am) and the 1½-2h queues that very quickly form, limit its value. The ride, however, is breathtaking as it rises over 2,000ft in a single, unsupported lift, sometimes passing through valley mist to come out above a sea of cloud.

Valdeón

Valdeón is a good valley base for activities in the Vega Huerta sector of the Western Massif and the Liordes sector of the Central Massif, and is also the natural start to the descent of the Cares Gorge. Though a difficult valley to get to, the effort is well-rewarded by pleasure of staying there. The usual approach is from Cangas de Onis via the Desfiladero de los Beyos and the Puerto del Pontón (N-637), or from Potes as indicated above. Scenically, both approaches have a lot to recommend them. On foot Valdeón can be reached from Fuente Dé as previously described, or from Sajambre via Vegabaño and the Collado del frade. Valdeón lies in the same rain shadow area as Potes and so enjoys equally good weather.

Accommodation:	Hostals, fondas, and bars in Posada de Valdeón. Fondas and bar in Cordiñanes (the once popular Fonda Rojo is now closed. The owners now run the Hostal Corona in Posada). Small campsite in Soto de Valdeón (guide service); a second in Santa Marina de Valdeón.
Services:	Bank, Post Office, supermarket, National Park visitors centre and First Aid Post in Posada. Land Rover hire in the 'Bar Picos de Europa' - Posada. Taxis in Posada and Soto.

Sajambre

Of limited value as a base for mountain activities, both Oseja and Sajambre are good rest spots, whilst the latter provides access to Vegabaño and marks the start of the Senda del Arcediano. As with Valdeón, this is an area with access problems for those on foot, though buses do run daily from Cangas de Onis to Oseja de Sajambre, the district capital. From Oseja, the village of Soto can be reached on foot or by taxi.

Accommodation:	2 hostals in Oseja, one on Soto (the 'Peña Santa', run by mountaineers; guide service). No campsite.
Services:	Bars and simple shops in both centres, plus an excellent baker's ('panadería') in Oseja whose bread keeps fresh for days.

Cangas de Onis

A small town (actually granted the status of City for historical reasons), Cangas de Onis offers all the services one might expect. Despite the above, it is not an especially good base, being expensive and crowded during the summer. The hostals and campsites in the villages along the valley of the River Güeña are perhaps of greater use to the visiting mountaineer. Fairly regular buses link Cangas to Oviedo, Sajambre, Covadonga, Los Lagos de Enol (summer only), Benia, Arenas de Cabrales and Panes.

Accommodation:	Cangas: 1 hotel and 5 hostals. No campsite. Soto de Cangas (3km E of Cangas; main entrance to the Covadonga National Park): hostals and a campsite. Avin (2km E of Benia; 20km E of Soto on the C-6312): the Casa de la Montaña provides bunkhouse accommodation (guide service). Campsite 'Picos de Europa'; well-run, swimming pool, etc. Very receptive to English speaking visitors.
Services:	Banks, Post Office, garages, restaurants, etc. Mountain guide's office, Tourist Information Office, Civil Guard Post with Mountain Rescue Team. National Park Information Office (ICONA, Plaza del Parque).

Arenas de Cabrales

Arenas is a small, rather commercialised town. Situated at the entrance to the Cares Gorge, it is more important as an entry point to the Central and Eastern Massifs than as a base. The town, which is rightly famous for the district's blue, 'Cabrales' cheese, has strong ties with El Naranjo de Bulnes which, to the chagrin of locals and tourists alike, is not actually visible from the town itself. Regular bus service west to Cangas de Onis and Oviedo, east to Panes.

Accommodation: Hostals, fondas, and a well-run campsite 2km E of the town (guide service).

Services: Bars and simple restaurants. Tourist Information Office. Petrol. Taxis. Mountain Rescue at Civil Guard Post in Carreña de Cabrales some 3km east of Arenas.

For reasons of space numerous smaller villages have been omitted from the above brief guide to valley bases. Almost every village, however, has some form of simple accommodation as well as a bar that often doubles for the local shop as well.

MOUNTAIN BASES

The enormous height differences in the Picos de Europa make it difficult to tackle the majority of climbs, and a good many of the high mountain walks and scrambles, in a single day from the valley bases, so the use of a hut, a tent or a bivouac is almost obligatory in order to tackle these routes effectively.

The number and quality of the huts in the Picos has grown significantly in recent years, and the range is now well-equipped in this respect, although, as is the case in all major areas, crowding is to be expected in the summer months, especially July and August. The larger huts are similar to their alpine counterparts, with permanent wardens, simple meals service, etc. The smaller huts usually have part-time wardens and more limited facilities, self-catering being the norm. All the huts will be found to be cheaper than in the Alps, though generally less well-organised. Silence is normally imposed at around 11pm (!), whilst hut wardens, it is worth noting, are not accustomed to waking people up in the morning.

Camping has the advantage of being independent of hut regimes, and of being free. The ground in the high mountains is often hard, however, and good pegs and a hammer are useful. Camping is usually possible near the huts, but alternatives have been given as necessary. Within the National Park (the Western Massif), camping in the high mountain is officially limited to 'bivouacs' above 1,600m – a bivouac being defined as a one-night stay, the tent being put up 1h before sunset, and taken down 1h after sunrise! In practice, discrete camping in places like Vega

35

Huerta (where there is no hut) does not seem to draw too much attention. When camping, water is available at the springs supplying the huts, or as otherwise indicated.

In stable, good weather a true bivouac has much to recommend it. A number of popular bivouac sites exist near the main climbing areas, and reference has been made to them in the following descriptions of the mountain bases. For both camping and bivouacs a good 2/3 season bag will be found sufficient in summer.

MACIZO CENTRAL

El Cable Hut 1,845m. (1)
Refugio del Cable. A small, modern building, connected to the upper télèpherique station by a concrete gangway. Useful for early starts, but currently in poor condition and threatened with closure. 16 places. No permanent warden. Keys and details in bar at upper station. Camping possible to the S in the Hoyo de Lloroza, but water is a problem.
1. When the cable car is not working the hut can still be reached on foot. Leave Fuente Dé by the miner's track to Liordes. When it begins its zig-zag ascent stay on the path that continues R. Below the cableway, strike off diagonally L through scrub (poor path), aiming for the deep gully that splits the amphitheatre wall L of the upper station. Enter the gully, and scramble up to the top (hard with big sacks; one chockstone pitch early on). The huts lie some 200m E of the gully. (2½h).

Though a last resort as a way up, the *descent* of the Canal de la Jenduda (1½h) is a far better end to the day than waiting in the cable car queue, being cheaper and quite possibly faster in the height of summer (see also Route 34). A second alternative to waiting in the queue is that of drinking in the cafeteria until the cable car staff indicate that the last cabin is about to go down!

Veronica Bivouac Hut 2325m. (2)
Cabaña Verónica. This diminutive hut, once part of an American aircraft carrier, lies S of the Collado de los Horcados Rojos. Of little value as a base because of its size and the proximity of better huts. 6 places. Warden (!). Drinks and snacks in summer. Emergency radio. Water from snowmelt only. No camping. Bivi cave below the S Face of Horc. Rojos.
2. From El Cable, follow the jeep track to just before the Horcadina de Covarrobres. Bear L and follow a track NW below the walls of Peña Olvidada. When it doubles back (La Vueltona), continue NW on a good path over scree. After switchbacks swing W to pass below the S Face of the Torre de los Horcados Rojos. Soon after, the path veers N to Horcados Rojos, but abundant signs go SW up a rocky crest to the hut. (1½h from El Cable; 2h from Aliva).

Aliva Hut 1670m. (3)
Refugio Nacional de Aliva. Situated below the impressive SE Face of

Aliva and the SE faces of Pêna Olvidada (L) and Peña Vieja (R). The Espolón de los Franceses takes the minor buttress to the R of the central snowfield.

Peña Vieja, above the large alpine meadows known as the Puertos de Aliva. Despite its name and its excellent situation, the building will be of little or no use to mountaineers due to a recent renovation which upgraded it to hotel status (restaurant, H&C water, TV, etc.) Private and expensive, it is to be hoped that it is the last of this type of 'hut' to be built in these mountains.

Aliva is a popular area for camping, particularly the area near the Chalet Real. Several springs.

3. Follow Route 2 to the Horcadina de Covarrobres, staying on the main track to swing NE below the SE Face of Peña Olvidada. The hotel is the lower (and much larger) of the two obvious buildings which stand below the SE Face of Peña Vieja (the first is the 'Chalet Real', a private hunting lodge), lying close to the Sotres-Espinama jeep track, (45 min. on foot. Land Rover service from El Cable and Espinama in summer – expensive).

Collado Jermoso Hut 2060m. (4).
Refugio de Collado Jermoso. A small, but beautiful hut in a situation which does justice to its name (hermoso = beautiful). Though limited to use as a base for activities in the Llambrión sector, the hut warrants a visit for its position alone. Warden from June to Sept – details from campsite in Soto de Valdeón. Drinks and meals. Radio. 12 places, though no one is turned away. Spring 100m from hut, a little below approach path. Camping is difficult here, but easy (and delightful) in Vega Liordes, a good alternative base for activities in this area. (Spring some 400m SE of small hut – protected from animals by stones.)
4. From Fuente Dé. Climb the Tornos de Liordes (a good but interminable mule trail below the S wall of the Padiorna) to the Vega de Liordes (2h). Go round the N side of the vega, a former mining area, to a

broad col (Cdo. de Padiorna) where an exposed path heading NW (the Sedo de la Padiorna) breaks through the enclosing walls to the R of the col. The path, well signed with cairns and paintmarks, leads to the hut without difficulty, offering excellent views of Valdeón and the Western Massif, particularly in the late afternoon (2h; 4h from Fuente Dé). A variation on this approach is to reverse Route 33 to enter Liordes via the Canal de Pedabejo and so join the Route 4 at the Sedo de la Padiorna. This makes little difference to the overall timing, though is probably marginally longer.

5. From Fuente Dé via El Cable. From the upper télèpherique station follow the jeep track until it swings sharp R (E). Drop down L from the track, and head W past ruins, picking up a path which climbs up into the Canal de San Luis. At the head of the canal, turn S (L) and scramble up through trackless broken terrain (small cairns) to the broad, airy Colladina de las Nieves (2226m. 1½h), from where an ascent of La Padiorna can be easily made. Head W from the col (no path, occasional cairns) until it is possible to work a way down through the walls guarding the N side of the Vega de Liordes, and so join Route 4 just above the Cdo. de la Padiorna (30 min). The hut is reached in a further 1½h (3½h from El Cable).

6. From Valdeón. Leave Cordiñanes heading NE (path vague at first), traversing in improbable positions below and round the walls which dominate the village, and entering the Canal de Asotín (1¾h). On entering the majada a large scree fan (the Argallo Berón) will be seen on the L. Ascend this (laborious) until grass terraces allow one to traverse R (SE) to gain the upper half of the Argallo Congosto. (The ascent of the lower section of the Arg. Congosto is NOT recommended, despite appearing on several maps.) Scramble up the bed of the gully to the spring and so to the hut (1¾-2¼h; 3½-4h from Cordiñanes). Very hard with a full sack, this approach makes a fast and spectacular descent to Valdeón.

A difficult but interesting path starts from the Collado Jermoso hut, linking it to the Jou de los Cabrones, and to Cabaña Veronica.

7. Follow the Liordes path for 10 mins. to a sign. Yellow paintmarks now lead up (N) over screes and slabs to the Hoyo del Llambrión. Work up into the top R corner of the hoyo, then enter the obvious gully (I+) that falls between Pt. 2621 and the N Ridge of the Torre de Llambrión. Scramble up the gully (I+), first on the true L side, then in the gully bed (loose rock) to gain the Tiro Callejo, the col between Pt. 2621 and the Llambrión (1½h from the hut). (The Te. de Llambrión is the second highest summit in the Picos and is easily tackled whilst in this area – see Route 78.)

From the To. Callejo, descend in an easterly direction (patches of hard snow) until below the N wall of To. Tirso, from where it is possible to drop down NE to the Cda. Blanca (30mins). From here the Cabaña Verónica can be easily reached in a further 30 mins. (2½h from Cdo.

Torre de Cerredo from the summit of the Tesorero. The Hda de Caín and Hda de Don Carlos (in shadow) are visible to the R of the photo, and the SW face of the Torre del Coello to the L.

Jermoso). Alternatively, Route 8 leads to the Cabrones hut in 3½-4h (5½-6h from the Cdo. Jermoso hut).

"José Ramón Lueje" Hut   (Jou de los Cabrones) 2100m. (5)
Refugio "José Ramón Lueje". Situated in the heart of one of the most rugged areas of the massif, the hut is a good base for activities in the Torre de Cerredo sector. Warden from early June to late September. 24 places. Drinks and very simple meals. Emergency radio. Limited camping possibilities. Some bivouac possibilities. Spring. Recent summers have seen the area invaded by foreign caving teams, the caves in the immediate vicinity being amongst the deepest in Europe.

8.   From Fuente Dé. Follow Route 2 to the Cabaña Verónica. From here traverse W over broken ground, skirting the N side of the Hoyos Engros, to gain the Callada Blanca (30mins). Now traverse NW (R) below the walls of the W Ridge of the Pico Tesorero to gain a small saddle yielding excellent views of El Picón, a prominent rock pillar above the deep Hoyo Grande Cimero. From the R side of the saddle descend slabs (I) and screes into the bed of the hoyo, then leave heading N, passing a huge block and so reaching narrows at the head of a scree fan. Bear diag. R now and pick up a narrow path which leads, still on scree, to the Horcada de Caín (Arenizas Baja – 2344m. 1½-2h from Cab. Verónica). Leave the col on the L, and follow a vague path over scree and broken ground to the Horcada de Don Carlos (Arenizas Alta – 2422m.) and good views of the Torre de Cerredo group. Descend to the bed of the Hoyo Cerredo, which is crossed to a rocky col below the Torre Labrouche. Continue N without losing height to a second, broad col by the slabby East Face of the Agujas de Cabrones (1½h). From the extreme R side of the col pick up an easy gully which drops down into the Jou de los Cabrones and so to the hut (4-4½h from the Cab. Verónica; 5-6h from El Cable).

This approach to the Cabrones hut crosses the wildest and most isolated areas of the Central Massif. Not recommended as an approach with full sacks, it is certainly worth incorporating into any walking tour undertaken in the sector.

9. From Poncebos. From the last bar in Poncebos follow the track up the Cares Gorge then drop down left and cross the river by the medieval 'Puente de la Jaya'. The path now enters the Canal del Texu, crosses the river low down, then climbs impressively up the true R side of the gorge, to come out at a small grassy area with a small bridge off R. Here the main path continues by the river to lower Bulnes (La Villa 650m – 1½h from Poncebos – bars), whilst a smaller path crosses the river (Puente Colines) and climbs up to Bulnes de Arriba (710m). Either way leave Bulnes de Arriba heading W, crossing an area of huge boulders before the path makes its way up the Canal de Amuesa (spring at the top). Leave Amuesa heading N, and so ascend a broad, grassy slope by its L side. At the top (small, flat grassy area below rock step – locate with care; several false trails), traverse SE (L) below the walls of the Cuetos del Trave, keeping high up and close to them, and crossing an awkward spur at one stage. The tortuous, but interesting, path (occasional cairn/paintmarks) eventually leads to a small col overlooking the Jou de los Cabrones (Excellent views of the Pico and Agujas de Cabrones). (2½-3h from Amuesa. 5-6h from Poncebos.)

"Julian Delgado Ubeda" Hut (Vega Urriellu) 1950m. (6)
Refugio "Julian Delgado Ubeda". Built in 1954, and enlarged ten years later, this is the most important hut in the range from the climber's point of view, given its privileged position below the great west wall of El Naranjo de Bulnes. A popular base for activities in the northern half of the massif. Warden from early June to late September. 40 places but presently being much enlarged. Drinks, meals, cigarettes, gaz, etc (all very pricey). Emergency radio. Camping, plus a number of well-established bivouac sites under boulders down from the hut. Spring next to hut.

10. From Fuente Dé. Follow Route 2 towards Cabaña Veronica, avoiding the final rocky crest and staying on the path N to the Horcados Rojos col and one of the classic views of El Naranjo. (1½h) At the col traverse E gaining height very slightly at first, and so pick up a fixed cable (paintmarks). Drop down (awkward in places) into the Jou de los Boches, from where a narrow path leads N into and then round the Jou Sin Tierre. A col is gained (awkward step) and crossed to yield a sudden, imposing view of 'El Picu'. Vega Urriellu and the hut are clearly visible and reached very soon after. (3-3½h).

11. From Sotres. From the junction at the hairpin bend below Sotres pick up the Aliva jeep track. This is followed for some 200m until it is possible to drop down and cross the River Duje. A recent, wide track climbs up from the river and is followed laboriously to open meadows a short distance below the Pandébano col (1h). Motor-vehicle access to the track is limited to local farmers, though sadly many Spanish visitors choose to ignore this fact.

Continue from the track to the broad Collada de Pandébano, then bear S up grassy slopes to pick up a path that leads SW past two isolated shepherd's huts and, in 100m, to La Terenosa hut (25-30mins). Pick up a recently constructed path from above the climber's hut, and follow it easily to the Cdo Vallejo (1,540m) and a first view of El Naranjo (2h from Sotres). The new path works its way monotonously across the bed of the Canal del Vallejo and then up the E side of the Jou Lluengu to come out in Vega Urriellu. (3½h from Sotres. 2½ in descent.)

The construction of the 'track', of its numerous branches in the Cdo Pandébano area, and of the polemical path from La Terenosa (see Appendix B), has robbed this route of almost all of the tremendous charm it once had. Indeed, anyone at one time familiar with the old goat path from La Terenosa to Vega Urriellu will feel distraught on seeing the damage the new path has caused. It is a great shame that the lessons being learned elsewhere in the world with regard to mountain conservation, are not being applied in the Picos.

12. From Poncebos. Follow Route 9 to Bulnes. Cross the village, passing by the Albergue, to pick up a narrow path that crosses grassy slopes, then climbs up to the L of a waterfall (good views of Bulnes) to enter the hidden, and initially very narrow, Canal de Balcosin. This opens out and is followed comfortably until, at the far end, a rocky step is surmounted to reach the Jou Bajo. Here the path swings R and enters the Canal de Cambureru with a welcome spring at half height. At the Majada de Cambureru (shepherds cabins), the path trends L to gain the Jou Lluengu (excellent views of El Naranjo, especially in the late afternoon). Screes, then broken ground, lead somewhat arduously to Vega Urriellu. (5-6h from Poncebos).

This classic though hard approach is rapidly falling into disuse because of the new path from La Terenosa (see Route 11), many people going to Pandébano from Bulnes. Given the state of abandon of the path it would be wise to check the current situation in Bulnes or Vega Urriellu before using it.

A somewhat difficult but nonetheless important path connects Vega Urriellu with the Jou de los Cabrones, making it possible to undertake certain activities in the Torrecerredo group whilst based in Urriellu.

41

Bulnes, perched precariously between the last and next centuries.

13. Vega Urriellu – Jou de los Cabrones Connection. From the hut
walk directly away from El Naranjo to pick up a vague path which goes
mainly NW over slabby, broken ground to reach screes below the N
Ridge of the Neveron de Urriellu (many small cairns, intermittent path).
Climb the screes diag. R (path) until a shallow, easy chimney gives
access to a narrow col. (The Corona de Raso. 2253m). Walk up the ridge
a few metres, then pick up a vague path to contour round below the N
slopes of the Neverón de Urriellu to the Horcada Arenera (2283m.
1-1¼h). Drop down into the jou beyond the col, cross it heading SW
(diag. L), and exit R at a small col offering first views of Torrecerredo and
the Pico de los Cabrones. Do NOT follow a vague path heading SW (L)
from the col. Instead, bear first NW (R) then W to contour around a deep
depression and so gain a broad col (pt. 2257m) which yields good views
N into the Jou de los Cabrones. Enter a broad, easy gully found at the far
E (R) side of the col and so descend to the hut (2½h). An irregular path
through austere terrain. Not recommended in poor visibility without
prior knowledge.

As an alternative approach to the Cabrones hut from Fuente Dé,
Routes 10 and 13 can be combined, though there is little advantage to be
gained in doing this. Routes 11 and 13 can also be joined with similar
results.

Amuesa Hut 1418m. (7)
Refugio de Amuesa. Situated in the Vega de Amuesa, the hut makes use

of an old shepherd's cabin. Currently in a very poor state. 20 places. As with the following two huts the beauty of the position is far greater than its utility as a base. Water at the head of the Canal de Amuesa. Spring sometimes dry in late summer. Camping possible.

14. Follow Route 9 to Amuesa. The hut is in the far R-hand corner of the majada. Water, which can be scarce in the late season, is at the small spring at the head of the approach gully. (2½-3h).

Bulnes Hut   650m. (8)

Albergue de Bulnes. One of the houses of the lower village, tastefully converted into a small but very comfortable hut. Limited as a base, but a 'must' as an overnight stop. 20 places. Warden. Meals, etc. in the hut or village.

15. Follow Route 9 to Bulnes. On crossing the bridge that leads into lower Bulnes a bar is reached, the hut being just beyond to the L (1¼h). Camping is difficult in Bulnes, a possible site being a relatively flat area beyond the upper village, at the entry to the Canal de Amuesa (spring).

La Terenosa Hut   1330m. (9)

Refugio de la Terenosa. Originally a shepherd's hut, recently refurbished and in good condition. Small, but attractive, offering good views of Bulnes and Pandébano. An interesting overnight stop during a walking tour, La Terenoso is not, however, a particularly good base. Moreover, the Pandébano area seems destined for major tourist developments (see Appendix B). 30 places. Warden, drinks and food. Camping possible lower down on the broad Pandébano col.

16. Follow Route 11 as far as La Terenosa. The hut lies some 100m beyond the shepherd's twin cabins, slightly below the main path (1½h from Sotres).

Las Vegas de Sotres Hut   1060m. (10)

Refugio 'Las Vegas de Sotres'. Of recent construction, the hut will, in the future, be a possible base for ascents of the main summits of the Eastern massif, as well as in the Valle de las Moñetas area. Not open at the moment. Camping possible, but avoid the enclosed fields, which are for hay.

17. Leave the Poncebos-Sotres road at the hairpin just before the final steep climb to the village of Sotres (parking). A track drops down from the hairpin and follows the R bank of the R Duje, the hut being in the middle of a group of shepherds' cabins (less than 1h on foot. With care, cars can usually negotiate the track).

MACIZO OCCIDENTAL

Enol Hut   1080m. (11)

Refugio de Enol. Originally built for the shepherds of the area (marked

'Casa Municipal de Pastores' on some maps), the building was converted into a hut in the early 80s. Attractively situated in the Vega de Enol. 30 places. Permanent warden. Restaurant service and bar. Emergency radio. Often fully booked by youth groups, especially during the summer.

18. On reaching the Lago Enol from Covadonga, leave the road to take the wide track that skirts the W side of the lake to enter the Vega de Enol. The hut is clearly visible to the R, some 400m away.

The National Park authorities, who over the last few years have worked very hard to make the park truly worthy of its designation, allow camping in the Vega de Enol as well as next to the nearby Lago Ercina. It is hoped, however, to put both sites together in a single site near the old Bufarrera mine workings next to the Ercina site, offering full facilities (the present sites have none). Camping at the moment is free, but limited to a maximum of 3 nights, a permit being issued by the patrolling park wardens.

Vegarredonda Hut 1510m. (12)

Refugio de Vegarredonda. A completely new hut opened 1986. The normal base for activities in the NW sector of the massif, though perhaps too far away to be a good base for activities in and around the Jou. Santu, for which a bivouac may prove interesting. 68 places. Permanent warden. Restaurant service. Radio. Camping possible near the old hut, a little higher up the valley. Spring at both huts.

19. Follow the jeep track of Route 18, going past the Enol hut and so reaching a fork in the track (Pan del Carmen – 30 mins. from the Lago Enol). Take the left fork and follow the track past a small, circular, meadow (El Pozo del Aleman), across a bridge, and up past large boulders and several shepherds' cabins (Vega la Piedra). A well-marked path leaves the vega climbing SE, crosses a flat meadow, then climbs again to reach another collection of cabins (La Redondiella – 1380m). A final short climb leads to broad Cdo. Gamonal (1460m) and a view of the hut which is reached in a further 10 minutes (2-2½h from the Lago Enol).

An important connection links Vegarredonda to Vega Huerta, the best base for activities on the S Face of Peña de Castilla.

20. Leave the hut and head S on a good path going past the old hut. The path climbs up towards a series of pointed towers (Los Argaos), dividing just below the first of them. Take the R fork and pass below an imposing rock pillar (El Porru Bolu), before climbing up in zig-zags, always on a good path, to La Mazada (2030m), an ample grassy col with excellent views N and W (1¼-1½h). The path, still very good, winds its way around a rocky spur and then below the SW Face of the Torres de Cebolleda (Huge cave above L; small spring below path to the R). The most marked path now climbs up W to the Horcada de Santa María. Do NOT follow it. Instead, work down over difficult terrain (occasional cairns; vague path) to skirt round the W side of the Torrezuela and so enter the Hoyo de las Pozas, which is crossed heading SE to reach the Horcada de Pozas (2030m. 1½h from La Mazada. It is also possible to reach this point by crossing the Horcada de Alba col immediately E of the Torrezuela, but this variant has a tricky descent into the Hoyo de Pozas). Beyond the col is the deep La LLerona hoyo, which is passed on its L. Yellow paintmarks are soon picked up, and lead below the Aguja de Corpus Cristi, through a boulder field, and over grassy slopes to Vega Huerta (4h from Vegarredonda). Here the only water is a spring about 50m E of the ruins of the old hut. It is covered to protect it from poisoning by animals, and usually sports a plastic tube to enable the water to be siphoned out of the small collecting well.

'Marqués de Villaviciosa' Hut   1580m, (13)

Refugio 'Marqués de Villaviciosa'. Situated in the very attractive Vega de Ario, this is another very well equipped hut, especially after the 1987 improvements. Of limited value as a base for climbing, the hut is well-situated for a number of interesting walking and scrambling activities. Moreover, as with certain other huts, the situation makes even a short visit worthwhile. 36 places. Permanent warden. Meals service. Emergency radio. Camping.

21.   From the Lago Ercina. Pick up the path which starts to L of the lake, and which is visible below rock walls to the SE of the car park. Follow the path comfortably past cabins, a yew tree, and several large boulders. Climbing gently into more open ground the path gains a broad col with good views of the Central Massif in the far distance. Now descend to a large majada (Las Bobias) with an excellent spring just beyond cabins (45 mins. from car park). Go R around the spring (FALSE path drops L) and climb up to cross rocky ground, then contour around head of a small valley (La Redondiella) following paintmarks. Cross the stream at the head of the valley, then follow steep zig-zags to leave the valley by true R bank. The path continues to climb, winding its way between small hoyos and rocky hillocks (paintmarks) to reach more open ground and views of the Cuvicente – Verdilluengua chain to the R (SE). A final steep section gains a broad col with excellent views of Central Massif, and a simple orientation table. (Las Bobias +1hr). Finally, swing L (N – path vague, but many paintmarks) and so reach the hut which stands in the back, left corner (NE corner) of the vega. (2-2½h from the Lago Ercina).

Vega Ario – Vega Redonda Connection. *A direct connection between these two huts is possible via the Vega de Aliseda. The path is very vague throughout, however, with only very occasional cairns marking the way. Moreover, the ground covered is complex and poorly represented on most maps. The connection is not recommended, except under optimum conditions. Those wishing to move from one hut to another would do better to do so via the Lago Ercina, combining Routes 19 and 21.*

The South face of Peña Castilla from the Camino del Burro path.

Vega Huerta Hut 2010m. (14)
The old hut, despite references to the contrary in several guides, now lies in ruins. The National Park authorities have a project for a new hut, though there is some suggestion that this may never be built because of the scarcity of water in the vega, and the negative ecological impact a hut would produce. Camping is allowed, however, and usually proves to be a wonderful experience.

22. From the Lago de Enol. Follow Routes 19 and 20, allowing between 6-7h if a sack is carried.

23. From Vegabaño. The normal approach for those able to get to Vegabaño (see 'Valley Bases'), and one of the most beautiful approaches in the range. Leave the Vegabaño hut and walk down the meadow. Cross a stream and skirt around a series of small fenced enclosures to pick up a path (wooden sign) that enters woods, crosses the Rio Dobra (limit of the National Park) and then works its way up the true R bank of the river, past a large oak (El Roblón). Shortly after a spring (last water) the path comes out of the wood at a grassy col (El Cueto. 1550m. 1¼h from Vegabaño) by a rocky knoll. Turn L (NE) and follow path through scrub to higher col with views of a small hut in the valley beyond (the Frade hut – owned by the park authorities but in bad condition). Do NOT cross the col, but follow a spur up R, first on its R side, then crossing L to contour round above the Frade hut to the Collado del Frade (views of Valdeón. 30 min). Now climb a broad grassy spur leading N until the path crosses L and swings round below big walls (Los Moledizos). The path climbs steeply to a small gap, then zig-zags up the screes of the Canal del Burro, coming out at the Collado del Burro (2100m. Views of the Central Massif. 45 min from El Frade). Abundant cairns and yellow paint spots mark the path which meanders north, first to the W of a series of minor tops, then to the E, before dropping down NE and skirting the W flanks of the Torres de Cotalbín to enter Vega Huerta (3h from Vegabaño).

24. From Soto de Valdeón. From the village pick up a path which climbs W up a long spur, then swings N to pass below the Pico del Cuerno before continuing up on a good track to the cabin (= chozo) at Llos (1680m. 1½h from Soto). Follow the path W below the S walls of Los Moledizos, swinging N towards the end to gain the Collado del Frade (2¼-2½h from Soto) and Route 23 (3½-3¾h total from Soto to Vega Huerta).

25. From Cordiñanes. Leave the village and cross the River Cares. A wide track leads N from just above the 'Mirador del Tombo', contouring above beech woods (go L at an early junction). A small bridge (water) is reached in less than 1h, the path continuing mainly level until a steep, exposed section cut out of the rock, signals the start of the real work. Hard climbing through the woods brings a momentary rest at the foot of a striped wall. The shade of the trees is now left for hazel-covered slopes, the path continuing to climb up always to the L of the gully bed. Shortly after the hazel dies out, Peña Santa de Castilla is glimpsed for the first time, whilst the path finally levels out and enters the gully bed (2h).

Cross the gully and climb steeply out R. When the path reaches the first slopes of Vega Huerta it dies out, so make for two large cairns on the skyline ahead and slightly L. The old hut lies just S of these cairns (1h; 4h from Cordiñanes, though with little chance to rest).

Hard work in ascent, the descent of Route 25 is a worthwhile alternative to Route 24 for those returning to a base in Valdeón. It is important, however, that when taken in this direction, the entry to the gully be correctly located. A large, 'waveform' wall (visible in part from the large cairns near the old hut) guards the entrance to the Canal de Capozo, the correct path down passing beneath this wall.

3:   TECHNICAL NOTES

TIMES AND GRADES

An overall time has been given in the guide for both walks and climbs, these times being based on personal experience and conversation with a broad spectrum of local mountaineers. Whilst the part times given do NOT take into account stops for rests, photography, etc, the overall times makes some allowance for such interruptions, and so are not necessarily equivalent to the sum of the parts. When in doubt, times given have erred in favour of being generous, **but all times assume that adequate training has been undertaken before coming to the range.** Though altitude is not a problem in the Picos, the differences in height are significant, often occurring over a relatively short distance. An estimate to height gain and loss has been given for the walks as this is more important than simple map distance.

The times for climbs do not take into account either approaches or descents, although when using the bases indicated for each route, these are seldom more than 1-1½h each. Times given for hut approaches assume a full sack, whilst those for walking routes and climbs assume only a day sack to be carried. As must be obvious, all times are approximate, and bad weather, problems of navigation, or the heat of good weather can make a mockery of them.

The walks in the guide have been given a grade from A to D in ascending order of difficulty. This has been determined by taking into account the **height gained or lost** during the route, the **nature of the terrain** crossed and the **problems of route-finding** that might arise. A **Grade A** walk presents none of these factors in a serious form, a **Grade B** walk presenting one of them, a **Grade C** walk two of them and a **Grade D** walk all three. The preamble to the route will indicate which factors determine the grade of a given excursion.

Grading climbs is always a thorny and worrying aspect of writing a guide, and one which has been complicated in the case of the Picos by recent changes within Spanish climbing circles. Originally, the UIAA system was used throughout the country. However, with the growth of sport rock climbing in Spain over the last few years, a switch to French grades has occurred. This has led to a certain degree of confusion, with the two systems being applied to new climbs in accordance with the preference of the first ascensionists.

In an attempt to remedy the situation, the authors of the Spanish definitive guides opted to use the French system, which had more or less imposed itself on Spanish climbing by the late 80s. The grading of climbs given in this guide is based on that used in the definitive guides, any differences being the result of personal experience. As will be seen in the table of comparative grades below (Table 1), the two systems begin to differ above IV, and it is possibly still true that pre-1980 Vs and V+s will be found easier than their modern counterparts. Most moves above V+ are post-1980, however, and so here the homogeny of the lower grades is regained.

TABLE 1

SPANISH (used in guide)	BRITISH	U.I.A.A.	WEST GERMAN	U.S.A.
I		I		
II		II		
III		III		5.4
IV	4a	IV		5.5
V	4b	V		5.6
	4c	V+		5.7
V+	5a	VI−	VIIa	5.8
		VI	VIIb	5.9
6a	5b	VI+	VIIc	5.10a
6b	5c	VII−	VIIIa	5.10b
		VII	VIIIb	5.10c
				5.10d
6c	6a	VII+	VIIIc	5.11a
7a		VIII−	IXa	5.11b
				5.11c
		VIII	IXb	5.11d
7b	6b	VIII+	IXc	5.12a
			Xa	5.12b
7c	6c	IX−	Xb	5.12c
		IX		5.12d
				5.13a
8a		IX+	Xc	5.13b
		X−	XIa	5.13c
8b	7a	X		5.13d
		X +		
8c	7b	XI−		

Whilst the individual pitches of climbs are given a numerical grading, the climb itself has been given an overall adjectival grade of the type commonly in use in other mountain areas. The basic significance of these grades is shown below (Table 2):

TABLE 2

Grade	Meaning
F	Long routes with moderately difficult moves
PD	or
AD	Short routes with moves up to IV
D	Long climbs with some difficult moves
TD	Short climbs with some very difficult moves
ED	Long climbs with moves of great difficulty
	Short climbs with continuously difficult moves

The subdivisions EDinf and ED, have been used to resolve the problem of grading long, technically reasonable climbs, and shorter, technically very hard climbs. The interpretation of each is:

EDinf – Long (500m+), steep climbs with certain very difficult moves, or shorter climbs with a high proportion of hard moves. Such climbs are well-equipped (belays, runners) and will rarely require a bivouac.

ED – Long climbs with abundant hard free and aid moves which are not necessarily well-equipped and may require a bivouac.

A number of climbs of EDsup exist on the west wall of El Naranjo, but all of them involve significant amounts of hard aid climbing and none have been felt worth including in the present edition of the guide.

Though every attempt has been made to guarantee the accuracy of grades, it would seem wise to begin on routes both shorter and easier than those to which we really aspire. Over the last five years I have seen a significant number of foreign climbers (British in the main) arrive in Picos only to perform significantly below their normal grade.

EQUIPMENT

Equipment is a very subjective affair, but in general, at least in terms of walking and the easier scrambling, what would serve for Scotland in summer will serve for the Picos, too. Modern lightweight boots would seem to be ideal for the rough high mountain terrain, but whatever is finally chosen, it should possess good shock-absorbing properties, as descents can be long and steep.

The Scottish summer is also a fair guide as to clothing. Above 1500m, a summer's day in the Picos can be very cold or debilitatingly hot. Worse still, it can be both in the same day. Shorts and T-shirts (and good sun-cream) are a wise inclusion, though obviously sweaters, tracksuit bottoms and/or polar wear are essential in poor weather. Rain gear is more problematical. When it rains it rains hard, but quite often we are enveloped in a fine, wetting mist known locally as "orbayu" (see Weather notes). Non-breathable waterproofs are intolerable in such weather so we can either suffer, buy breathable garments, or adopt the local solution of carrying an umbrella. Some people also claim that a cyclist's cape is a useful item. Strangely enough, a water bottle is an essential item. Water in the high mountains is limited to a handful of springs, some of which are not easy to find.

In a normal year snow can be a problem until mid-June. Consequently, anyone visiting the area from December to the beginning of May should bring full winter gear (see Chapter 7). From May to mid-June an ice-axe is a sensible precaution, whilst anyone nervous about moving over old snow may want to include a set of instep crampons. Full crampons are not really necessary outside the winter period, and nor is an ice-axe from mid-June to mid-October.

Equipment for climbing will vary enormously according to the difficulty of the undertaking. For ridges and scrambles a single 9mm rope is sufficient provided that there are no long abseils. A handful of slings and krabs, along with a small selection of nuts, will be enough to protect these routes. Walking boots are adequate for most scrambles, specialist rock boots only being needed on full climbs. Where they are necessary, comfort should take priority as long days and long descents make tight boots agony to wear. Moreover, the natural rock friction is sufficient, except on the very hardest moves.

On middle-grade climbs 2×45m ropes are advisable, and in some cases essential because of abseil descents. Hardwear could well include a set of 'Rocks' (or equivalent), a selection of medium 'hexes', half-a-dozen quick draws, and two or three long slings. In addition, it would seem sensible, however abhorrent the idea may seem, to carry a hammer and a small selection of pegs (channels and blades). The rock in the Picos does not always lend itself to nut protection, and belays are only in place on the most popular routes. Fortunately, cheap mild-steel pegs are better than chrome-moly ones, being more able to adapt themselves to the cracks.

The harder rock climbs require all of the above with the smaller Rocks repeated. Friends will be of great use, and up to 15 express slings may be needed. If the route includes aid moves above A1, a pair of étriers will prove an asset, though in the few climbs where specialist aid-gear is necessary this has been indicated. Finally, a helmet would be wise on all rock climbs.

Equipment is still not as easy to buy in Spain as in Britain, but three shops in Oviedo, all in a very small area not far from the RENFE railway station, sell most of whatever might be needed in an emergency. They are:

i)   Deportes Tuñón, Campoamor 5-9.
ii)   Deportes Centeno, Nuevo de Mayo, 14-16.
iii)   Oxígeno, Manuel Pedregal, 4.

The last of these will be found to be very receptive to English-speaking visitors, some English being spoken.

Finally, 'La Casa de la Montaña', Autonomía 9, is easy to get to for those arriving via Bilbao as it is in the same street as the ANSA bus-station.

MAPS AND GUIDES

The growing interest of the last few years in the Picos de Europa has resulted in a considerable number of new maps and guides to the area. Unfortunately, it would not be true to say that this increase in quantity has been matched by an increase in quality. The majority of maps continue to be inaccurate in one way or another, whilst almost all the guides available are of only limited use to the mountaineer, being mainly written with the car-bound tourist in mind. Finally, almost all of the literature available is published in Spanish.

MAPS

1:100,000 Picos de Europa José Arias Corcho
Privately published but inexpensive sketch map with panoramas and general information on the back. Worth considering as an alternative to the Firestone 1:200,000 motorists' map of the area.

1:75,000 Picos de Europa Miguel A. Adrados
A privately published map intended for use with an accompanying guide of 48 walks in and around the Picos. Whilst the scale makes it of limited use to those requiring detailed mapping, the map is still a serious and accurate affair containing a lot of useful subsidiary information. Probably the best general map of the range and its immediate surroundings. The back offers a good pictorial representation of the·area. Readily available. Recommended.

1:50,000 Sheets 55, 56, 80, 81 IGN (Instituto Geográfico Nacional)

The official government maps. Accurate contouring but all to no avail due to serious deficiencies in the naming and location of features such as cols, huts and paths. Fortunately (!) these maps are not easily available.

1:50,000 Mapa de los Tres Macizos de los Picos de Europa FEM

Based on the IGN maps of the same scale. One of the better maps but the scale is inadequate for an area as complex as the Picos. Panorama and information (out of date) on the back. Somewhat cluttered and marred by the same errors for which the official maps are renowned.

1:50,000 Picos de Europa Plano de los Tres Macizos GH Editores

Originally sold with the excellent *Naturaleza y Vida en los Picos de Europa* (see below), but now available separately. Very good in its use of local names, and with accurate contours within the limits of the scale. Somewhat spoilt by the inaccuracy with which huts and paths are marked. Recommended.

The huts on the GH map are located as follows:
El Cable: correct
Cabaña Veronica: just N of the 's' of 'Hoyos'.
Aliva Hotel: correct
Jermoso hut: just W of 'J' of hut name on map.
Lueje hut: just N of '3' in 2350 spot height.
Urriello hut: just S of 3rd 'a' in 'Gargantada'.
Amuesa hut: correct
Terenosa hut: just S of 'io' in 'Refugio'.
Enol hut: just S of 'o' in hut name
Vegarredonda: on opposite bank of Rio Junjumia
Ario hut" just N of 'g' in 'Vega de Ario'.
Vega Huerta: just N of 'o' in 'Llago Huerta'. Although the hut lies in ruins, its correct location is of use when looking for the spring.
Vegabaña: just W of 'nt' in 'Arroyo de Valdelafuente'.

1:25,000 Picos de Europa I Macizo Occidental   Editorial Alpina
II Macizo Central + Oriental

Widely available and much used maps with accompanying small booklet of background information and excursions. Inexpensive but hopelessly inaccurate, being based on enlargements of the IGN maps. The contouring at times suggests slopes where there are cliffs. Not recommended.

1:25,000 IGN

The above 1:50,000 sheets each divided into four 1:25,000 sheets. Currently being re-issued. Contouring reliable, but based on 1978 air photography and so subject to inaccuracies. Location of place names, tracks and huts seriously deficient at times.

1:25,000 Macizo Central de los Picos de Europa   Miguel A. Adrados

Privately published but much more accurate than the other maps currently available. Easy to read. General information, aerial view, recommended excursions and summit index on the back. The only serious map of the massif. A second edition of this map (due out in 1993) will include the Eastern Massif. Strongly recommended.

1:25,000 Macizo Occidental de los Picos de Europa   Miguel A. Adrados
Another privately published map by this Picos expert, and one which is even better than that of the Central Massif. Pictorial representation of the area on the back. This 1:25,000 map of the Western Massif, together with the new edition of the map to the Central and Eastern massifs will solve the mapping problems of the Picos to a very great extent.

Throughout the guide the names and spot heights given will be those found on the 1:50,000 GH map or on the Adrados 1:25,000 map. References for the walks in the outlying areas are to the Adrados 1:75,000.

GUIDES AND BOOKS

All the guides mentioned below are written in Spanish and require a fair knowledge of the language. Despite this, some are worth buying either for their visual or their written content.

Los Picos de Europa José Ramón Lueje ''Guías Everest''
Widely available and inexpensive. Many colour prints. Very hard reading and in need of up-dating.

Los Picos de Europa (Guía de los 3 Macizos) Miguel A. Adrados & Jerónimo López   Privately published.
The definitive guide to the area for the climber. Currently being re-published in three separate volumes (one for each massif), of which only that of the Central Massif is available. Essential for those who wish to go beyond the scope of this present work, but expensive.

El Parque Nacional de la Montaña de Covadonga Cayetano Enrique de Salamanca   Privately published

Cabrales y Picos de Europa Cayetano Enrique de Salamanca   Privately published

Two well-produced guides with many black and white photos. Interesting to read and especially informative with regards the areas surrounding the mountains.

Guía del Parque Nacional de la Montaña de Covadonga E. Rico et al. Siverio Cañada (editor).
An attractively presented book with a lot of information not only about the National Park, but also about the surrounding area. Good photography and a well-informed text make the book of interest,

though it is much more a coffee-table edition than a guide.

Vida y Naturaleza en los Picos de Europa   GH Editores
The work of a group of Picos experts. A coffee-table book even for those with little or no Spanish. Abundant and reliable factual information and some excellent photos and line drawings make the book a collector's item.

The following books have all recently been published in facsimile re-editions. Each is a classic in its own right, and worth buying for those who read Spanish.

Por los Picos de Europa   Conde de Saint-Saud   Ayalga Ediciones
Recently translated from French, this book and the accompanying maps are of great interest to those who wish to know more of the early exploration of the range.

Picos de Europa   Pedro Pidal y José F. Zabala   Ediciones Noega
A classic work which, apart from describing much of the early exploration of the area, includes the contrasting but complimentary descriptions Pedro pidal and El Cainejo made after their historic ascent of El Naranjo de Bulnes. Essential reading for all Picos devotees.

Picos de Cornión   José Ramón Lueje
An interesting insight to the Western Massif (which Lueje knew better than anyone), but very heavy reading due to the author's rather baroque style.

MOUNTAIN RESCUE

Although the situation has changed for the better over the last few years, mountain rescue in Spain is not at the same level as in other European countries. It is, however, free, as is any subsequent hospital treatment, although it would be wise to consult the relevant NHS body as to the EEC forms to be completed to guarantee free medical treatment within the community.

In the event of accident, or should someone go missing, the course of action to take will depend on the whereabouts of the incident. In the high mountains it is best to inform the warden of the nearest hut, who will then pass on the relevant authorities by radio and/or organise first aid for the victim where necessary.

In the valleys the incident should be reported to the Civil Guard (Guardia Civil), who are responsible for mountain rescue, although the only trained group is in Cangas de Onis. There are Civil Guard posts in Potes (Tel: 730007), Cangas de Onis (Tel: 848056), Carreña de Cabrales (Tel: 845016). The campsites at Fuente Dé, Soto de Valdeón and Arenas de Cabrales are the bases for small groups of mountain guides who would also be of help in an emergency.

4: VALLEY BASED ROUTES

LIEBANA

With its great natural beauty, its reliable weather and its artistic and
cultural heritage, it is not surprising that this area should have become
the major tourist attraction in the range. The pull it exercised was further
increased by the building of the télèpherique at Fuente Dé in 1966, to the
point that today the district is beginning to suffer some of the negative
effects of its own fame.

The walking in the area falls into two broad categories, with those
outings which explore the valley sides and the minor summits giving
easier days, but providing a taste of the Picos which is just as valid as
that gained from the second group. These routes venture into the high
mountains and are strenuous but rewarding.

CUETO AGERO   1349m

The huge wall that dominates the La Hermida gorge opposite the village
of Lebeña never fails to impress those seeing it for the first time.
Moreover, its low altitude and southerly orientation make it a good poor
weather alternative for climbers based in the Liebana area. The classic
South Ridge is described here, information about the many other
climbs being available from local climbers, who, in an interesting move
aimed at conserving the area, have chosen not to publish details of the
crag at the moment.

Descent: Scramble down N from the summit to pick up the path that
leads easily down the obvious gully to the W of the ridge.

26   South Ridge
*A fairly logical line following a series of cracks and diedres up the centre
of the ridge. Good rock, though with some vegetation. First ascent: J.
Torralbo, J. Rodríguez and A. Cianca, 24 June, 1973. TD–, 300m, 4h.
Diag. p.57.*

Approach: From opposite the 'Bar Desfiladero' on the Panes-Potes
road, take the single-track road to the village of Allende. A track leads L
out of the village to a drinking trough. Bear R here through woods (path)
to the base of the wall and the climber's hut.

From just R of the foot of the main S Ridge, scramble up a vegetated
gangway diag. R, then traverse easily back L to a tree on a shoulder on
the skyline. A steep corner and easier ground leads to a system of cracks
that trend R to a steep corner with pegs. Climb this, then make a hard
traverse R to finish up a steep wall. Easier slabs and walls lead to the
summit.

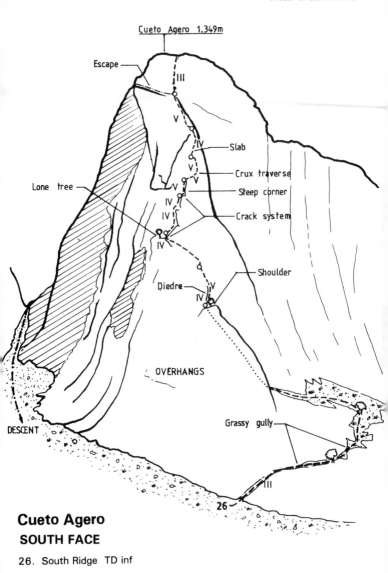

Cueto Agero 1,349m

Escape

III

V

IV — Slab

V

V — Crux traverse

Lone tree

V — Steep corner

IV

IV — Crack system

IV

Diedre

IV — Shoulder

IV

OVERHANGS

Grassy gully

DESCENT

III

26

Cueto Agero
SOUTH FACE

26. South Ridge TD inf

57

27 Bejas and La Hermida

This is a walk which is full of history, starting in Lebeña, with its tiny Mozarabe church, and ending in La Hermida, not far from the relatively recent, though now deserted spa. The walk is straightforward, and if the newly-made farm tracks distract slightly from the first part, this is more than compensated for during the second. Grade A, 900m of ascent and 1,000m of descent, 4½-5½h. Map: Adrados, 1:75,000.

Start near Lebeña at the 'Bar el Desfiladero' on the main Potes road. Be sure to visit the nearby 10th-century church with its curious mixture of Byzantine and Latin styles, and having done this, take the road opposite the bar and go up to Allende, picking up a track that crosses fields beyond the village, and following it to the obvious col to the L of the huge walls that dominate the valley (1h). From the col go past an attractive walled meadow, then an atrocious, low shed, from where the broad Cdo de Pelea is soon gained, along with good views of Beges and the way ahead (30-40 min).

From the col descend NW to the cabins of the Invernales de Panizales, then follow the track to Beges (35-45 min). The village has two parts, 'La Quintana' being the smaller one off to the R. 'La Aldea' lies on the track which connects the Andara cirque to the gorge. The track, a masterpiece of engineering, was built during the middle of the last century for the ox-carts which brought down the zinc ore from the mines. Once in La Hermida the ore was taken to Unquera for export to Belgium, Germany and England. The industry collapsed in 1929, in Picos as elsewhere, when Canada flooded the international markets with ore at much lower prices.

Follow the track up to the last houses in the village, then leave it for a path which goes up beneath the cliff immediately N of Beges. The path then makes its way up this barrier in spectacular positions, coming out at meadows that run along NE above the cliff (30-40 min). Follow a faint path as it goes from cabin to cabin, offering good views in all directions. Eventually a broad grassy col is reached (Cdo de Osina – 1h) to the R of an inaccessible crag. The col provides views E to the La Hermida gorge, and W to the remarkable path from Tresivso (hidden off L) to Urdón. From the col drop down through fields to a cabin on the L (6-7 min). From here a good track, cobbled in places and claimed by some to be of Roman origin, leads comfortably down to La Hermida (25-35 min).

28 Tour of the Eastern Massif (2 days)

This very complete outing, though possible in a single long day, is only flavoured to the full by including the overnight stop, for which a lightweight tent or bivi gear could be carried. The approach up the Canal de los Arredondas is long and hard, and so is best avoided during very hot weather, the same being true to a lesser extent of the descent. However, few people will be met during the tour as the Eastern Massif is not popular. Moreover, the views the massif offers and the sensation of solitude, along with the chance to explore some of the old mines, make this a memorable trip. Grade C – Day 1: 1,500m of ascent to bivouac, 4-5h. Day 2: Approx. 600m of ascent and 2,100m of descent, 8-9h. Map: GH Editores, 1:50,000.

Start in the village of Lon, where a good track leads N out of the village, staying to the R of the River Burón at first, then crossing it to come out later at a grassy esplanade with views of the Canal de los Arredondas and the long haul ahead (1¼-1½h). This area is known as Los Navarres, the platform having once been the site of mines buildings. The route now follows the old track that was used to bring down the zinc ore, and a thought might be spared as to just what was involved in driving ox carts up and down such terrain.

A short way above the platform cross to the true L bank of the river to pick up the old track. After some 30-40 min., swing off L to a grassy shoulder, then break back R, crossing steep, trackless ground for 30m, before scrambling up broken slabs to regain the main gully. Higher up this trackless section this is split by a rock buttress, the L fork being followed to the top of a promontory (30-40 min). Follow the old track again, the blank wall of the Silla del Caballo appearing on the L after half an hour. When more or less level with the base of this, a small platform is reached in front of an isolated mine entrance (1¼-1½h). Water can be found dripping from the roof some 40m inside the mine. At the end of the main tunnel lies a vertical shaft which provides a vivid insight into how the ore was extracted. The bivi site, the small platform, gives spectacular views of Potes and the Liebana area.

Day 2 begins with a 30-minute haul up to the col to the NW of La Rasa (2285m). Leaving the sacks here, scramble W below a minor summit to a second col. A track climbs away SW here, first L of a ridge, then R, before switching back L again to come out onto level ground which leads to views of the Jou del Jierru. This cirque, formed by the Pica del Jierru (2426m), Morra de Lechugales (2441m) and Silla del Caballo (2433m), also witnessed important mining operations. Red paint marks indicate the route along its N side to the summit of the Pica del Jierru ('jierru' refers to the slippery, tough grass that manages to survive hereabouts) and splendid views of the Central Massif (30-40 min. from sacks).

The highest summit in the massif, the Morra de Lechugales involves a short step of II- to gain the summit block. Walkers, then, will now return to their sacks, whilst those who wish to will descend easy ground S, following the ridge and red paint marks down and along the foot of the walls of the 3 minor summits of the Picos del Jierru. Abandoning the paint marks, gain a shoulder immediately E of the third summit, then swing round to the R (W) side of the main ridge to pick up a horizontal ledge which leads airily to a gap immediately N of the final summit block. Climb this by twin cracks on the R (25-30 min. from the Pica del Jierru).

Return to the narrow col just E of the 3rd minor summit and pick up the red paint marks again. They lead along a sharp ridge to the summit of the Silla del Caballo with one hard step down (I+; 10-15 min. from col). The name means 'horse saddle' and refers to the shape of the mountain as seen from the valley. To return to the sacks, double back to the first gap W of the summit, then descend diag. R down screes into the bed of the Jou del Jierru. Here an old track leads with 2 awkward steps (II) to the track from the col below La Rasa. This round trip needs 3-3½h.

The next section begins by traversing on a vague path below the SW walls of La Rasa to the col to its S (15 min). Now follow the ridge SE to gain the summit of the Pico de los Llambriales Amarillos (2261m) and superb views of the lower half of the Canal de los Arredondas (15 min). Leave the summit and follow the ridge E, taking in the Pico de San Carlos (marked 'Pico del Sagrado Corazón') if so desired. The Cdo de San Carlos, and the beginning of the long descent, is reached shortly afterwards (45 min).

The descent is steep at first, and the ground trackless. After some 45 minutes, however, the attractive Mda de Trulledes is reached, water being available in a small cubical construction opposite a highly unsightly concrete hut. From Trulledes a wide track leads down into oak woods, a promontory being reached after a further 35-40 minutes. The main track swings L, but a minor track is followed down R. At a T-junction go R again, and some 10 minutes later take a L fork which descends through woods to Argüébanes, and the end of a long day (2-2½h from the Cdo de San Carlos).

29 La Ruta de los Pueblos

Both sides of the Liebana valley are dotted with small villages. This reasonably gentle walk takes advantage of the tracks and paths connecting the settlements on the north side of the valley and, with the exception of the section between Argüébanes and Lon, travels over fairly level ground. Apart from the chance to visit these delightful villages, the outing provides excellent views of both the valley and the walls of the Eastern Massif. Moreover, the route can be lengthened or shortened at will. Grade A, 300m of ascent. Allow 2½h from Argüébanes to Brez, and another 2--2½h to reach Los Llanos. Map: GH Editores, 1:50,000. (No map currently available shows the tracks of this area correctly, but the contours on the GH map help general orientation.)

Follow the tarmac road into Argüébanes. The road narrows to a single track which divides shortly after. Take the L fork, and after 100m cross a bridge to pick up a wide track. Follow this for a couple of hundred yards until a smaller one drops away L. Take it and wind through woods before coming out above meadows. Go L at a junction to stay above the meadows and enter pine woods which are left on reaching an open grassy col (between pts 815 and 750 on the map). Descend W. cross a meadow and pick up a good track which meanders down to Lon 1½h).

In Lon cross a bridge and leave by the church, descending a little at first before climbing up through open meadows to Brez (1h). The village is famous for its smoked cheese, originally made in the Puertos de Aliva

and sold here, but now made in the village as well, though by strictly traditional methods. Smoke percolating through the tiles of small sheds indicates that cheese is being cured. For most people Brez, with its cobbled streets, is the most attractive village of the route.

Taken together, the above three villages make a very pleasant afternoon walk for most people, but those who wish can easily continue along the recently constructed road to Tanarrio. Here it is necessary to cross fields to reach Redo where another road is joined. This leads first to Mogrovejo and then Los Llanos del Rey.

30   Ascent of Pico Jano   1446m

This is the first in a series of ascents included in this guide to summits which lie outside the strict confines of the Picos, but which provide us with views which allow us to complete our knowledge of the range. This first ascent, although to a summit of quite modest altitude, rewards us with superb views of the Eastern and Central massifs, as well as of the whole Liébana area. Grade B, 900m of ascent, 4-5h. Map: Adrados, 1:75,000.

To the L of the main road, just S of the bridge at Los Llanos, lies the village of Bárcena. Go through the village and pick up a track which swings sharp L almost immediately and begins a sequence of steep zig-zags which end when the track levels out and goes R round a broad spur (15-20 min; ignore minor track off R at spur). Follow the track as it enters a valley, rounds a second, smaller spur, then rises up a second valley and enters an isolated meadow below a characteristic black slab (25-30 min). Cross the meadow and go up through the wood (faint track) until a major horizontal track is met. Go L along this to a col (15min). The track doubles back on itself and climbs a broad, wooded spur to a meadow. Soon after a second meadow is reached (30 min) with a track going off horizontally from the far R corner. This leads without difficulty to a broad col to the NE of the Jano summit (15-20 min), which is reached in a further 10 minutes. The minor N summit boasts the remains of an old mine.

The return is by the same route, although those who can may wish to make the ascent from Dobarganes, the village to the SSE of the mountain (see Adrados map), to make a complete crossing.

31   Pido – Cosgaya: forest walk

A straightforward walk along a fairly level track, but one which provides superb views of the villages in the upper Liébana valley and, in particular, of the walls around Fuente Dé. Grade A, 50m of ascent and 300m of descent, 12km. Map: Adrados, 1:75,000.

1½km below Fuente Dé the main road makes a long sweep L and a small track branches off R. The track leads S at first, then swings E, this section offering the best views of the Fuente Dé area. Next the path passes above Pido, then climbs a little to offer good views of the Pico Valdecoro and the course of the River Nevandi as it drops down from

An afternoon shower clearing off El Naranjo, viewed from the Mda de Camburero (Routes 12, 58, 168).

Aliva. The track levels out now and then enters deciduous woods where one's attention is given not to the views, but to the immediate surroundings, although a clearing in the trees just before two tight hairpins yields a delightful (and little known) view of Las Ilces. Half a kilometre later a cabin is passed as the track negotiates a gully. A path dropping down L here leads to Las Ilces, whilst a second track (not correctly marked) stays level for several kms before descending sharply to Puente Nueva, just before Cosgaya, where the restaurant of the Hotel del Oso provides a fitting end to the excursion.

32   Ascent of Coriscao   2234m

This is the second of the summits outside the range that have been chosen because of the perspective they offer of the Picos. The summit of the Coriscao provides superb views not only of the Central and Eastern massifs, but also of the Cordillera Cantábrica. The normal ascent is made from the Cdo de Llesba (see Adrados 1:75,000 map) but requires transport. The route given here, whilst involving a greater height gain, starts near Fuente Dé and, overall, is more satisfying. Grade B, 1,200m of ascent, 6-7h. Map: Adrados, 1:75,000.

Start as for the last route, but when the track swings E (large low cabin on the L), break off R (S) to follow a good track up the true R bank of the Rio Canalejas. After some 2-2½h in the woods, an open area is reached with an old cabin. This area and that above it form a series of stepped glacial cirques known as Salvorón. In the second step there is a small tarn. Go up the bed of the cirque to gain the NW Spur of the Coriscao, which is followed SE to the summit (3½-4½h from the road).

The return can be made by the same route, or by descending the N Spur until above the old cabin in the first clearing. Descend to this and so join the track back through the woods. 2-2½h should be sufficient for the descent.

33   Tour of the Peña Remoña group

A classic walk despite the hard work involved in climbing the Tornos de Liordes. Some varied scenery and the chance to visit one of the most beautiful vegas in the Picos. Grade B, 950m of ascent, 4-5h. Map: Adrados, 1:25,000.

Cross the field behind the Parador and pick up the track which, with its 38 unforgiving hairpins, climbs the Canal del Embudo in impressive positions beneath the south walls of La Padiorna. The torture ends with the sudden but memorable arrival in the Vega de Liordes (2-2½h, spring), which is crossed to a small cabin below the Torre de Salinas. A welcome rest will give time to observe the many rebecos that can often be seen in the vega. Climbing S to the Cdo. de Remoña (the ascent of the Torre de Salinas is now possible – see Route 88), the path is followed down on the R of the Canal de Pedabejo, a short section of scrambling leading to easier ground. Continue to descend SE to pass the Mda de Pedabejo and pick up the jeep track that leads E back down to Fuente Dé.

This route can be taken in the opposite direction. This alleviates the long haul up the Tornos de Liordes, but removes some of the drama of the arrival in Vega Liordes. Another variation would be to follow Route 85 to La Padiorna, then descend into Liordes.

34 The Collado de Valdecoro and the Canal de la Jenduda
This unusual outing explores the huge back wall of the Fuente Dé cirque, taking advantage during the ascent of what is thought to be one of the oldest paths in the range, and descending down what must surely be one of the most spectacular gullies. As an alternative to the téléphérique for those who simply wish to visit Aliva, it has a lot to recommend it. Grade C, 800m of ascent, 4-5h. Map: Adrados, 1:25,000.

Follow Route 1, staying on the main path to pass below the téléphérique cables. An old cabin is reached by the workings of the old El Buitrón mine (1h). Once past the mine the path deteriorates, and it becomes necessary to scramble up steep, grassy slopes to come out level with, and a short way to the left of, the Cdo de Valdecoro (1778m). Traverse across to this and turn to admire the views of Fuente Dé, views seldom seen even by local mountaineers.

From the col a good path rises gently NE to the Collado de la Juciana (1858m – 'juciana' = gentian) and views of Aliva (1h). By working NW over pathless but easy terrain the Cdo de Covarrobres is reached (30 min). Follow the jeep track down towards the cable car, but at the first L bend leave it and head W to reach the top of the Canal de la Jenduda (15-20 min). Descend this to Fuente Dé (1½-2h. See Route 1 for details).

VALDEON

With the exception of the descent of the Cares Gorge, walking in the Valdeón area is about going up into the high mountains. Long ascents up steep gullies, most of which have been of great importance in the past to the shepherds, characterise these routes, which in general are more exacting than those of the Liébana district. The perfect location of the valley allows us to choose freely between the Central or Western massifs, whilst the ascent of the Gildar provides a more complete picture of the area.

35 Tour of the Torre del Friero group
The summit of the Torre del Friero draws one's attention from many places in the Valdeón area, and particularly from Soto. It is hardly surprising, then, that this was the mountain the Casiano de Prado climbed in the mistaken belief that it was the highest summit in the range. This circular tour offers us a chance to explore the Friero group and, as is the case with all the walks that begin and end in the valley, takes us through a variety of scenery. Grade C, 1,220m of ascent. 5-6h. Map: Adrados, 1:25,000.

From Posada walk down the road to Cordiñanes (30min), from where a small path (hard to find) climbs up to and then traverses below the walls that dominate the village to the NE (see Route 6). The path now traverses in impressive positions above the Riega de Asotín to gain the Vega de Asotín (2h). This is the base for winter ascents of the great northern gullies of the Torre del Friero, and it is below these that the path now continues, entering the narrowest section of the Canal de Asotín.

When the gully opens out again branch off SE (main path bears away L), then work back SW to cross the spur which descends from the Torre del Hoyo Chico (no path), thus gaining the easy, open slopes that lead to the Cdo de Chavida (2160m; 1¼-1½h). It is possible to climb the Torre del Friero from here – see Route 91.

When ready, descend S down the stony Canal de la Chavida, passing the only reliable spring the route offers at the Mda de Chavida. From here Posada is clearly seen and quickly reached (1¾-2h).

36 Ascent of the Gildar (2078m)

As with Routes 30 and 32, the ascent of the Gildar takes us out of the wood to let us see the trees – in this case the SW quarter of the Central Massif, and the Bermeja group. The route described begins at the Panderruedas col, and is a pleasant walk to a summit that is seldom visited, but which gives ample rewards for a relatively easy day. Grade B, 630m of ascent, 5h. Map: Adrados, 1:75,000.

From the car park at Panderruedas a track goes off SE, with another branching off R immediately over grassy slopes. Take this and enter beech woods, the track becoming a path as it rises gently up a broad spur. At one point the path becomes vague, but is located a few metres on to the R side of the spur, along which it continues to rise until the wood is left behind for broom and heather slopes (35 min).

Staying below the spur, continue into a cwm, eventually gaining the well-used col at the back L of the cirque, with good views now of the Gildar. Leave the path and climb up on to the ridge to the R of the col, following it throughout to a second col below Peña Cebolleda, the traverse of which involves airy scrambling over an exposed, narrow ridge (avoidable by traversing below the NW walls of the peak). The Gildar is quickly reached from the Cebolleda/Gildar col (2½h).

After deciphering the views from the Gildar, descend E, crossing a long, flat col until it is possible to descend an awkward talus slope into the upper cwm of the Arroyo de Cable valley. A path leads NW out of the flat, grassy cwm bed, then works back R to cross a stream by a small hut (45 min). Leave the hut (path vague) on the R bank of the stream and cross hay fields to pick up a track which descends into woods to a major jeep track (35 min). Turning L leads back to Panderruedas in about an hour. Alternatively, go R, dropping down on a footpath leading to Soto just before the track ends.

37   Tour of the Bermeja group
A full but satisfying day which includes a visit to Vega Huerta. The ascent of the Canal de Capozo is steep, but it is sheltered from the worst of the sun and offers unusual views of both the Central Massif and Peña Santa de Castilla. Grade C, 1,400m of ascent. 7-8h. Map: GH Editores, 1:50,000 (though the Adrados, 1:75,000 map is better over the section from the Chozo de Llós).

From the campsite at Soto de Valdeón walk down to Cordiñanes and the Mirador del Tombo just beyond the village (1h). Locate a path that goes off N from the road some 100m above the monument and follow this above and then in beech woods to a small footbridge and water (30 min). Continue along the path until a section cut into the rock signals the start of a hard climb through woods to a rest below a striped wall (30 min). The woods are left behind for more climbing up hazel covered slopes, the path levelling out and finally entering the gully proper as Peña Santa is glimpsed for the first time (1h).

Cross the gully bed and climb out steeply R immediately. After a while the path levels out and the great South Face of Peña Santa comes into view, though the col (and a well-earned rest) are still some 30 minutes away. It is best to approach the col via a dominant white slab below and R of two large cairns seen on the horizon.

Leave Vega Huerta on the path heading SW below Pt. 1930 on the GH map. Cairns and paintmarks indicate the way S to the Collado del Burro, from where the route descends the broad Canal del Perro, swings L below the walls of Los Moledizos, and drops down to the grassy El Frade col (1¼h). Contour E from here to a grassy shoulder clearly visible from El Frade. Beyond the shoulder drop down to an area of high pasture with two large boulders, one of which protects a small hut. Leave the hut heading E, crossing a stream to immediately pick up a good track at the beginning of woods. In an hour the track reaches Caldevilla, Soto being some 10 minutes further on.

38   Tour of the Palanca group
This two-day tour passes through some of the highest and wildest terrain in the Picos de Europa, the second day being especially long if transport back up the Cares from Caín can not be arranged. The descent of the Hoyo Grande and the Canal de Dobresengos passes over some difficult and trackless ground, and care is needed to find the best route. Grade D – Day 1: 1,200m of ascent, 5h. Day 2: 460m of ascent and 2,000m of descent, 6-7h. Map: Adrados, 1:25,000.

Follow Route 6 from Cordiñanes as far as the Vega de Asotín, then continue up the Canal de Asotín to gain the Cdo de la Padiorna overlooking the Vega de Liordes (3h). From the col follow Route 4 to the Cdo Jermoso hut (1½-2h).

From the hut follow Route 7 to Cda Blanca (2h), then continue N into the Hoyo Grande Cimero (30 min). Cross this and then the Hoyo Grande Bajero and so enter the Canal de Dobresnengos. At first this is reasonably wide, but later it becomes much narrower, at which point it is important to descend diagonally L, looking for a very narrow, N-facing gully which gives access to a small majada with a spring. From the majada a vague path leads down towards the Cares, but by staying up on the L bank towards the bottom it is possible to cross a rocky spur and gain Caín without descending all the way to the river (3-4h from the Hoyo Grande Cimero).

39 Descent of the Cares Gorge
This is undoubtedly the most popular walk in the Picos de Europa, the combination of a relatively level, graded path and magnificent scenery attracting thousands of people each year. By making the descent mid-week and/or in overcast weather, the worst of the crowds can be avoided. Late May is perhaps the ideal time to visit, the vegetation being at its best then. Whatever the crowds and whatever the weather, the Cares Gorge should come high on anybody's list of priorities. Grade A, 700m, 5-6h. Map: Adrados, 1:25,000.

From Posada follow the road past Cordiñanes to Caín. After the steep descent beyond the Mirador del Tombo, a popular viewpoint, be on the lookout for Chorco de los Lobos and the Ermita de Corona. The first is an ancient wolf pit recently restored, and the second a small chapel on the spot where Pelayo was crowned by his soldiers (see General History). The road now enters the first section of the gorge, coming out quite suddenly at Caín (1½-2h), a village which has seen many changes since the arrival of the car, though the National Park authorities are now working to eliminate those which have proved detrimental. This first section can be covered by car, though the approach on foot is more in keeping with the day.

Leaving Caín, cross the river by a small dam and enter a series of tunnels to come out in the gorge proper. The dam serves the aqueduct which runs parallel to the path until near Poncebos, where the water feeds into a small hydroelectric plant before continuing to a second plant in Arenas de Cabrales. The footpath was cut into the rock in the 40s by the 'Electra del Viesgo' company, although the hydroelectric scheme itself dates from the early 20s.

The Cares is crossed twice by metal bridges, first by that of Los Rebecos, the scene of countless photographs, and shortly after by the Puente Bolín. The canal de Trea joins the gorge path here, and a short scramble up the path provides good views of the route ahead.

If this first section of the gorge impresses because of the sheerness of the walls, it is the second half, when the gorge begins to open up, that reveals the true magnitude of the canyon. Passing Culiembro and La Viña, the path now makes what for many day-trippers is an agonising climb up Los Collados, with the enormous Murallón de Amuesa, a 1,200m rock wall, keeping us company on the other side of the gorge. A final sudden descent brings us to Poncebos, and a welcome drink if the weather has been at all hot.

VEGABAÑO

Although difficult to get to without private transport, the Vegabaño area offers a small number of fine walks and the chance to camp in the attractive meadows which give the area its name. The walks here vary from simple outings such as that to the Pico Jario, to hard and problematical routes such as the ascent of the Torre Bermeja. All of the routes pass through the extensive beech woods which cover the area, and this gives them a special appeal, whilst in Routes 40 and 41 the transition from grassy meadows amidst dense forests to the stark, grey mountain limestone, is particularly striking.

40 Ascent of Peña Bermeja   2400m

Peña Bermeja, the highest summit in the Bermeja sub-massif, offers splendid views of the Cordillera Cantábrica, Valdeón and the whole of the South Face of Peña Santa de Castilla. Indeed, it was after seeing Peña Santa from the summit of Peña Bermeja that Saint-Saud resolved to return to climb it. The ascent involves some simple scrambling in the final gully, and requires a certain degree of experience if the descent described is to be followed without problems, though both parts of the outing are considered part of a classic Picos day, one which can also be tackled from Valdeón. Grade B (C if the alternative descent is undertaken), 1,100m of ascent, 5-6h. Map: GH Editores, 1:50,000; Adrados, 1:75,000.

Follow Route 23 to the Cdo del Burro (2-2½h). Now rise gently SE up the broad spur descending from the Moledizos-Bermeja ridge. Stay to the L side of the spur looking for the opportunity to leave it about two-thirds of the way up, and to cross uneven ground E staying below the walls of the Bermeja ridge. Scramble up the fourth (heading E) of the gullies on the R and so gain the ridge itself, which is followed without difficulty to the summit (1h).

The descent can be made by the same route (2½-3h). Alternatively, descend into the Hoyos Llorosos which lie to the SE of the summit. Go down the stoneshoot of the Canal del Bufón (not marked on either map – *bufón* refers to a huge cave that creates a whooshing sound in windy weather). At the bottom of the gully (25 min. from summit) go up R (W) to the Cdo Verde (10 min). Traverse W crossing a small gap (scrambling). Eventually, close to the Hda del Frade, three grassy shoulders are reached, one on top of the other and separated by rock walls. Take the middle shoulder and so gain and descend steep, awkward screes to join Route 23 at the Hda del Frade (1½-2h).

For those based in Valdeón Route 24 can be followed to El Frade where the present route is joined. The descent can then be made via the Canal del Bufón, at the bottom of which turn L (E) and gain the grassy Cdo de Pambuches from where the descent E and then S to Valdeón is evident (well-marked on Adrados map; allow 7-8h).

41   Vega Huerta and Valdecarombo

A long but memorable walk which takes in one of the most attractive approaches in the Picos (that to Vega Huerta) and combines it with a hard descent down the trackless Valdecarombo. The outing also permits those with sufficient energy to tackle the summit of La Bermeja and/or Los Moledizos. Grade C, 1100m of ascent, 5-6h. (1400m, 7-8h if Bermeja included). Map: GH Editores, 1:50,000.

Follow Route 23 to the Cdo del Burro (2-2½h), then continue along the same route to Vega Huerta and a well-earned rest (30 min). When ready leave heading W, then trend SW to enter a long, narrow hoyo with a path along the L side. This leads to a small col beneath the Punta Extremero (Pt 2150 on the map; 30 min. Do not follow the main La Duernona hoyo NW). Descend over difficult, trackless ground to enter a stony, V-shaped valley which is followed until it narrows and deepens. A junction is reached where the gully drops away steeply L and a path goes off R (cairn – 1h). Go down the gully, but when this situation repeats itself lower down, go off R over a col to gain grassy slopes, the gully being a dead-end. Descent to cabins on the L and then on to a bridge over the R Dobra (25min). Cross this and climb a broad, wooded valley to pick up a jeep track which swings SW around the summit of La Cotarra to enter Vegabaño (30 min).

42   Ascent of Pico Jario   1910m

A short and straightforward ascent to an apparently insignificant summit which turns out to be a remarkably good viewpoint for the SW sectors of the Western and Central massifs, as well as for a large part of the Cordillera Cantábrica. Very much an outing in the style of Routes 30 and 36, and a classic of the Picos. Grade B, 600m of ascent, 4h. Map: GH Editores, 1:50,000.

Start behind the Vegabaño hut (incorrectly marked) and cross the stream then a meadow to join a jeep track at the point where a muddy minor track goes up SW. Take this for 50m to a junction, then follow the R fork and go up the true R bank of the Valdelafuente stream. After several hairpins the track bears left and levels out. Follow it, and when it dies out go up the broad spur on the R, coming out of the woods at a meadow with good views of the route ahead (30mins).

Cross to a small copse and so continue up the spur. When the trees die out make for the broad col to the R of the Jario summit. This provides unexpected views S and SW, a further 15 min. being sufficient to reach the summit itself (1¼-1½h from Vegabaño).

From the summit descend E (difficult) to a col and then gain the next summit E. The descent from this by the crest involves three difficult steps, all of which can be avoided on the L. From a narrow grassy col (15-20 min) avoid the next summit on the R, and the one beyond that by rocky ground on the L. A short stretch of crest ends at another col below the Pica Samaya which is easily climbed and proves rewarding (15min).

Descend to the NNW then pass E below the summit walls to gain a col crossed by several paths (10 min). Go down NE to the Puerto de Dobres col (1-1¼h from Jario).

From the col descend L to a stream. Cross this and pick up a good, but partially hidden path that enters the woods and leads back to Vegabaño without further complications (45 mins).

43 The Senda del Arcediano and the Upper Dobra

The Senda del Arcediano was built in the 17th century at the initiative and expense of Pedro Díaz de Oseja, the Arcediano (= religious dignitary) of Villaviciosa in Asturias. The track, which followed the route of an old Roman road, linked the east of Asturias with Castilla, the road through the Desfiladero de los Beyos being a recent affair. Historically important, the Senda passes through some very beautiful surroundings, which makes it all the more sad that the tiny hydro-electric power station in Amieva has been allowed to place posts so close to certain parts of the path. For many local mountaineers the descent to Amieva is a classic outing. Combined with the return to Vegabaño via the upper reaches of the Dobra, as is done here, the outing becomes a full, but rewarding day. Grade B, 800m of ascent, 7-8h. Map: GH Editores, 1:50,000.

Start at the point where the track from Soto de Sajambre first enters Vegabaño. Facing the meadow (E) strike off L into the wood, passing a low, grey-roofed hut and keeping NNE to connect with a good track after some 50m. Follow this NW through the woods to the col due W of the summit of La Cotorra, where a smaller track goes off NW through a clearing which offers views of Peña Beza, the main track dropping away R (15 mins).

After 10 mins the track reaches a clearing and dies out and a small path is picked up. This begins to drop down W. Follow it past scattered cabins, heading W to join the Senda del Arcediano, the wide track visible to the W from just beyond the clearing (20 min). Follow the track as it climbs up and round the W of Pt 1590 (ignore GH map), before heading NE to a drinking trough (1h).

The path climbs to a gated wall, then descends to the Toneyo majada. Shortly after Toneyo a col is reached with ample views of the Ordiales-Cotalbín chain (30 min). From here the path, often cobbled, descends to Angón in fine positions, first above the River Toneyo, and later high above the River Dobra, the unmetalled road from Amieva to the hydro-electric plant being joined at El Cuetu (810m).

Follow the road to the plant (40mins) then cross the river to enter the National Park. A good track rises gently at first by the true R bank of the Dobra, then more steeply through wooded slopes to come out at a small clearing (Bellanzo) which allows us to look back over the Dobra at the route we have followed earlier (1h). The track ends soon after at the workings for the Jocica dam, where a small, exposed path contours above the dam, later going in and out of woods until it eventually drops down and crosses the Dobra (1-1¼h). This is the wildest part of the whole route, and the memorial plaque halfway along this section is a reminder of the need to take care here.

The last section of the route follows the true L bank of the river until level with Valdecarombo (no continuous path; approx 30 min). Once here (it is tempting to strike off R too soon) follow Route 41 back to Vegabaño (40-50 mins).

GÜEÑA VALLEY

The great attraction of the walks based on the Güeña Valley is the way in which they bring out the relationship between the valley and the mountains, providing at the same time a good opportunity to come into contact with some of the varied flora and fauna detailed in the first chapter. Moreover, due to the geology of the Picos the routes, in the main, approach the heights over relatively gentle slopes and pastures. Sudden and surprising views of the massifs to the south are typical of these outings, which make use of the ancient paths connecting the villages to the summer pastures, and which in some cases are still used.

44 Covadonga and the Vega de Orandi
The visit to Orandi is a classic outing for local mountaineers, though many of them are quickly tempted back to the restaurants in the valley, and so do not get to see the unusual views of the Torre de Santa María that the second half of this walk offers. At Fana Route 49 can be joined, the combination making a very attractive route between Covadonga and the Vega de Enol. Grade B, 750m of ascent, 5-6h. Map: GH Editores, 1:50,000 or Adrados, 1:75,000.

Immediately after the start of the road from Covadonga to Los Lagos, a path strikes up through the wood to come out at the Colladín de Orandi (650m). This is the point where the River Mestas disappears into a huge cave, to re-appear later in Covadonga.

Now follow the valley, first S then SE, the path climbing up through deciduous woods before coming out at a col with excellent views of the high peaks of the Western Massif (2-2½h).

Head E to a second col just S of Pt 1050 (GH map) and so descend to Fana (940m). Pass the ruined forestry house and pick up the track that leads to the road to the lakes. Follow this N, but as soon as possible break off E to enter the Vega de Comeya (1-1½h). In Comeya pick up the old track and follow it NW out of the vega and down to the road (40 min), from where just over an hour's walking should be sufficient to reach Covadonga again.

The final section can be avoided by following the ridge which runs NW from where the road is joined to the Cruz de Priena (725m). This adds another, 1-1½h to the total time, but offers good views of Covadonga and a more satisfying end to the outing. To do this, go down the road some 800m to pick up a path (the Camino Molledo) which goes off R by cabins. The path gains height to reach the Mda de Tarañodiós, where it crosses to the N side of the ridge, and continues essentially NW, descending past Pts 701 and 722 (GH map) to the col immediately SW of the Priena summit. A track descends from the summit to Covadonga.

45 Vega Comeya from Gamonedo

A circular walk, beginning in the attractive village of Gamonedo, and covering a wide variety of terrain, as well as providing unexpected views of the Western Massif. A very good outing for an easier day, or for when poorer weather makes the high summits an uninviting proposition. Grade B, 600m of ascent, 5-6h. Map: Adrados, 1:75,000 or GH Editores, 1:50,000.

From the last hairpin before the village of Gamonedo (car or taxi from Mestas de Con), walk up the road until the water deposit, a small concrete building just off the road to the L, marks the start of a muddy path between fields. Take the path, and follow it round below a white rock bluff to a fountain (20 min), from where a narrow path rises gently across the hillside, then climbs steeply up a small burn (faint in places) to join a better path. The new path climbs gently L across the hillside, always below the summit of the Canto el Utre, to gain a broad col with views of the immense Vega Comeya, and, in the distance, the central summits of the Western Massif (1¼h). From the col, drop down into the vega and explore the valley flora and fauna.

A waterfall by the remains of the old mines indicates the way. Scramble up to the L of it until, when all seems lost, a man-made path leads us through a small tunnel. After the tunnel either follow the stream bed to the Lago Enol, or break away from the stream, following first a faint path above a small cave, then an old track, to reach the Bufarrera mines (2½-3h from Gamonedo).

From the N end of the Lago Ercina head E, cross a broad col and pick up the track that descends E to the Mda de Belbín which is left going NE over a grassy spur (20mins). Just beyond the spur bear NNE across a series of small meadows which lead to a wide cobbled path. This is the 'camino real' (Royal way) along which the shepherds of the Gamonedo area have gone back and forth for centuries to their summer pastures in the Ario/Vega Maor sector of the massif. The path climbs at first, then levels out as it swings around the W side of the shapely Cantón del Texu; 15 mins.

To the NE of the Cantón del Texu lies a broad col called Soñín de Abajo. Gain this, with good views across Vega Comeya en route, and then rise gently NW to a second col (30 mins), from where the path leads easily down open ground at first, then through a holly and beech wood to a broad, muddy col (drinking trough) with good views across to the Canto el Utre, and the path taken earlier in the day (45 min). Drop down now on a wide path, cobbled at times, to enter a beech wood, then descend with zig-zags to a small wooden bridge (45 min). From here the path winds up to come out of the wood near a small chapel (below R), the village being reached shortly after (1¾-2h from Soñín de Abajo).

46 The Cabeza de Pandescura and the River Casaño

A walk that is seldom undertaken, but one which allows us to explore the upper reaches of the River Casaño, having first contemplated them from the summit of the Cabeza Pandescura (1001m). If the first section of the walk is straightforward, the descent into the Casaño is anything but. The ground is steep and pathless, giving the outing a sense of adventure. Grade C, 500m of ascent and 700m of descent, 4-5h. Map: Adrados, 1:75,000.

Start from the village of Demués (4km from Benia; taxi), taking a track which rises gently L amongst the first houses encountered on entering the village. The track levels out and passes an old chapel. After 250m take a smaller track that climbs steeply L to a false col (Cdo de la Veguina; 35-45 min). A few more minutes' climbing up a broad spur leads past a drinking trough to a col with two cabins and excellent views of the Western Massif (Las Cabezas on map). Now follow the main spur to a point just below the W walls of the Cabeza de Pandescura. From an obvious gap scramble up L to the summit (1h).

Back at the gap, descend SW to a cabin by a stone wall. Go past this, then descend to a col with woods and the Casaño to the L (30 min). Follow a track which contours through the wood above the river gorge to end at a rocky promontory. A path continues now, but when this too dies out descend steeply through the wood to join the river at a simple tree-trunk bridge (35-45 min).

It is possible to follow the river by its R bank now, but the path is vague and the undergrowth thick, so climb out from the riverbed and gain a man-made path cut into the rock some 50m above. The path dates from the construction of a small hydroelectric plant further downstream. After some 15 minutes the way is blocked, so drop back to the valley floor where a good path leads downstream, crossing to the L bank, going past the power station ruins, then, at Santianes, crossing back to the R bank via a rustic, gated bridge. Circular, stone enclosures for storing chestnuts can be seen near the cabins here, whilst on the R, just after the bridge, stand a number of small, stone shelters called 'cubiles', which once housed pigs (1¼-1½h from simple bridge).

After some 15 min, the path arrives at a narrowing, with the river resounding ominously in the depths of a short, deep canyon. Cross the river and take a cobbled path up L to the village of La Molina, where a good track climbs to Ortiguero (40-50 min).

47 Ascent of the Hibeo 870m

As with the ascent of the Torbina (see Route 54) this simple walk allows us to survey the complexities of the northern side of the Picos from a vantage point beyond the range. The view of the Western Massif is especially good. Grade A, 650m of ascent and descent, 4-4½h. Map:

Adrados, 1:75,000.

Start in Benia and follow the lane towards Pedroso for some 2km, looking out on the L for a small, painted bridge which crosses the Rio Ayones by a house. This part is possible by car.

Cross the bridge and pass between the house and the river, then head NW towards a small wood. Swing NE on entering the wood and continue NE over fields, with a dominant crest on the L. On reaching two abandoned houses turn NW again, climb onto the broken, limestone crest and follow it N. The final slopes are avoided by a detour first W to join a track from Silviella, then back E to the summit.

Return by the same route or descend SE to the Cuesta de Tebia (756m) and so to the village of Pedroso.

48 Ascent of the Cabezo Llorosos 1792m

Despite its relatively modest altitude, the Cabezo Llorosos (1792m) commands superb views of the Central and Western massifs, as well as of the whole of the Cares Gorge. The route described below saves these views until the very summit of the mountain is reached, at which point the agonies of the long ascent are immediately forgotten. Grade C, 1460m of ascent, 7-9h. Map: GH Editores, 1:50,000 or Adrados, 1:75,000.

From just S of the Altos de Ortiguera (bar/hostal) take the track that descends to La Molina. Staying above the houses, pick up a cobbled path that goes down to the Puente de Pompedro, a small hog-back bridge claimed to be Moorish in origin (45 min).

Cross the bridge and work S up a narrow valley to gain a col just S of the Cuetu Pandu. A good path works up the steep hillside in zig-zags, passing a single shepherd's cabin before the final cobbled section which ends in a small grassy bay. Leave this on the R and so gain open pastures with the summit of Peña Jascal due S (1½-2h).

The Valle Teyeres (GH map only) goes off L (SE) here, its R side being formed from the rock walls of the ridge coming down NW from the Cabeza de las Vacas. Continue S, however, over the grassy spur that descends from these walls, and so gain access to a valley running parallel to the last one. Pass through small majada (Mda de Ceribios – incorrectly marked on the GH map) with a hidden spring on slopes to its R, and follow the valley up and round a small jou. Now aim for the col between the Cabeza de las Vacas and the Cabezo Llorosos, the summit soon being reached by scrambling up S (1½h).

The descent can be made down the same route, and the time given is calculated for this. The Adrados map shows a route to Puente Poncebos via Ondón. This long descent (1570m; 2½-3½h) is tiring but truly rewarding as it yields excellent views of El Naranjo de Bulnes. Taxis and accommodation are available in Poncebos.

ENOL SECTOR

Together with the Fuente Dé area, the Vega de Enol (and the nearby Lago Ercina) is one of the most visited areas of the Picos de Europa. The proximity of Covadonga and the ease of access, coupled with the fact that lakes are few and far between in Northern Spain, accounts for the enormous popularity of the place. The vast majority of visitors, however, are content to wander around near the lakes, without ever getting too far from either their cars or the small bars which are still sadly part of an otherwise superb mountain landscape. It is relatively easy, then, to escape from the crowds, and of the walks given below only that to Ordiales could be said to be popular.

49 The Vega de Comeya and Los Lagos

This walk exemplifies what has been said above about escaping from the crowds, whilst at the same time allowing us to appreciate the impact of three historically important human activities in the Picos: shepherding, mining and tourism. Grade B, 300m of ascent, 5-6h. Map: GH Editores, 1:50,000.

Start at the N end of the Lago Ercina. Climb up E to a broad col then follow a track which descends mainly E to the Mda de Belbín (25 min), still very much a working majada. Leave going NW over a spur, just beyond which swing L (NNE) and follow small meadows to a wide cobbled path (See Route 45). Follow this, taking the L fork when it splits to enter a small jou (20 min). From its N edge descend NE (no real path) to a stream which is followed W into the upper section of the Vega de Comeya. The stream goes underground by a cabin and the path descends into the main section of the vega. This ample, marshy plain is a place of great botanical and geological interest. Home to a number of important plant species, it is also a fine example of a circular depression enlarged by karstification, a process which has proved fundamental in the forming of these mountains. The old buildings and overgrown waste heaps are the product of mining for iron and manganese by English and, later, local companies.

Leave Comeya by its SW corner, climbing up to the road just S of the Cabeza del Elefante (1h), so-named because of a strange, natural arch which gives the rocks the form of an elephant's head. Follow the road S for 100m, then branch off R along a track which leads to Fana. Cross the majada SW staying to the L of the walls to reach a small col dominating the ravine of the Pelabarda (20 min).

Now go down L for 50m then branch off SSW into woods on a narrow, well-used path which eventually comes out of the trees between small hoyos. Go S to a clearing then descend SW into a deep hoyo, from where a valley rises SE to the col between Points 1234m and 1161m on the map (1h, but move off R about halfway up the valley to gain unexpected, but spectacular views of the River Beyera canyon and, in the background, the Torre de Santa María). From the col drop down S and locate a small path that cuts through a problematical rock band and then leads E to the Vega de Enol (25 min).

Leave the vega going S from near the hut. Cross an area of limestone pavement and follow the path as it contours E below the foot of the Pico del Mosquital, swinging NE just before entering the Vega del Bricial, from where it contours to a col at the SW end of the Lago Ercina (25 mins). A further ten minutes is sufficient to return to the starting point, which is a classic example of the more negative aspects of man's presence in the mountains.

50 Ascent of Peña Ruana 1505m

The summit of Peña Ruana seems of little significance alongside the much more spectacular Peña Jascal. Its privileged position above the gorge of the Río Casaño, however, means that it commands fine views over the NW quarter of the Western Massif. The ascent of Peña Ruana, when combined with the subsequent descent to La Molina forms a very satisfying traverse. Grade B, 500m of ascent and 1,200m of descent, 4½-5½h. Map: GH Editores, 1:50,000.

Follow Route 49 to the Mda de Belbín (25 min) and cross the long spur to its E then descend SE, cross the Arroyo la Güelga and turn E to enter the broad pastures of Brañarredonda. Cross these aiming for Pt 1066 (GH map only), then climb ESE up the Valle de Espines (not marked), passing to the S of the Porra Estela to come out at the open meadows of Camplengo (not marked; 1h). Now ascend steadily N to the Mda La Beyuga from where the summit of Peña Ruana is soon reached (40-50 min).

From the summit return to the majada and descend NE into the fittingly named Brañarredonda de Cabrales (30 min). By continuing NE Route 48 is joined and followed down to La Molina (2-2½h).

51 Vega Maor and the Majada de Arnaedo

A pleasant walk, passing through various vegas and majadas of great importance to local shepherds in the past, and which still give a good idea as to what life was like in these summer pastures. The first and final section of the walk follow well-used paths and do not present problems. The section from Ario to Vega Maor is pathless and requires some care. Grade B, 700m of ascent and descent, 5-7h. Map: GH Editores, 1:50,000.

Follow Route 21 to the hut in Ario. The next section follows small cairns and stone arrows on the ground to reach the Pozo de la Cabeza Muxia. Leave the hut and skirt round the NW flanks of the Cabeza Julagua. The cairns, arrows and occasional red paint marks left by cavers lead to a huge cave entrance to the N of the Julagua. Here an animal track is picked up and followed down into Vega Maor.

There is a spring to the SE of the main group of cabins, whilst by the cabins themselves the spoon-shaped remains of an ancient 'bolera', or bowls pitch, can be made out on the ground. Such 'boleras' were a common sight in the major vegas and go some way to indicating their previous level of activity. Upwards of 25 families regularly spent their summers together in places like Vega Maor.

Leave Maor by going round the W side of the hillock to the N of the cabins. As the path begins to rise to the col to the SW of Pt 1482, pass close to an impressive, and apparently bottomless cavern. Cross the col (1430m; excellent views back towards the Central Massif) and drop down to the Arnaedo majada (not marked on the GH map, but SE of Pt 1306; 30-40 min). At least one shepherd can still regularly be found here, and those lucky enough to be able to do so should not hesitate to engage him in conversation.

Skirting round the E of Pt 1306, cross a level, pathless area to locate the path again at the head of a tiny valley which is descended W to a majada with a handful of cabins (La Güelga). Leave this by the course of an irregular stream which leads N, the path being absent. When the stream enters a V-shaped valley, climb out NW to gain and cross a long, N-S running spur, and so enter Belbín (45 min-1h). A good track leaves from the NW corner, passing old mines before rising to a col which brings the Lago Ercina into view (25 min).

52 Vega de Aliseda and Riosecu

A counter route to the last, heading west from Ario instead of east. Though the first part of the route covers well-known ground, the second half ventures deeper and deeper into seldom-visited areas before coming out in a surprising manner close to the Vega de Enol. A rewarding outing, even if the middle section follows poorly defined paths. Grade B, 800m of ascent and descent, 5-7h. Map: GH Editores, 1:50,000.

Follow Route 21 to the orientation table at El Jito (1¾-2h; not marked). It is not necessary to continue to the hut but there is no more guaranteed water for quite some time. From El Jito the route now goes off SW, skirting the NW side of the deep Jou de la Cistra (not named) and then rising steadily to pass close to the Pico Gustuteru to the N (ignore map) and enter the Vega de Aliseda (¾-1h).

Cross Aliseda following a small path and leaving heading SW to climb to the col to the S of the Pico Conjurtao (45 min). The next section covers some fairly remote ground. From the col descend NW and enter the narrow valley head. A small path descends to the valley floor, and this is followed past numerous pools until beech woods are entered (1-1¼h). The path comes and goes, but it is sufficient to follow the river and enjoy the surroundings. The Riosecu is a very attractive valley which even many local people do not know about.

At the very end of the valley, when just above the Vega del Brial, the river bed is abandoned for a muddy gully located some 50m to the L. The gully provides a way down to the Brial, from where the Lago Ercina is reached in a further 15-20 minutes.

53   The Mirador de Ordiales
The visit to Ordiales is one of the most popular outings in the Picos de Europa, partly because of the superb views this natural balcony offers to the S and W, and partly because of the historical significance of the place. The Marquis of Villaviciosa, founder of the Covadonga National Park, is buried at Ordiales in accordance with his own wishes. This is an easy walk along a good path, the hut at Vegarredonda providing midway rest and refreshment for those who feel the need. Grade A, 600m of ascent and descent, 5-6h. Map: GH Editores, 1:50,000.

Follow Route 19 to Vegarredonda (1¼-1½h). The path to Ordiales goes off W from just behind the hut, then climbs up a wide gully (Cuenya Cerrada) before coming out on level ground (Campos de Torga) which is crossed to a point where the path winds back and forth then enters an open grassy area with a disused hut. The viewing platform and the tomb of the Marquis lie at the far end of this meadow (1h).

The inscription on the tombstone reads: *Enamoured of the National Park of the Covadonga Mountains, we would wish to live, die and rest eternally here, but the latter in Ordiales, in the magic world of the rebecos and eagles – there where we knew the joy of the sky and the earth – there where we spent hours in admiration, emotion, dreams and transports of delight – there where we worshipped God in his work as the Supreme Craftsman – there where Nature appeared to us to be truly a temple.*

Return the same route, although the adventurous may wish to try Route 130.

ARENAS/PUENTE PONCEBOS

In marked contrast to the nearby Güeña Valley, this area provides a number of hard walks over rugged terrain. Poncebos stands at a mere 218m above sea-level, so steep ascents and descents are the order of the day as the abruptness of this northern entry to the Central Massif makes itself apparent. Three of the walks given here climb out of the Cares Gorge from Poncebos, one to a maximum height of 2,400m, whilst the ascent of the Torbina, a classic day, is another chance to contemplate the Picos de Europa from beyond the confines of the range.

54   Ascent of the Torbina   1315m
A simple, though fairly steep ascent to a summit which offers exceptional views both north and south due to its privileged position between the Picos and the sea. Most of the walk follows well-used paths and tracks, but because of the trackless nature of the final section the route cannot be recommended in poor visibility. Grade B, 900m of ascent, 4-5. Map: Adrados, 1:75,000.

The walk starts near Arangas, a picturesque village 4.5km NE of Arenas de Cabrales. A track goes off L (N) some 500m beyond the village, at a R-hand bend over a bridge. Go up the track until, after about 10 min. it is necessary to double back to three cabins. Go past the cabins on a narrow path and come out into open, scrubby ground which is ascended between walled fields until it is possible to traverse R to a minor spur characterised by a single cabin on the crest of the spur (20 min).

Climb the spur (NE) on a vague path, and when this dies out continue over heathery slopes to gain a good path crossing the hillside (15 min). This path now zig-zags steeply up the slope before climbing off R to gain level ground (40 min).

Go N for a short distance, then head E below a conical hill to reach the Mda Piedra del Oso (10 min). The summit of the Torbina can be seen from the far side of the majada to the NE. Leave the majada heading NNE over difficult terrain (occasional sheep tracks), looking for and entering the large hollow immediately S of the Torbina. Scramble up the SW slopes to the summit (¾h-1h).

Return by the same route (1½-2h).

55   Arenas to Tielve via the Calzada de Caoru

A varied walk with some spectacular views of Cabrales and Tielve, as well as of the Central Massif. As an added attraction the first part of the route follows an ancient cobbled path. Traditionally taken in descent, the route is described here from Arenas, the views being more rewarding in this direction. Grade C, 1,200m of ascent and 600m of descent to Tielve. 5-7h. Map: GH Editores, 1:50,000.

Start on the Arenas-Poncebos road at a hairpin bend immediately after the last house in Arenas. A path climbs up L between chestnuts, crosses an aqueduct, and climbs up a burnside. After passing stone enclosures once used to store chestnuts for winter pig-feed, a grassy col is reached to the R of the castle-like rock (40 min).

Leave the col R to pick up the cobbled path immediately. Held to be Roman, it leads comfortably through hawthorn woods, giving good views of Arenas when these die out. A steep section and open beech woods (path vague) lead up to the ample Majada Trasmialma (1-1¼h), which is left by the top R corner heading SW (intermittent path). At a junction by a wall swing L (SE), then contour round the R side of a depression and climb to a pathless open area which is crossed to enter a maze of limestone pinnacles ending at a col (abandoned cabins) overlooking a large, deep jou (40 mins).

A path contouring ESE leads off from the far side of this jou, passing a second smaller jou, to gain a broad col with a drinking trough 100m further on (30 min). Head SE over heather slopes, moving R over rocky ground to a V-shaped gap (Pt. 1,170m) with unexpected views of Tielve. Now go E over level ground to the col N of Pt. 1,324m, and so gain Tordín, a delightful majada with a huge cave in the NW corner (45 min).

Leave Tordín going S and cross the Jorcao la Torzal (views of the Central Massif), picking up a mule-path leads easily down to a broad

The Majada de Arnándes *clings to the mountain slopes above Bulnes.*

grassy col (Valfrio). Descend W to cabins and locate a comfortable path (concrete posts mark the start) leading down to Tielve (1-1¼h), from where it is an easy matter to hitch back to Arenas.

56   Ascent of Peña Maín   1609m
Traditionally, the ascent of Peña Main is tackled from Sotres following Route 11 to Pandébano. Unfortunately, the numerous new tracks in this area have removed a great deal of the pleasure from this approach, and so an alternative, beginning in Tielve, is offered here. Although longer, and involving more height gain, this new start passes through some attractive terrain, avoids the scars of the jeep tracks and keeps the best of Peña Maín's views until the end of the ascent. Moreover, it combines perfectly with the last route, making a very complete two-day outing. Grade C, 900m of ascent and 1,400m of descent, 6-7h. Map: Adrados, 1:25,000. Adrados, 1:75,000.

Start at an old pack-horse bridge some 300m below Tielve on the main road. Cross this and follow a comfortable mule path past switchbacks then two cabins. Continue along the path until a group of three cabins appears on the L. Hidden below and to the L of the first is a smaller path which is followed until it divides by a large ash tree. Take the R fork and follow it up between two cabins, past a third and then below a power line and soon after a telephone line. The path now climbs steeply to the obvious col just L (E) of the Cueto Vierro (1-1¼h from Tielve).

From the col follow the path as it skirts S outside the stone enclosure wall, then swings W to reach a point due S of the Cueto Vierro pinnacle. After a further 10 min. the path dies out in a tiny clearing. Turn L and rise SE, passing behind a rocky hillock on a vague path. This soon improves and is followed as it climbs steadily SE amongst beeches to reach a rocky col (¾h-1h from Inv. de Vierro).

Cross the col and descend R to pick up a well-used path which rises S, traverses briefly W (vague), then climbs steadily SW towards the lower Maín summit and a commanding view of the northern sector of the Central Massif (1590m: 30 mins). From the main summit (1605m) descend S for 10-12 min, then SE down a tiny valley from where a majada is reached with several old cabins and two reconditioned ones. Leave here going S and quickly reach good views of Pandébano. Descend steeply (pathless) towards the col (1h).

Follow a good path W past cabins, but when it begins to descend into a small ravine, stay high and so traverse across to the Mda de Arnandes, and one of the classic views of El Naranjo de Bulnes (15-20 min). The path away is by the first cabin met on arrival. Follow it down and across fields to regain the main path by a cabin above a stream. A cobbled path descends to Bulnes (30-40 min) from where Route 12 is reversed to Poncebos (1h).

57 Amuesa and the Canal de la Raíz

Slowly but surely the old shepherds' paths are beginning to disappear. This full day makes use of one such path to make what for some is an awesome descent from Amuesa to the Cares gorge. As these old paths become popular again as walking routes, it is to be hoped that they will be recovered and become easier to follow. Grade C, 1240m of ascent, 7-8h. Map: Adrados, 1:25,000.

The excursion follows Route N on the Adrados map. Route 9 is taken as far as the Mda de Amuesa (3-3¼h), the spring on leaving Bulnes de Arriba being the last reliable source of water until almost down in the Cares gorge. From Amuesa traverse west gaining height very gently and picking up a path some 50m above the Monte Llue woods. The Cdo de Cerredo, in practice no more than an inclined shoulder on the spur dropping to the Cares from the Trave summits, gives access to the Canal de Piedra Bellida.

The broad and trackless expanse of scree is taken on the L, staying close to the Trave walls. At the bottom a slightly more awkward section leads into the Canal de la Raiz (also known as El Pando). Follow the gully down to the Mda de la Raíz (spring next to first cabin). Below the majada descend a good zig-zag path and cross the Cares by an ancient bridge (2-2¼h). Climb up to the main path, which is followed easily back to Poncebos (Route 39: 1½-2h).

58   Tour of the Albo group (2 days)

A classic outing taking in some of the most impressive scenery on offer in the Central Massif. As with a number of two-day routes given in the guide, this excursion could be done in a single, long, hard day. This, however, would seem to be straying into the dubious realms of masochism, and has little to recommend it. Grade D – Day 1: 1800m of ascent, 6-7h. Day 2: 250m of ascent, 2050m of descent, 6-8h. Map: Adrados, 1:25,000.

The route is a combination of approach marches to the huts in the Jou de los Cabrones and Vega Urriellu and the whole outing is marked on the Adrados map as Route Ñ. On Day 1 follow Route 9 to the Lueje hut. The arrival in the early evening will mean that the Pico de los Cabrones group will be seen at its best.

The second day involves following Route 13 to Vega Urriellu (3h), from where Route 12 is reversed to Poncebos. The view back towards El Naranjo from the Mda de Cambureru (1½h from Urriellu) is one of the classic shots of the mountain, which is at its best in the late afternoon. It is also worth saving film for the arrival in Bulnes (2½-3h from Urriellu), which appears quite suddenly as the narrows of the Voluga de Casti-sierra are left.

59   Poncebos to the Lago de la Ercina via Vega Maor

A full and varied traverse which contrasts the rigours of an ascent of one of the Cares gullies with the pleasures of visiting some of the most attractive vegas and majadas of the Picos. As with a number of routes in this area, this walk brings us into close contact with the life of the shepherds, the majadas visited still being in use. Grade C, 1,110m of ascent and 450m of descent, 5-6h. Map: GH Editores, 1:50,000.

From Poncebos pick up the main Cares gorge path (be sure not to stay on the lower track which is a dead end) and follow it to Culiembro where a narrow path climbs off R immediately after a cabin by a lone poplar (40 min). The path climbs steadily but comfortably up the broad gully, passing below a huge cave at two-thirds height, then entering a narrow, subsidiary gully which comes out on grassy slopes, the pastures and cabins of Ostón being reached soon after (1¼-1½h from Culiembro).

Leave Ostón following the path which rises NW alongside the enclosure wall, then work up broken ground to the L of a broad, shallow valley coming down from Vega Maor. Just below an outcrop of white rocks visible from Ostón enter the valley, which narrows considerably as it enters Vega Maor (40 min; drinking trough).

In Vega Maor Route 51 is joined and followed to the Lago de Ercina (2-2½h). Alternatively, follow Route 51 until just before the long spur is crossed to enter the Mda de Belbín. Now pick up Route 49 and follow this down into the Vega de Comeya (40-50 min) where Route 44 is joined and taken to the Covadonga road (¾h), the sanctuary being reached in a further 1¼-1½h (9-10h from Poncebos).

LAS VEGAS DE SOTRES

Las Vegas de Sotres is an area which has been largely ignored in the past with the exception of organised summer camps, and it is true to say that all of the activities suggested below can be tackled from a base in the Arenas de Cabrales area provided private transport is available. However, for those who do not have the advantage of their own vehicle, or for those who wish to stay for more than a day without having to journey up and down from Arenas, this quiet vega has its attractions. It is, moreover, an ideal base for an ascent of Peña Castil, as well as for anyone wishing to climb on the slabs of Peña Fresnidiello.

A privately-owned hut is projected for the area, but is not as yet open. Camping is easy, though must not be done within the walled fields, where hay is grown for winter feed. It would be better not to drink water from the Rio Duje. The grey deposit on the river bed is sediment from the mining operations in Aliva. A good spring supplies a small drinking trough between the river and the cabins.

PEÑA DEL FRESNIDIELLO   1477m

The 300m wall of the Peña del Fresnidiello lies off to the R of the track up the Duje valley, about 1km from the beginning of the track just below Sotres. With its double summit and the enormous sweep of its compact, grey slabs, the crag never fails to impress first-time visitors. Despite its appearance, however, climbing here has been a very recent affair, the first routes being put up in 1983.

The rock, as has been suggested, is invariably excellent, and the climbing is relaxing, enjoyable, and at a very reasonable standard. Natural threads abound, some being very big. As a result, it is useful to carry a good selection of slings, including one or two old ones which could, if necessary, be used to reinforce the abseil points.

There are over 10 climbs at present, with scope for more. The three given here have been selected as being representative of climbing at Fresnidiello, whilst the first, *Elixir Para Calvos,* coincides with the abseil descent from the North Summit.

Descent: Though it is possible to scramble down NW from the main summit to a broad, grassy col (III+), from where a long, grassy gully leads back to the foot of the Route 60, most climbers prefer to abseil back down this route.

60   Elixir Para Calvos
The most popular climb on the crag and a good introduction to the climbing as the only difficult moves come early on and the route follows the line of descent closely. A fairly direct line to the North Summit, the climbing being varied and with all the belays in place. FA: F. Herrero, J. López and A. Villar, March, 1985. TD-, 315m, 3h. Diag. p.83.

Pena del Fresnidiellu
EAST FACE

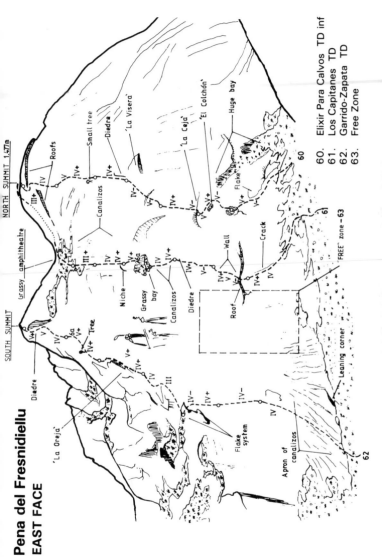

NORTH SUMMIT 1.477m

SOUTH SUMMIT

60. Elixir Para Calvos TD inf
61. Los Capitanes TD
62. Garrido-Zapata TD
63. Free Zone

83

Start below and L of a huge, grassy bay. Climb the L-side of a flake and then the wall above. Go round El Colchón, a grassy niche, and gain a stance below a long, narrow roof (ceja = eyebrow). Go over this and up towards a second, smaller roof. Cross this trending diag. R to gain an indefinite diedre above and L of La Visera, a prominent roof. Climb this, then continue past a small tree to gain compact slabs below the final roofs, the first of which is avoided on the R, the second on the L.

61 Los Capitanes
The route takes a direct line up to the central amphitheatre, with some difficult climbing to get out of the bay in the centre of the wall. The climb is dedicated to the pilots of a helicopter which crashed in this area when bringing down an injured British caver. FA: I. Arregui and A. Villar, 4 Nov, 1983. TD, 270m, 3h. Diag, p.83.

Start below the R-hand end of the long roof which characterises the centre of the face. Climb the roof on excellent holds. A wall and a 60m section of *canalizos* leads to the grassy, central bay. This is left with difficulty on very steep rock which soon relents as a second section of *canalizos* is gained. From the upper amphitheatre 60m of easy scrambling leads to the N Summit.

62 Garrido Zapata
This was the first climb to be put up at Fresnidiello and, as might be expected given this circumstance, it looks for obvious features on what, in general, is a fairly blank wall. Good climbing, with the hard moves saved for the second half, in sharp contrast with Route 60, FA: I. Arregui and A. Villar, 21 Jan, 1983. TD, 315m, 3h. Diag, p.83.

Start at the base of a huge grooved slab directly below the obvious flake/diedre two-thirds of the way up the wall and just L of the summit line. Go easily up (60m) to the first belay, then continue (belays in place) to gain the flake/diedre. The next pitches are the key to the climb. Climb the diedre (pegs) and then head for the small tree, beyond which lies the crux slab (bolts). Finally go diagonally R on poorer rock to gain and climb a well-defined diedre which leads to the summit.

63 Fresnidiello "FREE"
To the L of Route 61 is an area of slabs which, whilst perfectly climbable, is steep enough and blank enough to make progress difficult, if not impossible. Local climbers have used this area to establish a number of bolt-protected, 2-pitch slab routes, varying in difficulty from V– to 6b. These climbs make an entertaining complement to their longer neighbours, though any aspirants to the harder lines would do well not to 'over-test' the protection: a good many of the bolts are of the home-made variety. Diag, p.83.

Listed below are the names, lengths and difficulties of the climbs, ordered fro R to L.

Destroyer. V–, 80m.
La Voletade. 6a, 85m.
Fuxa Dos Ventos. 6a, 50m.
El Nalón. 6a, 80m.
Atmósfera Chunga. 6a, 70m.
Si lo sé no vengo. 6b, 70m.
La Lija. 6a, 70,m.
La Morca. V–, 80m.
Galaica. V–, 80m.

64   Ascent of Peña Castil   244m

This is one of the most interesting, and consequently most popular, ascents in the Central Massif. The mountain's privileged position (the first ascent was made in 1865 by a team of military surveyors) mean that it provides excellent views of the surrounding area, especially of the N Face of El Naranjo de Bulnes, which seems but a stone's throw away. A long ascent, though nowhere very steep. Grade B, 1,400m of ascent, 6-8h. Map: Adrados, 1:25,000 (see Route P).

Start as for Route 11 and follow this as far as Cdo Pandébano (1h). Go up the slopes to the S of the col, continuing up these instead of going W to the Terenosa hut. The slopes turn into a large gully which finally comes out at the Mda de las Moñas (1¾-2¼h). The angle decreases now, and another 30 minutes is usually sufficient to reach the Cabeza de los Tortorios and good views into the Canal del Fresnedal and the Duje Valley.

After dropping down W from the summit, descend SE into the Valle del Agua to gain the Hda Camburero, where it is possible to leave sacks if so desired. The way ahead lies up the unforgiving slope to the south, an hour being par for the course (3½-4h from Pandébano).

The descent is either made down the same route, or, from the Hda de Camburero, E via the Canal del Fresnedal. Steep and trackless at first, this leads to the Mda del Carbonal. Here a vague path zig-zags down, crosses the gully bed to the R side where it continues to descend steeply to Las Vegas de Sotres (2-2½h).

65   The Canal del Vidrio and the Moñetas Valley

A relatively short walk, but one which passes through some wild terrain in its descent of the lonely Moñetas valley. Grade C, 1,200m of ascent, 4½-5½h. Map: Adrados, 1:25,000.

Start at Las Vegas de Sotres by following the jeep track until this begins to climb up and away from the Duje (20 min). Stay with the river and follow it to the mine at Aliva, going round this to gain the start of the Canal de Vidrio (1¼-1½h). The name of the gully comes from the

Over 1,000m above sea-level Sotres is the highest village in the Picos. Peña Castil peers out of the cloud.

abundant, high-quality galena (Lead sulphide ore) which the local shepherds used to collect here to supplement their meagre earnings. This was then used in the production of glazes for earthenware pots and other ceramics.

Scramble up the first section of the gully to come out suddenly at the base of a long, evenly-angled slope. This proves to be an unaccommodating mixture of grass and stones, and leads laboriously to the Coteras Rojas col (1-1¼h).

Stretching out below to the NE is the Valle de las Moñetas, whilst Sotres is visible in the distance. There is no good path down the valley, which is representative of some of the rougher terrain in the Picos. In general aim for the base of the Cuchallón de Villa-sobrada, looking for the easiest way down amid the maze of small hoyos. Lower down small paths are picked up to the L of the valley bed. These lead more easily back to Las Vegas de Sotres (1¾-2¼h).

66 Circo de Andara

The Eastern Massif is the smallest and most compact of the three, the majority of the summits forming a huge cirque centred on the Vegas de Andara. Walking this cirque proves an attractive outing offering excellent views, first of the Liebana area and later of the Central Massif. The best base for the route is in Andara itself, just beyond the Pozo de Andara tarn. There is a spring at the old lake head, the tarn being no more than the remains of a lake which was drained during the mining operations of the last century. The base is reached from Sotres by following the jeep track to the Jito de Escarandi (see Adrados 1:75,000 map) Go S here and follow the jeep track to the Casetón de Andara (1h) The Pozo de Andara lies some 10 mins away to the SW. Grade C, 900m of ascent, 6-7h. Map: Adrados, 1:75,000 and GH Editores, 1:50,000.

From the Pozo de Anadara go SW then S, crossing the pastures of the Majada del Redondal with its curious 'cave-like' cabins. In the past these were used by the shepherds from Tresviso, who spent their summers living here while they tended the sheep. During the middle of the last century one of the cabins was home to La Osa de Andara (osa = female bear). The 'bear', it turns out, was a women called Joaquina López, who had chosen to live apart from Beges, her birthplace, ashamed of the copious hair which covered her body.

Beyond the Redondal go up a ravine and cross a shoulder to enter a cwm. Contour round to the S and climb up to the Cdo de Valdominguero (1½h). Now cross the broad, grassy campos de Valdominguero, to an awkward col (II–). A final, stony slope leads to the summit of the Pica del Jierro (30 min), and excellent views of Aliva, the Central Massif and the lower land to the N.

Scramble down E along a broken ridge and pick up a good track which winds gently N before crossing a ridge L then R to come out at a narrow col. A short traverse east round a hillock ends at a broader col crossed by a track (Cdo del Mojón; 30-40 min).

From the Cdo del Mojón continue the traverse E on a vague path, passing below the S walls of La Rasa to gain the col to its SE. From here the summit of the Pico de los Llambriales Amarillos is easily gained (30-40 min), and is another excellent viewpoint, especially of the Canal de las Arredondas and the Cordillera Cantábrica.

To the NW, along an obvious broad ridge, stands the Pico del Sagrado Corazón with its huge statue of Christ (30 min), and beyond this is the Cdo de San Carlos from where another broad ridge rises NE to the summit of the Pico de Samelar (¾h-1h). The Samelar is the third good vantage point the cirque offers.

To finish the day return to the Cdo de San Carlos. A good track descends NW into the Vega de Andara and crosses this to the Casetón de Andara at the foot of the Mancondiu (1999m), whose double top offers fine views of the whole cirque.

67 The Canalón del Jierru

A number of steep gullies descend from the Eastern Massif to the Duje valley, of which the Canalón del Jierru is the most impressive. Coming out at a narrow gap between the Pica del Jierru and the Morra de Lechugales, the gully provides a hard, but challenging way of ascending these summits from Las Vegas de Sotres or Aliva. Grade C, 1,400m of ascent, 5h (6h if Lechugales ascended). Map: GH Editores, 1:50,000.

From Las Vegas de Sotres follow the jeep track until it zig-zags L then R shortly after crossing the river. From the second bend strike up the hillside following the obvious broad gully (25 min). The route is obvious and determination rather than ability is the key to the descent. Tiring though the ascent of these gullies is, they form an integral part of mountaineering in the Picos de Europa.

At around 1800m the gully divides and the L branch is taken. This steepens and becomes looser, with occasional scrambling being necessary (I+) to reach the narrow Cdo del Jierru (2h from road). The summit of the Pica del Jierru lies five minutes away to the N, whilst that of the Morra de Lechugales is gained by traversing S below the E side first two of the three minor Picos del Jierru summits, then ascending a broken slope to gain a col to the S of the third. Locate and follow an exposed ledge going S from the col along the W side of the ridge. This ends at a second col by the summit block of the Morra de Lechugales, which is climbed using twin cracks (II+) on the R (25 min from Cdo del Jierru; 3-3½h from Las Vegas de Sotres).

The descent can be made down the same route (2-2½h from Cdo del Jierru). Alternatively, reverse Route 66 as far as the Cdo de Valdoming-uero (II–) where the Canal de Jidiello can be descended (I+) to the Duje valley (2-2½h from Pica del Jierru).

5: MOUNTAIN ROUTES

PART I: THE CENTRAL MASSIF

EL CABLE/ALIVA SECTOR

For most people arriving in the Picos de Europa from Britain the El Cable/Aliva sector provides their first contact with the high mountains. As such, the area has a number of advantages, not least of which is the presence of the télèpherique at Fuente Dé and the consequent reduction in approach times. Equally important for the newly arrived, however, is the range of routes available, from simple walks to long, alpine-style ridges and walls, allowing newcomers to introduce themselves steadily to the style of mountaineering on offer.

Accommodation for the area, as has already been pointed out in Valley Bases, seems to hinge around camping in Fuente Dé or hostals in Espinama, but for those who wish to avoid the almost permanent queues for the cable car, however, camping in the Puertos de Aliva can be recommended.

EL JISO (Pico Pozán)   2130m

This elegant ridge is clearly visible from many parts of the Liebana valley including Potes, and provides not only the best route in the Eastern Massif, but also one of the classic rock climbs of the range. Though actually in the Eastern Massif, the climb is always approached from Aliva via the Cdo de Cámara.

Descent: From the summit go N to the col between El Jiso and Prao Cortés, then scramble down the obvious gully to Aliva.

68   South Ridge
A good climb in excellent positions and mainly on good rock. The difficulties are limited to El Faraón, a pillar at the base of the ridge proper, but by following the crest throughout, especially in the upper section, the grade is maintained. The ease of access and escape make this a good training route. First ascent: E. Conde and G. Lastra. 4&5 June, 1969. TDinf, 600m. 5-6h. Diag, p.93.

From Aliva go E to the Cdo. de Cámara, then follow the path NE and down to an inclined, grassy shoulder from where it is possible to contour E to a second, ill-defined shoulder. A small path continues below rock walls to ochre-coloured broken slabs which lead up to a chimney-corner to the R of the South Ridge (Allow 1h).

Climb slabs then the chimney-corner to the amphitheatre which is crossed easily to a cave at the foot of the ridge. A pitch up grooves to the

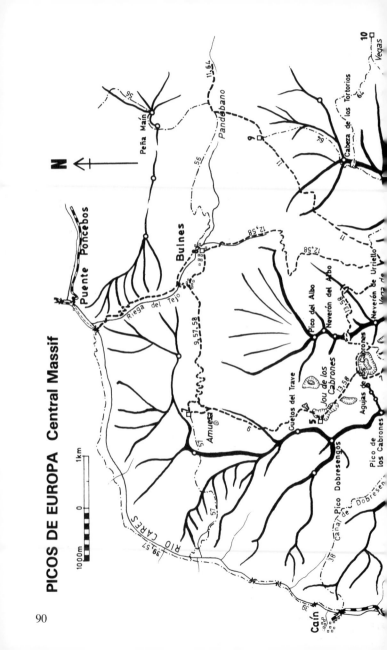

PICOS DE EUROPA Central Massif

1km

1000m · 0

N ←

Puente Poncebos

Peña Maín

95

11,64

Pandébano

56

9

79

11

Bulnes

Riega del Tejo

9,57,58

12,58

12,58

Cabeza de los Tortorios

6

10
Vegas

Pico del Albo

Neverón del Albo

13,58

Neverón de Urriellu

Vega de

Amuesa

6

57

Cuetos del Trave

Jou de los Cabrones

13,58

Agujas de los Cabrones

5

Pico Dobresengo

Pico de los Cabrones

57

57

RIO CARES

39,57

Caña Pico Dobresengo

Canal de Dobresen

38

38

Caín

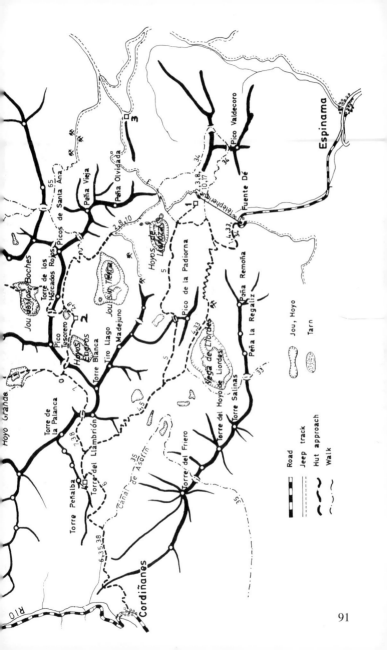

Espinama

Pico Valdecoro

Pico Deñe

Fuente Dé

teleférico

Peña Olviada

Peña Vieja

Picos de Santa Ana

Torre de los Hórcados Rojos

Jou de los Boches

Hoyo Grande

Torre de la Palanca

Torre Peñalba

Torre del Lliambrión

Pico Tesorero

Jou Sin Tierra

Pico Llago

Hoyos de los Llagos

Hoyos Negros

Tiro Llago

Madejuno

Pico de la Padiorna

Vega de Liordes

Peña la Regaliz

Peña Remoña

Cañal de Asotín

Torre del Hoyo de Liordes

Torre Salinas

Torre del Friero

Cordiñanes

RIO

65

2.8.10

6

9

7.38

6

6.35.38

35

4.33

5

4.5

35

7.8.

10.17

34

12

3a

4.33

33

5

	Road
	Jeep track
	Hut approach
	Walk

Jou, Hoyo

Tarn

91

left of a square-cut chimney leads to the arête proper. A sustained pitch taken first on the crest, then up steep cracks to the R, leads to a stance below a crack with slab. Climb this (hard) to easier ground. The route now follows the arête, with occasional hard moves, escape being possible L at two-thirds height. Staying on the crest after the escape ledges keeps the standard at V, though easier ground is always available L.

PICO VALDECORO   1841m

An impressive wall when viewed either from the village of Espinama, or from the Invernales de Igüedri on the Espinama-Aliva track. As with the Cueto Agero, the low altitude and southerly orientation mean that climbing is possible here even in poor weather.
   Descent: From the summit follow a vague path down (NW) into a broad valley. Either descend this to Igüedri, or go up to the Cdo. de Valdecoro (excellent views of Fuente Dé), then double back NE to gain the Cda. de la Juciana and the Puertos de Aliva.

69   South Face: Original Route
The climb takes a bold line up the centre of the face, the positions making up for the occasional vegetation. Good rock, especially in the central section. All pegs and belays are in place, with étriérs helpful though not essential. First ascent: G.Lastra, E.Conde, M.A.Herreros and E. Muñiz. 6&7 June, 1969. TDinf, 330m. 4h. Diagram, p.94.

From the Invernales de Igüedri follow a narrow path that contours round above extensive beech woods to the huge buttress that lies against the base of the wall.
   Start just L of buttress. Scramble up slabs to a chimney-crack and the start of the climbing. Three pitches, the first taking the chimney-crack and the last an awkward, rising traverse R, lead to a stance below the centre of a long narrow roof clearly visible from the foot of the climb. Two airy pitches, involving most of the hard climbing on the route, lead up to and then past the R of the roof, before trending diag. L over slabs to a corner. Leave the corner on the L and climb straight up in two pitches to a stance by a large cave. Go R from the stance and up a vague corner to the summit.

PEÑA VIEJA   2613m

An excellent viewpoint, Peña Vieja is also one of the most popular summits in the Picos. Access for walkers, though straightforward, is limited to the north side, whilst the SE Face is a complex mass of walls and buttresses that rise some 800 metres above the Aliva meadows, the SW Face dominating La Vueltona in similar style. Unfortunately, the rock on Peña Vieja is not generally good, for which reason few of its routes have been included here.

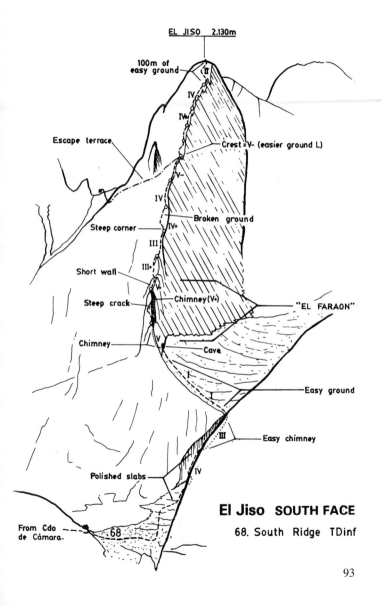

EL JISO 2.130m

100m of easy ground

II

IV

IVw

Escape terrace

Crest = V− (easier ground L)

V−

IV

Broken ground

Steep corner

IV+

III

III+

Short wall

V

Steep crack

Chimney (V+)

"EL FARAON"

Chimney

V

Cave

Easy ground

I

III

Easy chimney

Polished slabs

IV

El Jiso SOUTH FACE

68. South Ridge TDinf

From Cdo de Cámara

68

93

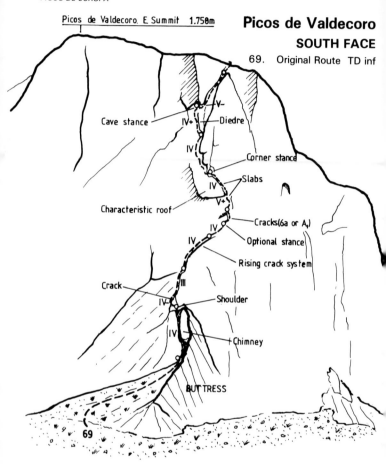

Picos de Valdecoro. E Summit 1.758m

Picos de Valdecoro
SOUTH FACE
69. Original Route TD inf

Cave stance

V−

IV+ — Diedre

IV — Corner stance

Slabs

IV

V+

Characteristic roof

Cracks(6a or A₁)

IV — Optional stance

Rising crack system

Crack

III

IV− — Shoulder

IV — Chimney

BUTTRESS

69

70 North Face (Normal Route)

A walk, with the exception of the very last section. Straightforward and popular. First ascent: Saint Saud, P. Labrouche and C. Soberón, 9 July, 1890. Grade B, 800m of ascent, 1½-2h from El Cable. Map: Adrados, 1:25,000.

From the upper cable car station follow Route 2 to the switchbacks, then follow the R fork into a broad gully (the Canal de la Canalona). At the head of the gully (Collado de la Canalona; 1½h) bear R (SE) on a

94

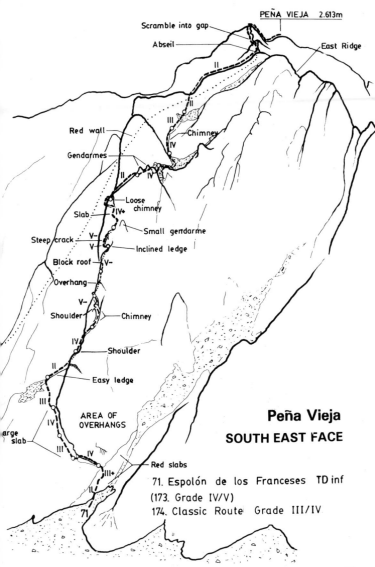

PEÑA VIEJA 2.613m

Scramble into gap

Abseil

East Ridge

II

II

III

Chimney

IV

Red wall

Gendarmes

II

IV

Loose chimney

Slab

IV+

Small gendarme

Steep crack

V−

V

Inclined ledge

Block roof

V−

Overhang

V−

Shoulder

Chimney

IV

Shoulder

II

Easy ledge

III

AREA OF
OVERHANGS

IV

arge
slab

III

IV

Red slabs

III+

Peña Vieja

SOUTH EAST FACE

71. Espolón de los Franceses TD inf
(173. Grade IV/V)

174. Classic Route Grade III/IV

71

well-worn path that swings round to, and then climbs the N slopes of the mountain (2h).

Descent: By the same route. Alternatively, go NE from the Cdo. de la Canalona to gain the broad col of Coteras Rojas. Now drop down E, but always staying L, to the start of the Canal del Vidrio which is descended to Aliva from where Route 3 leads back to El Cable (Grade C, 4½-5h).

NB: the start of the Canal del Vidrio is difficult to locate in descent and involves some awkward terrain (I+). Because of this it is better taken in ascent in combination with Route 63 to provide a circular tour of the mountain.

71   SE Face: Espolón de los Franceses

A long, alpine-style route up a large and attractive wall. Clearly divided into two sections, with good climbing on the main buttress followed by a long, airy scramble up to the summit. The climb is a classic of its grade, which, whilst never technically hard, nevertheless demands a certain degree of mountaineering experience. Good rock (except near the twin gendarmes) and belays make this a popular climb. First ascent: P. Forn and B. Trouvé, 18 Aug, 1967. TDinf, 800m, 6-7h. Diag, p.95.

Start at reddish slabs to the R of the line of the spur, just L of the gully which descends from the Intermediate Cirque. Climb the slabs until steep walls force a traverse L over grey slabs to a belay on the L of the main ridge. Three pitches up slabs lead to a ledge going R to the ridge itself. This is followed for several pitches of good climbing, difficulties being turned mainly on the L. The last pitch, a slab capped by a broken wall, finishes L on an easy arête going up to twin gendarmes taken on the R. A chimney-gully to the R of a large orange wall leads to a broad ridge, which goes easily R to a junction with the East Ridge at a deep gap. Abseil into the gap and descend L a little before scrambling back to the ridge proper. This is followed, airily at times, with several short scrambles down into further gaps, turning most difficulties on the R.

PEÑA OLVIDADA   2406m.

Peña Olvidada stands as a satellite peak to the main mass of Peña Vieja, and, as its name suggests (olvidada = forgotten), it is often ignored because of the fame and importance given to its near neighbour. Unlike Peña Vieja, it has no easy route and no easy descent, its inaccessibility adding to its unpopularity. The S and SW faces are impressive but the rock is generally poor, and only one route has been selected here.

Descent: Follow the broad crest leading N towards Peña Vieja until it narrows considerably, and broken, scree-covered slabs allow a descent NW. Head down diag. R until a short scramble down good rock ends at a shattered col. A narrow chimney drops away to the R (N). Scramble down it for 5m to a hidden abseil point. Abseil to the scree above La Vueltona.

Aguja de Ostaicoechea SOUTH FACE

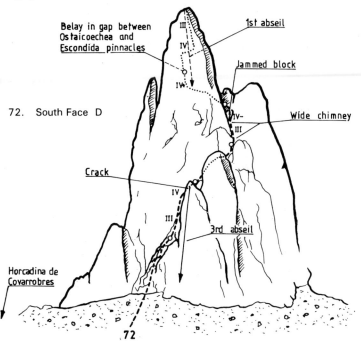

Belay in gap between Ostaicoechea and Escondida pinnacles

1st abseil

Jammed block

Wide chimney

72. South Face D

Crack

3rd abseil

Horcadina de Covarrobres

72

72 Aguja Ostaicoechea: South Face

This is the northernmost of a group of 5 pinnacles which descend from the S Wall of Peña Olvidada to the Hda de Covarrobres. It offers one pleasant climb on good rock, and this, along with the ease of access make it a good way of getting the feel of Picos rock. FA: P. Udaondo and A. Urones, 9 Jan, 1966. D, 90m, 1h.

Scramble up to the base of the pinnacle from the Hda de Covarrobres. Scramble up easy ground then take a crack to easier ground going diag. R to the foot of a gully. Climb this then pass round to the N Face and gain the gap between the Ostaicoechea and Escondida pinnacles. Climb the wall above to the summit.

73 SW Face: Las Placas

Las Placas is one of the harder recent additions that the Cantabrian climbers have made to this part of Picos. As the name suggests, the climbing is mainly on slabs. The rock is generally good, with the exception of some moves in the first half. The protection left by the first ascensionists is sparse and natural protection is difficult to find, which gives the climb a certain feeling of seriousness. FA: J. López, J. Rubio and J. Sáenz, May 1986. EDinf, 450m, 4-5h. Diag, p.99.

The upper half of the centre of the SW Face is characterised by a large red tower whose base is marked by a large ledge which runs across the face at half height. The ledge goes R to a hanging cirque, the route climbing to the R-hand side of the cirque, and then up the wall above. Start by gaining and climbing a corner, then continue beneath a yellowish roof, trending L until a short, steep wall is climbed and it is possible to go diag. R to the bottom, R-hand corner of the cirque.

3 pitches lead easily up past the cirque to the wall behind. This is climbed directly at first, but as it becomes more vertical it is necessary to make a series of traverses back and forth to find the simplest line.

AGUJA DE CANALONA

This attractive pinnacle, as its name suggests, dominates the approach to the Cdo. de Canalona (see Route 70). Despite its dimunitive size, it commands remarkable views of large parts of all three massifs. Climbs here are easily combined with others on the Aguja de Bustamante and the Picos de Santa Ana (see below). Such combinations, apart from providing a valuable introduction to climbing in the range, are useful during unstable weather because of the ease of access to these summits.

Descent: Two in-situ abseils back down the route to the base.

74   East Face (Normal Route)
A short climb with a very alpine feel for such an apparently insignificant peak. First ascent: J. A. Odriozola, A. Martínez and J. T. Martínez, 8 August, 1948. 80m, ADsup, 45 min.

Follow Route 70 to the Collado de la Canalona then scramble horizontally to the base of the tower along an exposed ledge which starts a few metres NW of the col, and ends in a gully that descends L below the SE face of the pinnacle.

Cross the gully and traverse L, crossing a short wall (III+) then a terrace which leads L to a belay below an obvious, deep chimney visible from the approach ledge. This is climbed (IV–) to a stance in a gap (abseil cable). The wall above is climbed up to, then awkwardly L past, a precarious block, to gain a diedre, which is followed to a ledge (IV–), and finally the summit.

75   Southwest Face: Capricho
A bold, modern route up the blank wall which overlooks the approach path. Very good rock on the hard pitch makes up for the protection, which is only average. First ascent: J. . González, A. Pelayo and J. Rubio, 10th July, 1983. 100m, TDinf, 1½h. Diag, p.101.

Peña Olvidada. SW. Summit 2.406m

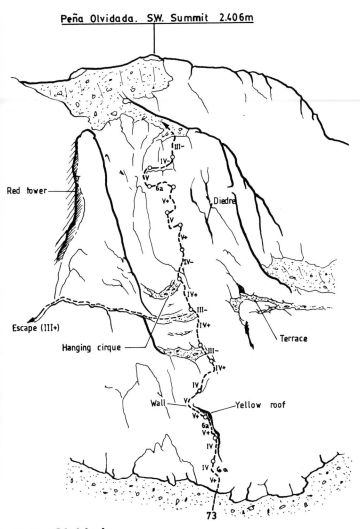

Red tower

Diedre

Escape (III+)

Hanging cirque

Terrace

Wall

Yellow roof

73

Peña Olvidada
SOUTHWEST FACE

73. Las Placas ED inf

From the base of the tower scramble up the R-hand of two gullies, moving R at the end to gain a small gap at the foot of the face. Climb the wall in front up to a small ledge below a diedre, then swing out L onto the face which is climbed moving L at the difficulties (protection from small nuts) to a stance overlooking the gap on Route 74. Gain cracks above and R, then climb easier ground before moving L to the summit.

AGUJA DE BUSTAMANTE

The lower and more westerly of two elegant pinnacles, the Aguja de Bustamante bears the name of the Potes photographer, a visit to whose shop is almost obligatory when in the town.

Descent: A 35m abseil to the gap N of the pinnacle. Abseil ring in place.

76   East Ridge
A short climb on good rock, the shortness being compensated by the positions. First ascent: F. Nuñez de Celis and J. A. Odriozola, 14 Aug, 1950. 60m, D, 45min. Diag, p.102.

Start below a short chimney just R of the ridge. Climb it, then move L to gain a corner which leads to an airy stance. Surmount the wide crack (crux) and the slab above.

77   East Face: Via Del Diedro
Slightly longer and harder than the previous route, tackling the obvious groove on the left of the East Ridge, and giving one fine pitch. First ascent: A. Cianco, J. Rubio and M. Torralbo, 18 Sept, 1983. 65m, Dsup, 1h. Diag, p.102.

Approach as for the last climb, traversing further L to the base of the diedre, which is climbed to a shared stance with Route 76. Leave this by surmounting the overhang on the L, and the slab above.

PICOS DE SANTA ANA   2601m.

The Picos de Santa Ana are the twin summits that form the continuation of the East Ridge of the Torre de los Horcados Rojos. The East summit, whilst slightly lower offers excellent views of the Duje valley, with the beaches of San Vicente de la Barquera visible on a fine day. The West summit has a small number of short climbs.
Descent: From the West summit scramble down the East ridge which is abandoned after a few metres. Scramble east down the north slopes of the mountain (easy slabs) to gain the Cdo. de Santa Ana. Alternatively, reverse Route 78.

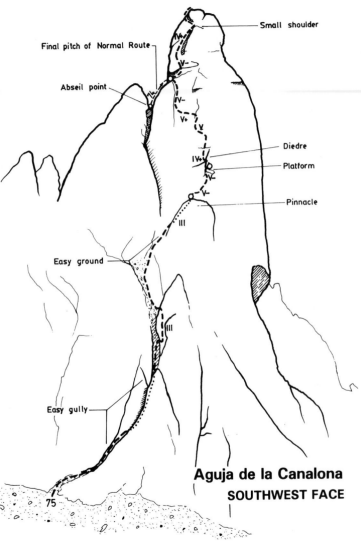

Small shoulder

Final pitch of Normal Route

Abseil point

Diedre

Platform

Pinnacle

Easy ground

Easy gully

Aguja de la Canalona
SOUTHWEST FACE

75

75. Capricho TD inf

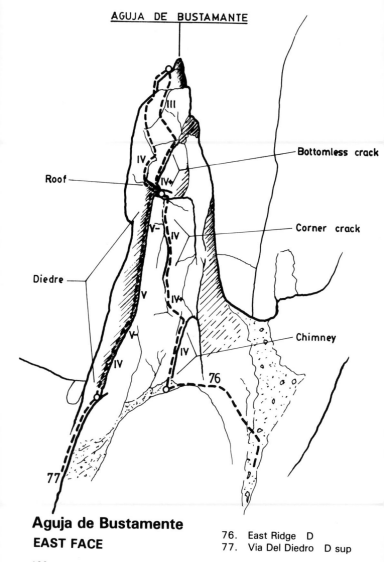

AGUJA DE BUSTAMANTE

Bottomless crack

Roof

Corner crack

Diedre

Chimney

76

77

Aguja de Bustamente
EAST FACE

76. East Ridge   D
77. Via Del Diedro   D sup

102

78 East Face (Normal Route)

An easy scramble up the eastern slopes of the East summit. First ascent: P. Labrouche, 29 July, 1892. Grade A, 750m of ascent, 2h from El Cable.

Approach as for Route 70 to the Cdo. de la Canalona. Go L on reaching the Cdo. de la Canalona and follow broken slopes NW past good views of the Aguja de Canalona to the East summit. (The West summit can be reached along the connecting ridge: III, broken).

79 West Face: Espolón Rojizo

This red ridge is clearly seen from the Jou de los Boches and provides a short, popular climb on good rock and in good situations. First ascent: A. Benito, R. Fernández and P. Udaondo, 7th Oct, 1965. ADsup, 150m,

Picos de Santa Ana
WEST FACE

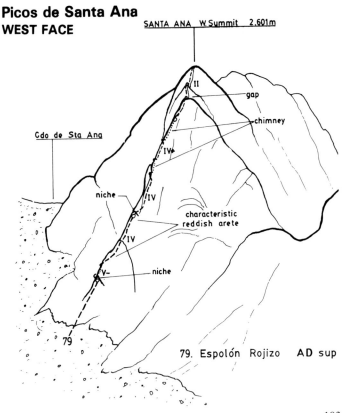

79. Espolón Rojizo   AD sup

1½h. Diag. p.103.

The climb is best approached by traversing N from the Cdo. de Canalona to the Cdo. de Santa Ana, then descending to the foot of the ridge. Scramble over brown rock to a niche, moving L to avoid the overhang above and going up good rock to a second niche. Go over this to a chimney which is followed to an exit R onto a buttress. Go L to a second chimney, after which a bréche is reached. Scrambling leads to the summit.

TORRE DE LOS HORCADOS ROJOS   2506m

The great red South Face of this summit seems to catch people's attention almost as soon as they leave El Cable. The wall possesses one classic climb, while the summit proves a worthwhile excursion for the walker, with good views north to El Naranjo de Bulnes.

80   West Side (Normal Route)
A reasonably straightforward walk, though a bit loose in parts through erosion. First ascent unknown. Grade A, 670m of ascent, 2h from El Cable. Map: Adrados, 1:25,000.

Follow Route 10 to the Horcados Rojos, then go easily up rocky slopes to the east.

81   South Face Direct
The ease of both access and descent make this route a good introduction to the longer climbs in this grade. The Direct variation provides a good line, with varied climbing on rock that is generally sound. A classic route in Picos. First ascent: J. M. Régil and C. García. 30 June, 1962. Dsup, 350m. 4h. Diag, p.105.

Follow Route 2 El Cable to the foot of the wall (1h). The climb starts at the R side of the huge pillar that leans against the centre of the face.

Easy slabs lead to a deep chimney on the R of the pillar. This is climbed strenuously, and not without certain difficulty, to a large platform from where a steep wall is taken on good holds. The final chimney has one hard section where it narrows to an awkward, steep groove (crux). An easy gully leads to the summit.

PICO TESORERO   2570m

The simple fact that this apparently modest-looking peak is the triple junction of the provinces of Asturias, Cantabria and Castilla-León should justify an ascent. If we add that it probably offers the most complete views of the Picos de Europa of any summit in the range, the ascent becomes obligatory. A popular outing.

Torre de Horcados Rojos
SOUTH FACE

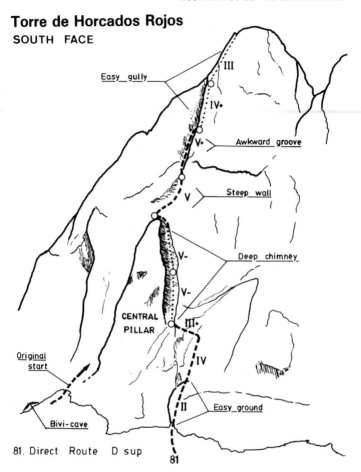

81. Direct Route D sup

82 Southeast Ridge (Normal Route)
A pleasant scramble up the SE Ridge on good rock. First ascent unknown. PD, 1h from Cabaña Verónica.

Follow Route 2 to Cabaña Verónica. From the hut climb NW towards the base of the SE Ridge, avoiding a rock bluff by trending R below it, and so passing around the L side of a small hoyo. Climb a steep gully on the L to gain the base of the ridge proper. Follow this on good rock to the summit (I+).

TORRE DEL LLAMBRION   2642m

The second highest summit in the Picos and an excellent viewpoint, the Torre del Llambrión was one of the earliest objects of exploration (see Climbing History notes). When Casiano de Prado was finally able to make measurements from the summit, believing it to be the highest in the range, he was dismayed to find that the Torre de Cerredo held that honour by a mere 6m.

The name 'Llambrión' is a derivation of the word 'llambria', a word used to describe the polished, holdless slabs left by the process of glaciation.

83   Northeast Face (Normal Route)
A relatively simple scramble up the NE Face of the mountain, the problems, if any, often arising from the negotiation of the snowfield that guards the foot of the wall. Ice-axe possibly useful. First ascent: Casiano de Prado and J. Boquerín, 12 August, 1856. PD, 2h from Cabaña Verónica.

Go W from Cabaña Verónica to reach the Cda. Blanca. Continue W to gain and cross (or avoid in late season) the snowfield that guards the Torre Tirso and Llambrión north walls, aiming for a point just R of the Llambrión summit (white survey post just visible). Gain a hollow and leave R by a gully that leads to the summit ridge.

The base of the NE Face can also be reached from Cdo. Jermoso by following Route 7 to Tiro Callejo and then traversing R. Finally, it is possible to scramble directly along the ridge connecting Tiro Callejo to the Llambrión summit (II).

PICO MADEJUNO   2513m

The summit of this mountain is formed by a chain of minor peaks (a *madeja* of summits – hence the name), that signal the start of one of the longest and highest ridge climbs in the Picos, stretching as it does over Tiro Llago, Torre Blanca, Tiro Tirso and the Torre del Lambrión.

84   Madejuno – Llambrión Traverse
This is one of the longest ridges in the Picos, and is probably the most popular as it is of relatively easy access, and can be abandoned without difficulties just before Tiro Llago (to the S), at Torre Blanca (to the NE) and after descending from Tiro Tirso (to the NE). The exact difficulty can be varied almost at will by tackling or avoiding the many subsidiary towers encountered, but at least one rappel and climbing up to III+ will be needed. FA: P. Udaondo, J. Rodríguez, A. Llorente and A. Fernández, 21 July, 1955. ADsup, 4-5h.

Gain the Tiros de Casares, the col to the SE of Pico Madejuno. This point can be reached in 1½-1¾h from El Cable by following Route 2 until 100m past La Vueltona. Now cross SW and pick up a small path

Approaching Tiro Llago on the Madejuno-Llambrión ridge. Flat, grey clouds scurrying in on SW winds indicate the imminent arrival of a frontal trough.

going round the S side of the Jou Sin Tierra and then below the N walls of the Pico San Carlos and the Torre del Hoyo Oscuro.

From the Casares col go up easily on the R of the main crest for some 40m. Head for a vague gully which later steepens to form a diedre which is climbed (III+) to a gully. Climb this, first direct, then towards the R. After a small step (II+), slabs lead to the summit.

Once on the crest follow it at will, an abseil being normal before Tiro Llago. From the summit of Torre Blanca descend to a level section and enter a gap (III). Climb out R (III+) and gain the Torre Sin Nombre (II) from where it is necessary to climb (III+) or abseil into a gap, then traverse a tower to another gap (III). Continue to the summit of Tiro Tirso then descend the W Ridge (II).

From the deep gap between the latter and the Torre de Llambrión climb a short chimney which narrows before exiting at a gap on the main SE Ridge (moves of III+). Scramble up the ridge (II+) to the summit.

PICO DE LA PADIORNA   2319m

A good walker's summit, offering a superb panorama of the Cordillera Cantábrica to the south of the Picos, and impressive views of Fuente Dé more than 1,200m below.

85 North Side (Normal Route)
A simple walk up the northern slopes of the mountain. First ascent unknown. Grade A, 500m of ascent, 1½-1¾h from El Cable. Map: Adrados, 1:25,000.

Follow Route 5 to the Colladina de las Nieves, from where a further 10 minutes leads to the summit. The descent can be made by following Route 5 into Vega Liordes, then returning to Fuente Dé by Route 33, this combination making a pleasant day (Grade B, 4-5h).

LIORDES/JERMOSO SECTOR

Despite the proximity of Fuente Dé and the coach-bound hordes, this remains one of the less-visited parts of the Picos, probably because of the effort required to get there. Those willing to expend the necessary energy, however, are almost always left with a strong impression of the special character the vega possesses. Liordes and the area below the huge Madejuno-Llambrión south wall, are excellent places to see rebeccos during the summer, often in large numbers.

The only hut is that at Cdo Jermoso, but camping in Liordes is a highly recommendable alternative. The Casetón de Liordes, a small hut meant for use by local shepherds, is also of use in an emergency.

PEÑA REMOÑA   2247m

Peña Remoña is the impressive triple-summited peak that towers over Fuente Dé, being especially attractive in the early morning light. Despite its appearance the mountain has no climbs of any significance on it, and continues to be a walkers' peak, as well as a superb backdrop to countless holiday snaps.

Descent: by the Normal Route.

86 North Face (Normal Route)
Equally impressive as the view of Peña Remoña from Fuente Dé, is that of the upper Deva from the summit of the mountain. A straightforward ascent which can be easily combined with Route 33. Grade B, 1,200m ascent, 3-4h from Fuente Dé. Map: Adrados, 1:25,000.

Follow Route 33 or cross the vega from the small shepherds' hut and so reach the Cdo. de Liordes from where it is possible to work S over grass and screes. A short section up steepish rock leads to the W summit, the highest of the three.

PEÑA LA REGALIZ   2196m

One of a chain of lesser summits running W from Peña Remoña to the Cdo. de Remoña. Of little significance as a summit, but offering one good slab climb on the face overlooking Vega Liordes.

Descent: By the normal route, which uses the obvious gully descending to Liordes to the R of the slabs.

87 Northwest Face: Divertimento

A pleasant slab climb up very good rock on the wall to the L of the gully that descends to Liordes from between the mountain's two summits. From the large central terrace (escape R) two finishes are possible. There is no in-situ gear but nuts and slings for threads will prove sufficient. FA: M. A. Adrados and E. Martínez, 7 July, 1985, D sup, 290m, 2h.

The wall is split by a huge terrace above which, to the left, is a large arch roof. Start below the R end of this roof, and climb a canalizo to a thread belay. Move R to a roof then go past a perched block. Two more pitches lead straight up to the terrace.

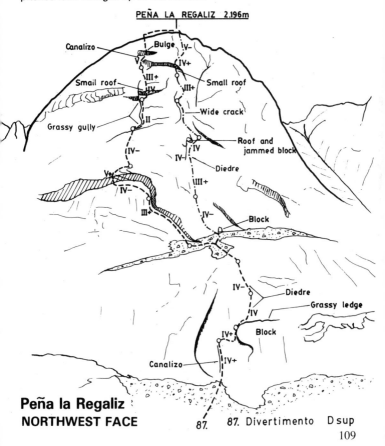

Peña la Regaliz
NORTHWEST FACE

87.   87. Divertimento   D sup

Climb slabs beneath the arch roof until a hard move allows this to be climbed at its highest point. Two easy slab pitches lead to a second, smaller roof and a belay by a third. Avoid this on the left, then gain and climb a bulge to gain the finishing slabs.

TORRE DE SALINAS 2446m

One of the first summits to be climbed in the Picos (though in the mistaken belief that it was the highest – see Climbing History), the Torre

Torre de Salinas
Northeast Face

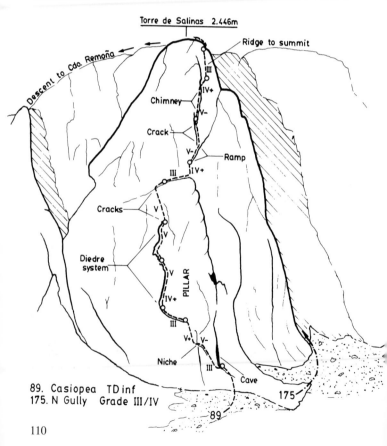

Torre de Salinas 2.446m

Descent to Cdo. Remoña

Ridge to summit

Chimney

Crack

Ramp

Cracks

Diedre system

PILLAR

Niche

Cave

89. Casiopea TD inf
175. N Gully Grade III/IV

de Salinas offers excellent views of Valdeón and Vega Liordes, as well as some good climbing on the N Buttress.

Descent: by the Normal Route.

88   East Ridge (Normal Route)
The route thought to have been taken by Casiano de Prado, who quickly saw that the Torre de Llambrión was higher. An easy ascent from the Cdo. de Remoña. PD inf, 400m of ascent, 45min. from col.

Reach the Cdo. de Remoña either from Fuente Dé (Route 33 in reverse – 2½-3h) or from Vega Liordes (30 min. from the Casetón de Liordes). Work W up the ridge, mainly turning difficulties on the L.

89   N. Face: Casiopea
An attractive and quite sustained route offering good crack and chimney work for those daunted by the bald slabs of other areas of the Picos. The rock is generally good, the situations making up for the occasional looseness. Route-finding is a little tricky in the central section. Pegs useful for belays. FA: J. Alonso, J. M. San Cristóbal and J. C. Tamayo, 18 Sept, 1978. TD inf, 300m, 4-5h. Diag, p. 110.

Start just L of the huge cave at the base of the pillar. Work out diag. L to a grassy niche (Pegs) and continue L to gain a small terrace. Go L to a large diedre and climb it (exit difficult) and the cracks above until it is possible to traverse back R to the crack system of the cave. Gain a ramp rising R, and climb it until it can be left for a crack leading to a chimney, and then the summit ridge.

TORRE DEL HOYO DE LIORDES   2474m

Despite being the highest point in the chain of summits running from Peña Remoña to the Torre del Friero, the Torre del Hoyo de Liordes is seldom visited. As with the neighbouring Torre de Salinas, it offers excellent views of the Cordillera Cantábrica, of Valdeón and of the Madejuno-Llambrión ridge. Moreover, being the highest summit in the group, it provides fine views west to the Western Massif. It has been suggested by some Picos devotees that this was the summit climbed by Casiano de Prado, and not that of the Torre de Salinas, which is obviously lower.

Descent: From the summit follow a broad ridge W until forced slightly R of the ridge into the head of two deep gullies, one straight ahead and the other to the R. Ignore both of them and follow cairns L (S) through a gap in the ridge, then down a fairly loose S-facing gully before moving R (W) to gain a platform back on the ridge. Descend a gully which divides almost immediately, the left fork being taken to reach a broad grassy col (25-30 min.).

Descend N into the Hoyo Chico and either follow this throughout to the path from Asotín, or contour round below the NW walls of the Torre del Hoyo de Liordes, and so reach Liordes more directly (1½-2h from summit).

90   NE Ridge and Traverse to Main Summit
A good ridge which is longer and more entertaining than it looks from the Vega de Liordes. The rock is generally good and is best when the climbing is hardest. The only real difficulties are limited to some 100m in the section from the first shoulder to the SE summit. The views grow in both quality and variety as height is gained. First ascent: Unknown. AD, 300m+traverse, 2½-3h from Liordes to summit.

The ridge, whose impressive E walls enclose the R-hand side of the Hoyo de Liordes (see Adrados map), descends towards Vega Liordes in two pronounced steps, the first of which is avoided by starting in the Hoyo de Liordes, some 150m to the L of the toe of the ridge itself. Scramble diag. L up easy angled slabs, then follow a small ledge diag. R to the shoulder above the first step (1h from Liordes). Go easily up to the second step which in the main is taken just R of the ridge with moves of III and IV. After a short, steep crack (IV+) the ridge lies back and easier scrambling leads over several small towers, with a final deep gap before the main summit, the gap being left up easy slabs to the R of the ridge proper (1¼-1½h).

TORRE DEL FRIERO   2445m
This complex and somewhat isolated tower offers fine views over Valdeón, the upper reaches of the Cares gorge and the Western Massif. In addition, the North Face of the Torre del Friero boasts the longest routes in the Picos up the ridges and gullies that plunge 1,000m down to the Vega de Asotín.

91   Normal Route
A short but interesting ascent which is easily tackled from Vega Liordes, or which can be combined with Route 35 to make a full day. Grade B, 450m ascent from Liordes, 2h. Map: Adrados, 1:25,000. (See also Diag, p.113.

From Vega Liordes head W towards the Canal de Asotín. Just past Pt 1984 contour round and into the broad gully descending from the Cdo. de Chavida. A little below this col a stony ramp runs up diag. R, narrowing at the top. Ascend the ramp to a shoulder, then gain loose gullies which lead to the summit.

92   North Ridge
A very long climb with a real alpine atmosphere about it, and superb views of the Western Massif. Not sustained, but with two harder sections, both on dubious rock. Some route-finding skills would be an asset. FA: J. L. Marquínez and J. M. Suárez, 1&2 Feb, 1975. D sup, 1,200m, 6-9h. Diag, p.113.

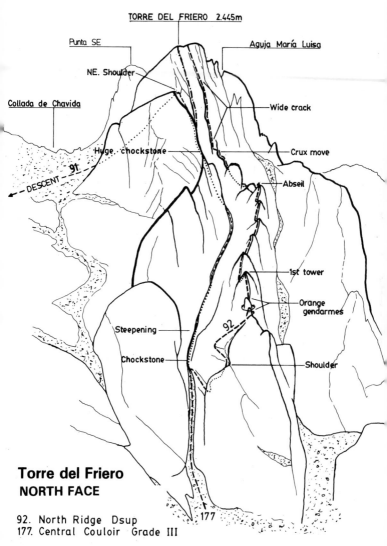

TORRE DEL FRIERO 2.445m

Punta SE

Aguja María Luisa

NE. Shoulder

Collada de Chavida

Wide crack

Huge chockstone

Crux move

DESCENT — 91

Abseil

1st tower

Orange gendarmes

Steepening

92

Chockstone

Shoulder

177

Torre del Friero
NORTH FACE

92. North Ridge Dsup
177. Central Couloir Grade III

Follow the Central Gully of the North Face until some 50m below a large chockstone, where a short move (IV+) gives access to a ramp rising easily R. Follow this, then move back L before going up to a small shoulder (IV+). From the shoulder climb up then L (IV) across obvious ground. By moving back R (IV−) the main ridge is gained just below 2 orange gendarmes.

Pass the first on the R (loose), and next either L or R (V−) to reach a grassy gap from where a slabby arête leads to the top of the first tower. Follow the ridge easily over several towers, then abseil off the last into a deep gap. From the gap pass several small towers on the L, then cross the ridge to pass a large tower below R and gain the shoulder beyond it, and below the crux wall.

A hard move up a wall (V) then an easy traverse L allow a wide crack to be reached and climbed to easier ground. Work up this using slabs and shallow grooves to reach the summit.

TORRE DE PEÑALBA   2442m

The Torre de Peñalba and the neighbouring peaks would be little visited if it were not for the hut at Cdo Jermoso. Indeed, all the routes on the mountain are posterior to its being built. The South Face is reasonably attractive, and the great diedre in its upper half draws the attention of all who pass that way. The full traverse from the Torre de Peñalba to the Torre de la Palanca (2614m) is another classic activity in the area.

Descent: a) From the S (lower) summit reverse the normal route down the West Face, descending first to the gap made with the main summit, then scrambling down L (W). Rock bands across the W Face are descended taking advantage of small gullies and ledges. Difficult route-finding. Not recommended.

b) From the main summit go N a few metres to find the first abseil point (bolts and loop). A 15m then a 40m abseil lead to the gap between the Peñalba and Ubeda towers. From here a third abseil leads to the Hoyo del Llambrión. The first abseil can be avoided by scrambling.

93 South Face: Gran Diedro
One of the classic climbs in the Picos, the present route is the result of various attempts to climb the eye-catching diedre of the upper half of the wall. The first attempt was that of F. Brasas, P. Acuña and S. Rivas in 1956, and even as late as 1985 climbers have attempted to straighten the line out, avoiding the poorer rock of the lower section at the same time. FA: P. Udaondo, A. Landa and J. M. Régil, 24 Sept, 1958. Good rock in general, especially in the diedre. Dsup, 300m, 4h. Diags p.115 & 116.

Start at the highest point of the scree and climb easy ground to a vertical wall with an inclined ramp to its R. Follow this to a large niche, then climb up to a large ledge which is followed R round a spur to a hidden ramp (1½h). This is climbed easily until it is possible to breach the overhanging R wall of the ramp (6b if done free) and so gain the

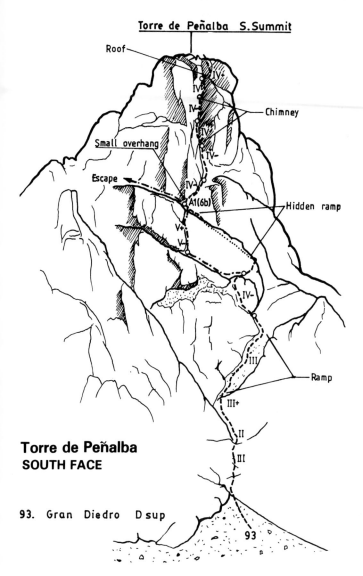

Torre de Peñalba S.Summit

Roof

IV+
IV
IV-
Chimney
IV
IV-
Small overhang
IV-
Escape
A1(6b)
Hidden ramp
V+
V-
IV-
III
Ramp
III+
II
III

Torre de Peñalba
SOUTH FACE

93. Gran Diedro D sup

93

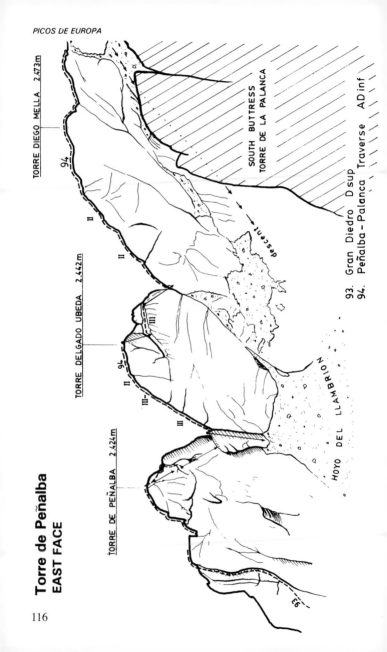

Torre de Peñalba
EAST FACE

PICOS DE EUROPA

TORRE DIEGO MELLA 2.473m

TORRE DELGADO UBEDA 2.442m

TORRE DE PEÑALBA 2.424m

SOUTH BUTTRESS
TORRE DE LA PALANCA

descenso

HOYO DEL LLAMBRION

93. Gran Diedro D sup
94. Peñalba - Palanca Traverse AD inf

main diedre. This is climbed first in the chimney, then by its R wall.

94 Peñalba – Palanca Traverse

A fine and entertaining traverse involving some quite technical scrambling and a number of abseils. The traverse makes a good complement to the previous climb, although it is described here with the Normal Route to the Torre de Palança, a perfectly viable alternative start. FA: Unknown. ADinf, 3-3½h. Diag, p.116.

From the hut traverse round to and then below the W Face to reach a short vertical step giving access to a horizontal ledge. Cross to a shoulder at the R end of the ledge, and so gain the gap between the S summit and the main summit. This section is indicated by occasionsl small cairns. The main summit is reached by climbing first a vertical section to the L of a detached block, and then a small bulge (1h).

From the summit abseil down to the gap with the Torre Delgado Ubeda (2 abseils, 15m and 40m). Scramble up the S Ridge of the Delgado Ubeda tower (III), then make a short abseil, a horizontal traverse (III), and a second abseil to gain the S Ridge of the Torre Diego Mella. Follow this (II) to the summit, and then on easily to the Torre de la Palanca.

From the Palanca it is possible to descend easily S into the Hoyo del Llambrión, and so return to the hut (1h).

HOYO DE CERREDO SECTOR

The Hoyo de Cerredo and the Hoyo Grande constitute the most remote sector of the Picos, approaches to the former requiring from 5-7h. The whole area, with its towers, pinnacles and ridges, has a wild, alpine feel about it, which fully compensates the efforts made in getting there. Though still not much frequented (the ascent of the Torre de Cerredo being the main attraction), the Cerredo sector has been busier in recent years due to the presence of large foreign caving teams exploring what are believed to be amongst the deepest caves in Europe (see Adrados, 1:25,000 map).

There has been talk recently of building a graded path to the area from Bulnes or Vega Urriellu. It is to be hoped that common sense prevails, for if it does not, the area will be robbed of its greatest asset; its remoteness. Accommodation is in the Lueje hut, camping around the hut being a common, though somewhat uncomfortable alternative due to the lack of level ground.

TORRE DEL COELLO   2584m

Insignificant when viewed from the Hoyo de Cerredo, the Torre de Coello presents an attractive 400m face to the upper end of the Hoyo Grande, the climb given below tackling this wall. The area can be approached from the Lueje hut by reversing Route 8 (2h), or from

117

Torre de Coello
SOUTHWEST FACE

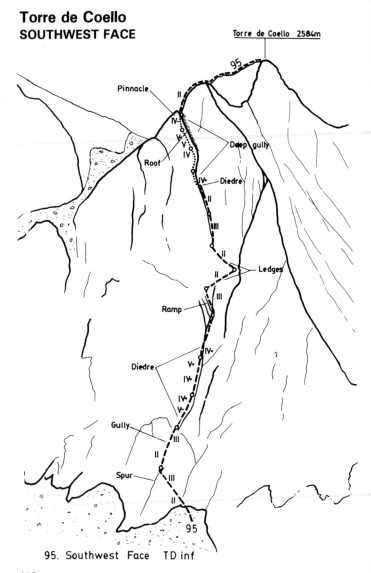

Torre de Coello 2584m

95. Southwest Face   TD inf

Fuente Dé by following Route 8 (2½-3h).

Descent: scramble down easy slopes NE to the Hoyo de Cerredo.

95 SW Face
The route climbs the centre of the SW Face, offering interesting climbing on a remote and seldom visited wall. Good rock except on some easier sections. FA: J. Alonso, R. Chávarri, J. M. San Cristóbal and J. J. Zuazua, 4 Sept, 1976. TD inf, 400m, 4-5h. Diag, p.118.

Start at the highest point of the scree, and climb diag. L to a spur which is crossed to reach a small gully. This leads to a diedre which is followed for 3 pitches to a ramp leading diag. L. A second ramp going R finishes on a terrace which is crossed L to the foot of the gully coming down from a large pinnacle. Climb the gully to the gap N of the pinnacle, then follow the ridge to the summit.

TORRE DE CERREDO   2648m

The Torre de Cerredo is the highest summit not just in the Picos de Europa, but in the whole of the Cordillera Cantábrica. Moreover, it is situated in one of the wildest parts of the range, and its ascent, whilst little more than a scramble, often feels a great deal bigger. The summit provides a perfect view of the Cares gorge some 1,500m below, as well as of the Western Massif.

Descent: by the Normal Route.

96 Southeast Face (Normal Route)
A reasonably easy scramble first up chimneys, then over slabs. Popular. An ice axe may prove useful until mid-season. FA: Generally credited to Saint-Suad and Labrouche, but their account suggests they actually climbed the East Ridge. PD inf, 90m, 45 min. from Jou de Cerredo. Diag. p.120.

From the Hoyo de Cerredo work up over broken ground to a short gully rising diag. R towards the NE Ridge from the bottom R side of the face (snow until late season). Climb the gully until forced to exit R (II). Regain the gully to exit L immediately on to the SE Face which is climbed rising diag. L via easy ledges separated by short steps (II).

97 East Ridge
The route used on the first ascent of the mountain. A very good scramble on excellent rock, and one which is easily combined with an ascent of the Risco Saint-Saud. FA: Conde de Saint-Saud. P. Labrouche, J. Suárez and F. Sallés, 30 June, 1892. PD sup, 120m, 1½-2h.
Diag, p.120.

From the Hoyo de Cerredo climb up to the gap between the Risco Saint-Saud and the East Ridge (moves of II). Ascend the exposed ridge, surmounting occasional steps on good holds (II, III).

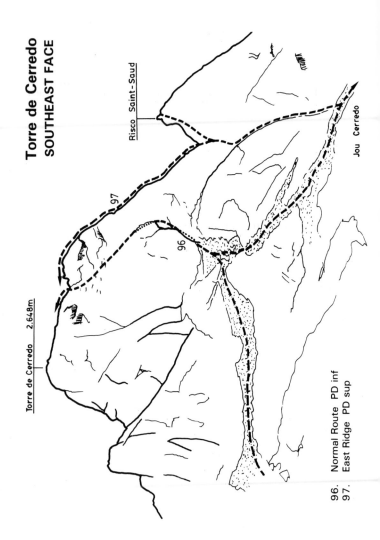

Torre de Cerredo
SOUTHEAST FACE

Risco Saint-Saud

Jou Cerredo

97

96

Torre de Cerredo 2.648m

96. Normal Route PD inf
97. East Ridge PD sup

98 North Buttress
A fine climb on excellent rock. Elegant and direct, it is the best of the climbs on this side of the mountain. FA: F. Bonales, J. Alvarez and P. Udaondo, 27 June, 1976, TD–, 250m, 3-4h. Diag, p.123.

From the Jou Negro scramble up to a point just L of the toe of the buttress. Climb steep rock for two pitches over several small bulges to a stance in a niche (V, IV+). Descend slightly and traverse R, crossing the main ridge (V) to a small shoulder from where the 'Gran Terraza' is gained (III). Leave this on the L (IV), climbing slabs for one pitch to reach a diedre (IV, V+, V) just L of the N Ridge. Climb this (IV+), then trend L to a crack followed by a second short diedre (IV). A final easy crack (II) leads to the summit ridge (II).

PICO DE LOS CABRONES   2553m

Despite its attractive appearance, especially when seen from the north, the Pico de los Cabrones proves to be of limited interest. Access for the non-climber is difficult, and the rock on the north side is poor in general, the wall being at its best in winter. The SE Face, on the other hand, has better rock, though its routes lack continuity, and is linked to the Torre de Cerredo by one of the best ridge climbs in the range.

The name of the mountain refers to an ancient breed of wild goats (goat = cabra) which at one time existed in the area.

Descent: Rather loose and somewhat intimidating, the best summer option being via the Normal Route. Follow the S Ridge down from the summit to the first gap (moves of II). Descend a gully to the E (L), then go down diagonally R (II+), looking for the best route between small steps, and moving back L towards the end.

99 SE Face
A mountaineering route up the rambling SE Face, the best of the climbing being concentrated in the second half of the wall which provides interesting climbing on excellent rock. FA: J. González Folliot and M. López, Dinf, 350m, 3h. Diag, p.123.

The climb takes a direct line from the foot of the face to the summit. The first half reaches the central snowfield over a series of ledges where care is needed with scree. From the snowfield a long crack is followed directly to the summit in four pitches of good climbing (III and IV).

100 NW Ridge
Along with the Normal Route (see descent) this is the most popular route on the mountain. An airy ridge, but one which needs care in places due to loose rock. AD inf., 2h from the hut. Diags, p.123 & 124.

Scramble up the back of the Jou de los Cabrones to Pt 2317 on the Dobresengos-Cabrones ridge. An initial tower is avoided on the L, then the ridge is followed throughout with several steep sections.

Of little value as a route in its own right, the NW Ridge is the ideal way

The Agujas (L) and Pico (R) de los Cabrones from the Lueje hut.

to reach the summit of the Pico de los Cabrones in order to start the next route.

101   Cabrones – Cerredo Traverse
A classic climb in fine positions on the airy ridge which joins the summits of the Pico de los Cabrones and the Torre de Cerredo. This attractive outing involves certain technical difficulties, and in winter is a major undertaking. FA: A. and J. M. Regil, 19 Aug, 1959. D. inf., 800m, 2h from the Pico de los Cabrones. Diag, p.123.

From the summit descend without difficulty to the first gap in the S Ridge. Climb the wall above this (III) and continue to climb back to the crest via the Jou Negro side. Shortly after gaining the crest descend on the W side (R) to a gap. Climb or turn various small towers, descending from the last of them on the Jou Negro side of the ridge. Follow the crest to its lowest point, then on until it narrows (poor rock) and slabs lead to the final difficulty – a short, steep wall. Climb the wall with one awkward move (IV, PR). A second step leads to the summit.

AGUJAS DE LOS CABRONES

These attractive pinnacles, especially when seen from the north with the neighbouring Pico de los Cabrones, form a very alpine scene, though as with the latter they provide little good climbing.

Descent: The safest descent is down the S Face into the Jou Negro.

122

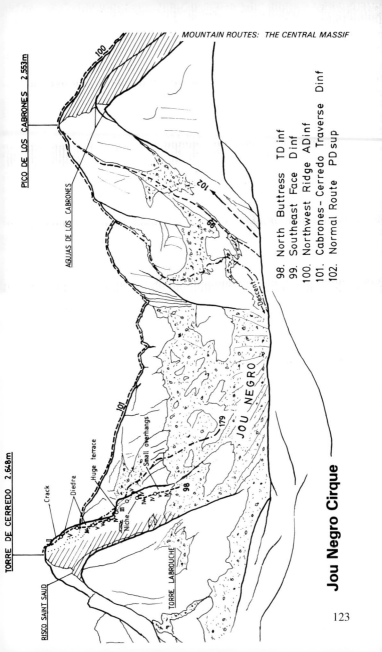

PICO DE LOS CABRONES 2.553m

AGUJAS DE LOS CABRONES

TORRE DE CERREDO 2.648m

RISCO SAINT SAUD

TORRE LABROUCHE

Crack

Diedre

Huge terrace

Small overhangs

Niche

Descent

JOU NEGRO

98. North Buttress   TD inf
99. Southeast Face   D inf
100. Northwest Ridge AD inf
101. Cabrones - Cerredo Traverse D inf
102. Normal Route   PD sup

Jou Negro Cirque

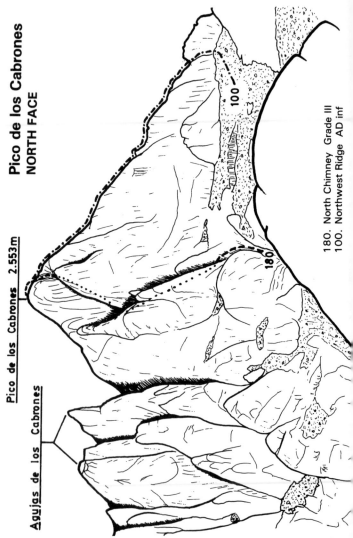

Pico de los Cabrones
NORTH FACE

Pico de los Cabrones 2.553m

Pico de los Cabrones

Agujas de los Cabrones

180. North Chimney Grade III
100. Northwest Ridge AD inf

Going over the crescent crack on the Martinez-Somoano,
a route of certain historical importance.
El Naranjo, E face. (Climber R. Walker).

124

Two or three abseils are usually sufficient.

102   Central and West Towers: Normal Route
The normal route tackles the slabs of the South Face to gain the gap between the two pinnacles. From here either summit can be reached without difficulty. The rock is good, though care should be taken with loose stones. FA: unknown. PDsup, 1h. Diag., p.123.

PICO DEL ALBO   2442m

This is the central of the three summits which make up the Albo group. Access to the peak is relatively easy, and the summit offers excellent views of El Naranjo, yet despite this the Pico del Albo, and indeed the group as a whole, is seldom visited.

103   West Gully (Normal Route)
The ascent taken is made via the wide gully which characterises the west side of the mountain, and which ends at the col between the Cueto Albo and the Pico del Albo. FA: T. Díaz and M. Serna, 1956. PDinf, 400m of ascent and 2h from the Lueje hut.

From the hut cross to and traverse around the S side of the Jou del Agua. Go up beneath the S walls of the W ridge of the Pico del Albo, then cross the gap between the Aguja de María del Rosario and the main ridge, to gain the West Gully. Follow this (snow in early season) to a gap

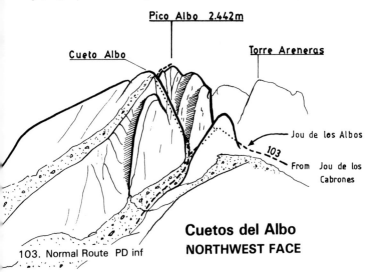

Two climbers finishing the huge 'rampa de canalizos' on the South Face Direct Route of Peña Santa.

on the Cueto-Pico del Albo ridge, then scramble S to the summit (odd moves of I+/II–).

It is a relatively simple matter to combine the ascent of the Pico del Albo with that of the Neverón del Albo (2445m). To do so, scramble along the ridge connecting the two summits (PD, 10min).

VEGA URRIELLU SECTOR

Vega Urriellu is the most important sector in the Picos with regards to rock climbing, being synonymous with El Naranjo de Bulnes. As a result, the majority of climbers visiting the area will want to spend at least part of their time here. Walkers, on the other hand, will find the vega of limited value, and though two attractive tours have been given below, most walkers seem to make a visit to Urriellu part of a longer tour.

The popularity of the area means that it is invariably crowded in summer, having been transformed from the haunt of dedicated mountaineers to the mecca of the thousands in the space of the last few years. A new path (see Route 11) has facilitated access, and the hut is being enlarged to accommodate (or create?) the expected increase in demand. Most British parties prefer to camp.

104 Tour of the El Naranjo group
A worthwhile tour which, when taken in the direction suggested here, allows each of the main faces of El Naranjo to be seen in the best lighting conditions. The section from Cda Bonita to Coteras Rojas is one of the less-frequented areas of the sector. The ascents of the Picos de Santa Ana (Route 78), Peña Vieja (Route 70) and the Torre de Horcados Rojos (Route 80) are easily incorporated into this tour. Grade C, 700m of ascent, 5h, Map: Adrados, 1:25,000.

Descend NE from the hut to enter the Canal de la Celeda which is followed up its L side to the Cdo de la Celeda. Go round the SE side of the Jou Tras el Picu until it is possible to break through the rock walls on the L, and so scramble up to Cda Bonita (2382m) and a classic view of the S and E faces of El Naranjo (2h from hut).

From the col scramble down and then R to an un-named col to the N of the Hoyacón de Villasobrada jou. Follow a vague path round the E side of the depression, then take the easiest line (many small cairns) S over slabby ground to the Coteras Rojas col, from where the Cdo de la Canalona is soon reached (1h). Descend the path to pick up Route 10 below the S Face of the Torre de Horcados Rojos, and follow this back to Urriellu, with increasingly good views of El Naranjo as the distances shorten and the sun moves into the western sky.

105 Tour of the Neverón de Urriellu group
A good walk, though one which covers a fair amount of rough, trackless ground, and which could be troublesome in poor visibility. The outing

South Face of El Naranjo from the Collada Bonita (Central)

can be easily modified to include the ascent of either the Neverón de Urriellu (see Route 106) or the Torre de Cerredo (see Route 96). Grade C, 700m of ascent, 5h. Map: Adrados, 1:25,000.

Follow Route 13 as far as the small col with the first views of the Torre de Cerredo (1½h – Route 106 goes off SE from here). Take the small path heading SW (L) away from the col, skirting below rock walls to a second small col amidst a maze of small jous. Cross this and follow cairns and a vague rising path diag. L onto a large rock dome. Descend off this NW at first, swinging SW at the end to pass by a large cave and gain the col at the N end of the Jou Cerredo (1h – Route 96 can be tackled from here).

Cross the bed of the Jou Cerredo and ascend to the Hda de Don Carlos up broken ground to the L of the col, then descend easily to the Hda de Caín (1h). From here a path descends diag. L (ENE) over scree. When this dies out work down over a boulder field to reach a grassy col overlooking the Jou Sin Tierre. Descend from this col (no path), trending L to join the path from Hdos Rojos at the Gta del Jou Sin Tierre. Vega Urriellu is reached in a further 15 minutes.

NEVERÓN DE URRIELLU   2572m

If only because of the way the dawn light plays on the walls of the East Face, the Neverón de Urriellu attracts the attention of all who spend any time in the area. Closer inspection reveals two climbs of interest, whilst the summit itself offers walkers superb views of El Naranjo and the Torre de Cerredo group.

106 Southwest Face (Normal Route)

*A reasonably straightforward but rewarding walk from Vega Urriellu.
Some care is needed, especially in descent, to find the best line up the
section from the Hda. Arenera. Best undertaken in the afternoon to see
El Naranjo's west wall at its best. Grade B, 600m ascent, 1½-2h from
Urriellu. Map: Adrados, 1:25,000.*

Follow Route 105 as far as the Hda. Arenera, then head S as for Route
105 to just before the small col immediately S of Pt 2350. Head SE up to a
small jou below the SW side of the mountain, which can be ascended
quite comfortably by small slabs and ledges.

In descent in poor visibility it is best to drop down SW to enter the
small jou before crossing N to the Hda Arenera.

107 East Face: Los Celtas

*Varied climbing with some hard moves in the upper section. Care is
needed with the rock on the first bulges and the terrace, but it improves
greatly for the main pitches. The Llambria de los Astures is poorly
protected. Not sustained, but worthwhile for the climbing and change of
scenery. FA: M. A. Mora and C. Sánchez, 17 July, 1980. TD, 300m, 4-5h.
Diag, p.129.*

Approach the start of the climb (snow patch till late season) from Vega
Urriellu in 35-45 mins. The first part gains and climbs the obvious diedre
(some loose rock) low on the R of the face, finishing on easy terraces
which are crossed to the central gully. Climb the gully to the foot of a
large blank slab (Llambria de los Astures) which can be climbed either
direct, or from the upper end of a small ledge rising R. The latter is
harder but has some protection. Either way reach and climb the wide
crack that descends from the summit, the crux being the exit from the
final chimney.

108 East Face: Sol Naciente

*A sister climb to the Via de los Celtas, being another product of the
fructiferous summer of 1980. Not as popular as Los Celtas despite being
more sustained. Again, the upper section provides the main difficulties.
Pegs useful. FA: J. Gálvez and T. Saelices, 13 Aug, 1980. TD, 300m, 5-6h.
Diag, p.129.*

Start some 40m L of the last route. After reaching and passing the
characteristic rising overhang, follow easier ground diag L. Climbing up
to the L of the central gully, a series of R-facing corners is reached. These
lead to the summit, with the main difficulties being concentrated in
pitches 5 and 6.

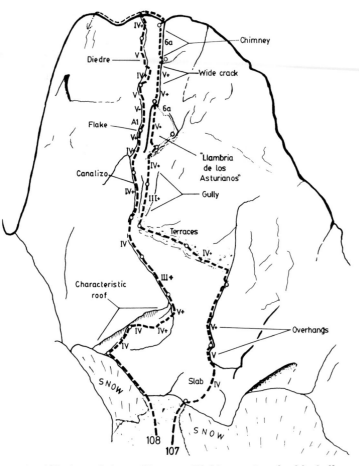

107. Los Celtas TD
108. Sol Naciente TD

El Neverón de Urriellu
EAST FACE

129

EL NARANJO DE BULNES (Picu Urriellu)   2519m

El Naranjo de Bulnes is undoubtedly one of the most famous mountains in Spain. Its illustrious history, along with the tragic events surrounding the first winter attempts on the West Face, have made the 'Matterhorn of Spain' a household name. Such is its fame inside Spain, that it seems quite remarkable that until recently it should have been so poorly known throughout the rest of Europe. The last ten years, however, have seen El Naranjo gain a much wider recognition, with climbers coming from all over Europe to try its climbs, particularly those on the West Face.

Known locally as **El Picu,** the present name is thought to come either from a reference to the colour it turns in the evening sun (naranja = orange), or, more probably, from the corruption of the word naranco (= small area of grazing land) by early French and German explorers. Nowadays most people, and in particular climbers, call the mountain quite simply El Naranjo, though the name Picu Urriellu appears on maps published in the regional language.

The rock, except in a limited number of places, is an excellent, grey, mountain limestone, where water-worn grooves (canalizos), solution pockets, or finger pockets (hueveras) are often the answer to apparently blank walls and slabs. Friction is invariably superb, though due to the compact nature of the rock natural protection is sometimes hard to find. Bolts have alleviated this problem to some extent, but on some routes long run-outs are still to be expected.

With more than 40 climbs on offer, those given here are but a selection. Anybody wishing to extend their knowledge of the mountain will find details of other routes either in the hut in Vega Urriellu, or in the definitive Spanish guide (see p.54).

SOUTH FACE

The shortest and the easiest of El Naranjo's faces, the South Face has, nevertheless, come up to date with routes like Espolon 'Why' and Anfepaz. The face is a suntrap, with all that this implies. An early start is recommended for the Direct Route as queues can form in mid-summer. When descending, an eye should be kept open for stones dislodged from the amphitheatre.

Approach: From the spring by the hut follow a small path NE, passing below the NE Spur of the mountain to enter the Canal de la Celada. Scramble up this exiting L to good views of the E Face. Continue SE over slabs to the Cdo. de la Celada. Allow 1h from the hut.

Descent: With the exception of some E Face climbs, all routes on the mountain descend via the normal route (see Route 110 below).

From the lowest point on the summit ridge scramble down an open gully. On reaching the lower slabs of the amphitheatre trend L to pick up deep canalizos. Follow them until final moves R lead to the abseil bolts.

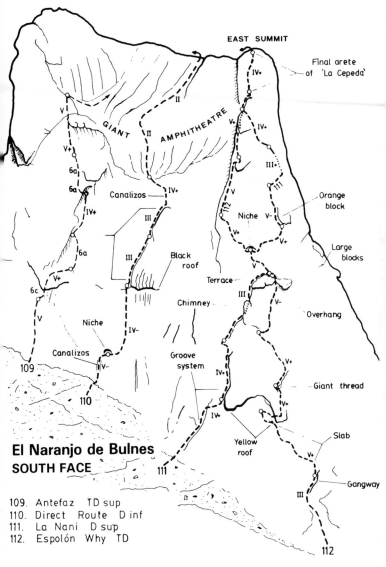

El Naranjo de Bulnes
SOUTH FACE

109. Antefaz   TD sup
110. Direct   Route   D inf
111. La Nani   D sup
112. Espolón   Why   TD

4 abseils (with 50m ropes the last two go in one).

109 South Face: Anfepaz
The hardest climb on the face, and very much in the modern idiom, the summit being an 'optional extra'. Sustained climbing, with one very hard move to start the second pitch. Bolt protection and belays mean that little gear is necessary, although a 'Friend 2' is useful. First ascent: T. Núñez, P. Aguado, 21 September, 1986. TD+, 150m, 2½h. Diagram, p.131.

Start some 20m L of the Direct South Face Route, below an obvious roof. The route goes up to the roof and through the middle of it (hard) before crossing diag. R. After two pitches more or less straight up, hard moves L lead to a difficult slab. An easier pitch to the left of an obvious roof leads to easy ground and the escape into the amphitheatre.
Descent: scramble down into the amphitheatre to the first abseil ring.

110 South Face: Direct Route (Sur Directa)
The most popular route in the area, if not in the Picos, and the normal route for El Naranjo. The first two pitches represent a variant to the original line which lies to the L. The long unprotected traverse of the latter induced a certain nervousness in the clients of the early guides, who promptly sought a more direct entry.

A pleasant climb on good rock, although the difficulties are limited to the first 120m, the rope being a nuisance in the amphitheatre. The stances coincide with the descent route and are equipped with bolts and abseil rings, though the route itself has no in-situ protection. The ability to climb canalizos is an asset. First ascent: A. and J. Tomás & 6 clients, 13 August, 1944. D–, 200m, 2h. Diagram, p.131.

Start below and slightly L of a large black overhang in the centre of the face. Long deep cracks descend from a large niche (abseil ring just visible). Climb the cracks with difficulty to a stance in the niche. Leave the niche on the R, gain cracks that lead directly to a stance at the foot of a large diedre. Follow the corner easily to the next belay ring, then continue in the diedre until it ends below a slab with deep canalizos. Climb the slab (awkward) trending L towards the end to reach the amphitheatre and the belay bolts. Scramble up the amphitheatre to the summit ridge.

111 South Face: Via Nani
An attractive line and a good introduction to the middle-grade climbing on the mountain. The rock is excellent and the protection good when it matters. First ascent: H. Llanos and A. Díaz, 23 August, 1974. D+, 300m, 3-4h. Diagram, p.131.

Start at a groove system below and to the L of a huge, yellow, inverted-V roof. Follow the groove to a stance by the roof, from where another groove and a chimney lead to a small terrace in the centre of the

The East face of El Naranjo. The Y-flake is visible bottom L, the ledges of the Schulze route running across the centre of the photo.

buttress. Climb up diag. L to a niche (difficult), from where a rising traverse R leads with one hard move (PR) to a stance by an orange block. Climb the L side of the block, then trend R to easy slabs going back L with difficulty to a stance overlooking the amphitheatre. Follow the crest to the summit.

112   South Face: El Espolón 'Why'

A route from the bumper summer of 1980. A counter climb to the 'Nani', going from R to L up the SE Buttress, but altogether more serious and more sustained, with some long run-outs. The rock, perfect over the lower half, deteriorates a little towards the end. Pegs might be felt necessary at some stances. First ascent: J. Gálvez and T. Saelices, 16 August, 1980. TD, 250m, 3-4h. Diagram, p.131.

Start below and slightly R of the R end of the obvious yellow roof. Scramble up to a gangway sloping diag. R. Belay as high up this as possible (poor belay – pegs). Climb a difficult slab to a stance below the yellow roof. Cross this with difficulty low on the R, then go up to a huge thread belay. A short gangway and a hard move lead to a long slab which is climbed to an intermediate stance. A second pitch finishes through easy overhangs on to the terrace of the 'Nani'. Follow this route to the niche, from where a vague line goes diag. L to a bolt stance on the edge of the buttress. Two pitches up the buttress (some poor rock in the final chimney) lead back to the 'Nani', and so to the top.

EAST FACE

The featureless nature of the East Face meant that climbing here was late in developing, the first significant route being the Martínez-Somoano. The arrival of specialist footwear and the willingness to use bolt protection changed everything, however, with the summer of 1980 yielding three good routes which are characterised by the vagueness of their lines, and the difficulty of their middle pitches as the face steepens and the superb friction begins to be insufficient. An early start to climbing is recommended to catch the morning sun and, more importantly, avoid any stones that might be sent down by parties on the Cepeda terraces.

Approach: As for the S Face to the head the Canal de la Celada from where the wall is clearly visible. 45 min. from hut.

Descent: All the climbs included here can be followed to the E summit of the mountain, from where the S Face descent is taken. From the final hard chimney of the Vía Cepeda it is also possible to pass directly through to the amphitheatre, thus avoiding the summit ridge. Alternatively, an abseil descent can be made down the E Face, beginning at the N end of the easy terraces of the Vía Cepeda. Convenient for routes such as Capricho and Amistad, the descent does tend to dislodge stones in its lower section.

113 East Face: El Cainejo
The hardest of the 1980 East Face routes. Fairly sustained climbing with two hard pitches. Excellent rock except for the roof on pitch 6. Mainly adequate belays and protection. First ascent: C. Sánchez, A. Díaz, 7 July, 1980. TD+, 300m, 3-4h. Diagram, p.135.

Start some 30m L of the Martínez-Somoano and directly below a long grey streak. Deep canalizos lead easily to a shallow scoop. Gain the scoop and then go straight up (unprotected) or trend R to a peg on 'Capricho de Venus', and then back L. Either way reach a small, broken ledge with poor belays (Large channel useful). Leave the ledge trending L to gain a shallow corner, which is followed until it is possible to move R, and gain a ledge by a final very hard move. Two easier pitches lead to a block belay below an orange bulge. This is climbed with difficulty (7a or A1) to easy ground. Trend diagonally R to the cave stance of the Cepeda Route.

114 East Face: Capricho De Venus
The first of the 1980 routes. Some good climbing, despite the wanderings of pitch 4. Excellent rock, Belays and protection adequate. First ascent: M. A. Mora, C. Marín, 6 July, 1980. TD–, 200m to junction with Martínez, 2½-3h. Diagram, p.136.

Start by scrambling to the terrace formed by a characteristic block in the centre of the face. Pass the flakes above the stance on the L, and

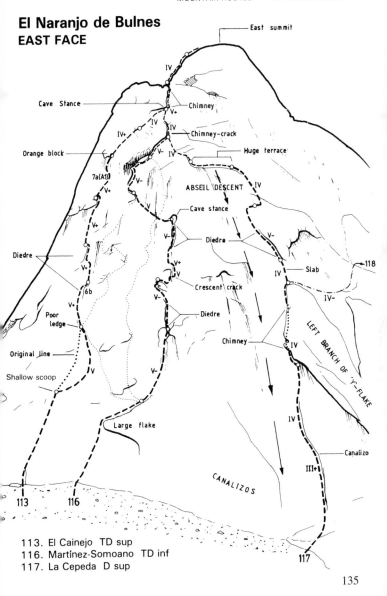

El Naranjo de Bulnes
EAST FACE

East summit

IV

Cave Stance — Chimney

V+

IV+

IV+

Orange block

7a(A1)

V+

V-

Diedre

V+

6b

V+

Poor ledge

Original line

Shallow scoop

V

V-

Large flake

113   116

Chimney-crack

Huge terrace

IV

ABSEIL DESCENT   IV

Cave stance

Diedre   V-

V-

V+   IV   Slab   118

V   Crescent crack   IV-

V-

Diedre

Chimney   IV

IV

Canalizo

III+

CANALIZOS

LEFT BRANCH OF 'Y'-FLAKE

117

113. El Cainejo TD sup
116. Martínez-Somoano TD inf
117. La Cepeda D sup

135

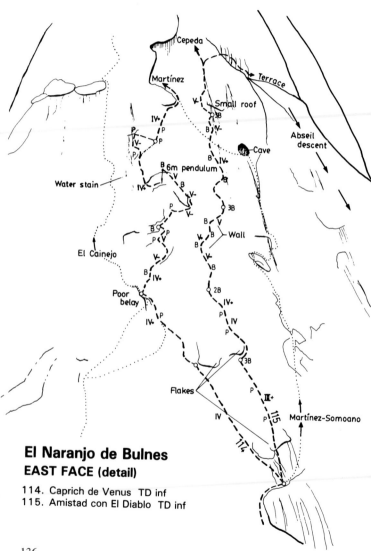

El Naranjo de Bulnes
EAST FACE (detail)

114. Caprich de Venus TD inf
115. Amistad con El Diablo TD inf

climb up to a stance just to the L of another small flake. Trend diag. L to the poor ledge of El Cainejo. Climb first diag. R, then up to a bolt belay. Cross R to an inverted flake and climb this, then back L to a bolt which allows a blank slab to be crossed. Up a vague groove (peg) to a peg in a small roof. Descend R to a poor belay on a slab. Easier climbing leads to the Martínez-Somoano.

115   East Face: Amistad Con El Diablo

The last of the 1980 crop but by far the most popular. Its direct line and the enjoyable, but never difficult climbing have made it a classic. Excellent rock throughout and good belays. The protection is well-spaced, but well-placed. First ascent: A. Iñiguez, C. Marín, 6 and 9, August, 1980. TD-, 200m to junction with Cepeda, 2½h. Diag. p.136.

Start as for Capricho de Venus. From the terrace climb straight up from the stance to a bolt belay below the R-hand of two small flakes. Pass the flake on the R, then up trending slightly L to another bolt belay. The slab steepens now, but one hard section (bolts) allows moves to be made up and R to the belay. Leave the stance trending L, then cross back R before climbing up to a small black roof, crossing the traverse of the Martínez-Somoano en route. Pass this on the L and so up canalizos to a large platform stance. Exit R to La Cepeda.

116   East Face: Martínez-Somoano

A bold effort in its day and a test piece until the arrival of rock boots and bolts took the sting out of the third pitch. Still a very good climb, certainly as worthwhile as its modern rivals. Excellent rock, with good protection and belays. First ascent: T. Martínez, J. L. Somoano, 14 August, 1974. TD-, 260m to junction with Cepeda, 4h. Diag. p.135.

Start as for Capricho de Venus. From the terrace work up diag. R to a stance below a shallow diedre. Follow this, then trend slightly L to a ledge just L of a characteristic, inverted crescent-crack. Pass the crack low down (awkward) to gain the slab to the R, which is followed with difficulty to a diedre (possible belay) which leads more easily to a cave. Make a slightly-rising traverse L to an obvious, large diedre (vague line, poor protection). Two pitches up the corner lead to the Cepeda.

117   East Face: La Cepeda

The first route of the face and the easiest. Not sustained, but providing some good climbing, with one hard move at the top. Mainly good rock and belays. First ascent: M. J. Aldecoa, J. Cepeda, P. Udaondo, 21 September, 1955. D+, 350m, 3½h. Diagram, p.135.

The climb starts just left of the base of the huge Y-flake that dominates the R side of the face. Slabs with canalizos lead to the Y-flake, which is climbed to a stance on top of the L branch. Three pitches up the wall behind the flake lead to easy terraces (abseil bolts) that are followed L to a cave stance with poor belays. Trending diag. L a chimney-crack is

The crux moves of Amistad Con El Diablo, the slabs steepening to make
138 *problems. (El Naranjo, E face. Climber: Eduardo Martínez)*

gained and followed to slabs and a second cave stance. Leave the cave with difficulty (crux) and follow a broken chimney (exit into S amphitheatre possible) to the SE Ridge, which is followed to the E summit.

NORTH FACE

Despite being the scene of the first ascent of the mountain, the North Face has been largely ignored in recent times, possibly due to the nature of the rock which is more broken than elsewhere. The ascent of the Original Route was an heroic affair (see Historical Notes), but no less so was the second ascent of the mountain made by Gustavo Schulze, a German geologist who climbed the characteristic Y-flake, then crossed to the foot of the north Chimney to join the Original Route. With slight variations in the chimney on the line taken by Pidal and the Cainejo, Schulze reached the summit, from where he descended via the South Face, making use, for the first time in Spain, of the then advanced mountaineering technique of abseiling.

118 Schulze Route
The better of the two original routes with easier route finding in the first half. Good rock in general, and some interesting and varied climbing which finishes up the entertaining North Chimney. First ascent: G. Schulze, 1 Oct, 1906. D+, approx 500m, 3-4h. Diag. p.140.

Start as for Route 117 which is followed to the top of the L fork of the Y-flake. The climb now crosses to the R fork then ascends to a large terrace which crosses the face to the foot of the North Chimney. Climb this over several bulges, the last of which proves the most difficult. (This bulge was named the Panza del Burro (Donkey's Belly) by the Pidal and El Cainejo. The intrepid pair, unaware of the abseil technique, down-climbed their route. On reaching the Panza del Burro, El Cainejo was obliged to lower the Marquis by rope, knot and jam the rope, then slide down before finally cutting off the section of rope he was unable to retrieve!) After the last bulge easy scrambling leads up a gully directly to the summit.

119 NW Spur: Regil variant
The best and most popular of the three early lines up the NW Spur, the Régil combines well with the upper section of the last route to provide a long climb with a strong alpine flavour and good views. First ascent: A. Régil and J. M. Régil, 14 July, 1955. TD–, 600m, 5-7h. Diags, p.140 & 141.

Start on the top L-hand of grass terraces below the slabs and walls of the W Face of the NW spur. An easy rising traverse is made over broken ground, followed by a slight descent to gain the very marked chimney/gully that comes down from the NW Spur. The chimney is followed, not without some difficulty, to the spur. Scrambling leads to the NW Shoulder, from where an exposed pitch up blank slabs, then an

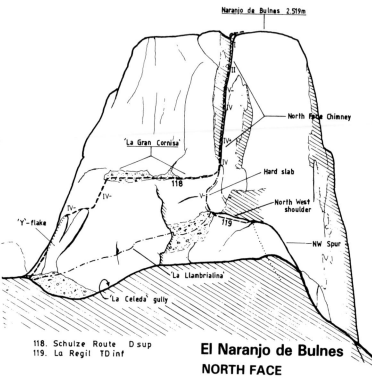

118. Schulze Route   D sup
119. La Regil   TD inf

El Naranjo de Bulnes
NORTH FACE

easier pitch up a crack and bulge, allow the chimney of the last route to be reached.

120   NW Spur: Esto no es Hawaii. ¡Qué Guay!

A route very much in the modern idiom. Put up from above and going nowhere, this bolt-protected line offers some very hard climbing-for-climbing's-sake. A popular test-piece, and 'fun' on rest days. Many parties abseil off after the hard pitch. First ascent: A. Merino and J. Olmo, Aug, 1983. ED–, 170m, ?h

Scramble up to the terrace of the last route, then take a ramp rising R to a belay in a niche. Climb the compact wall above and left of the niche (bolts) on excellent, pockety rock – 2 or 3 falls seem to be par for the course – before traversing R to a belay below a chimney crack. Follow this to the NW Shoulder, the first pitch being sustained and with

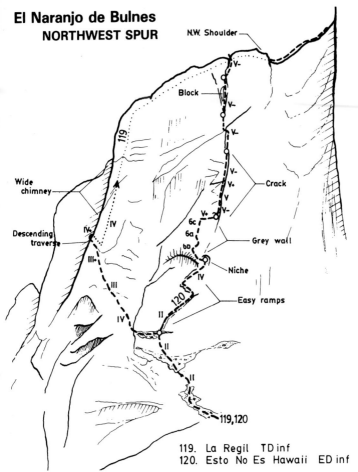

El Naranjo de Bulnes
NORTHWEST SPUR

N.W. Shoulder

Block

V-

V-

V-

V-

V-

V+

V-

V

Crack

V+

V-

6c

6a

Grey wall

bb

Niche

IV

Wide
chimney

119

IV

IV

Descending
traverse

III+

III

Easy ramps

120

IV

II

II

II

119,120

119. La Regil TD inf
120. Esto No Es Hawaii ED inf

apparently little convincing protection. An abseil descent can be made from the NW Shoulder, though the die-hard alpinists will continue to the summit via Route 119.

WEST FACE

500m at its highest point, the West Face of El Naranjo would be dwarfed by many faces in the Alps. Yet without a doubt, this elegant piece of rock possesses an undeniable attraction for many, including those for whom it is sufficient just to come and gaze. The view from Vega Urriellu is impressive, and though the face holds few secrets now, it is not without a certain anxiousness that most west-face parties steal out of the hut at the break of day.

The hardest climbs the mountain offers are gathered together here, and whilst two of them have been done free (Rabadá and Leiva), most require aid to some extent. It would be wrong to dismiss these climbs out of hand, however, as the aid climbing involved is often limited to a couple of pitches in an otherwise superb free-climb.

The routes given below have been selected from across the width of the face, avoiding climbs where aid dominates, except for Mediterraneo – a concession to those who still have not completely kicked the habit. Details of the other excesses with skyhooks and étriers will be found in the hut or the definitive guide (see p.54).

Approach: Obvious, but awful in the early morning. Routes 121 and 122 start on top of the plinth of grey rock on the L side of the face. The next two start at a small pillar resting against the face, below and slightly R of the Lastra Soldada. The Lieva starts some 50m R of the Rabadá, at a grassy bay below rounded overhangs.

Descent: Via the S Face (see p.130), though two important escape lines serve these climbs. The Murciana coincides with a series of rescue abseil rings set up by the Civil Guard in 1984. Apart from providing an easy escape from this route, the rings also make escape possible from Mediterraneo at Rocasolano, and from the Rabadá after the abseil pitch. The Rabadá, Almirante and Leiva can also be left at Tiros de la Torca, the huge bay on the R side of the wall.

121   West Face: Mediterraneo

A hard climb, the lower section of which ventures boldly up some exposed ground. Two long, difficult aid pitches require competence in artificial technique, and a lot (or total lack) of imagination. The free climbing, though never extreme, is always interesting. Apart from the gear recommended for the Harder routes (see Equipment Notes), skyhooks and some 15 pegs (small and medium channels, medium blades and leepers) are needed. Jumars ease the second's lot, though are not essential. The rock is good throughout, whilst bolt belays take some of the tension out of the aid. First ascent: M.A., J.L. and C. García Gallego and A. Ortiz, July, 1980 (climbing spread over 10 days; summit reached on July 18). ED/A3, 550m, 12-16h. Diagram, p. 143.

Start just below the top of the grey plinth, below a small niche and an obvious crack. Climb the crack to the top of the tower, then work diag. L for two pitches (the second 6a/b if the pendulum move is freed) to gain a large cave clearly visible from below. Leave the cave on the L – a mixture of pegging and skyhooking leads to a series of bolts, then more aid to a hanging stance. Difficult pegging off the stance gives way to easier aid,

El Naranjo de Bulnes
WEST FACE

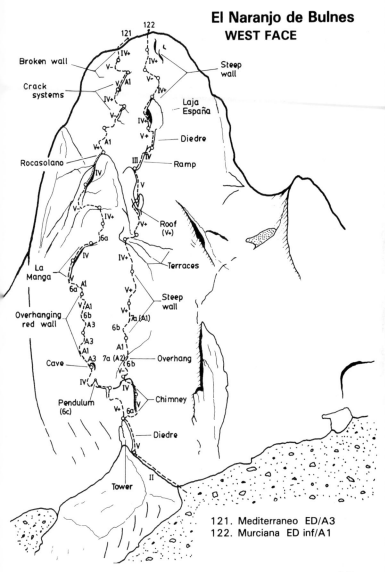

121. Mediterraneo ED/A3
122. Murciana ED inf/A1

143

with bold but easy free moves to reach the belay.

A few simple aid moves then a difficult, poorly protected traverse L, lead to a prominent crack system (La Manga). Follow this easily to a hard, steep wall which finishes at a wide ledge and the end of the main difficulties. Traverse L to another crack system that rises easily to large ledges (Rocasolano – escape possible up or down the Rabadá). From the top of the tower, the last five pitches link two vague crack lines by long traverses over slabs, the first pitch being the hardest. Ignore old bolts going diag. L after this pitch and go R instead.

122   West Face: Murciana

A superb climb which finds a direct but natural line up the face. The route has rapidly become a classic. Moreover, each summer sees the aid reduced further, the little that remains being straightforward, and adding to rather than detracting from the variety of the climbing. The rescue points make the route a safe undertaking even in doubtful weather. The rock is almost always perfect, and the protection sufficient. First ascent: J. L. and J. C. Gardía Gallego, J. C. Ferrer and A. Cerdán, August 1978 (9 days' climbing; summit reached on August 11). EDinf/A1, 530m, 8-12h. Diagram, p.143.

Start as for the Vía Mediterraneo. Climb the crack to the top of a small tower, then traverse R over poor rock (hard) to gain a deep chimney. Follow this to a ledge below a bulging wall. Hard climbing through the overhangs on the R leads to a bolt ladder and a hanging stance. Leave this heading slightly L, then back R to break through another bulge. The Gran Traversía of the Rabadá is reached after two straightforward pitches up superb, steep, pockety rock.

Climb an intimidating black wall, first trending R on good pockets (poor protection), then back L to finish boldly through a roof. A steep corner then an easy ramp lead to the foot of a 30m diedre. Climb this with a difficult final move, then make a long pitch up poor rock to a stance on top of the Laja España. The final slabs are climbed in three exposed pitches, going first R, then back L, before going up to finish slightly R up a broad groove.

123   West Face: Rabadá-Navarro

The first route on the face and still a classic of Spanish climbing. The first ascent was made by the Aragon pair, Alberto Rabadá and Ernesto Navarro, who were the first to use bolts on the mountain. Their attempt involved four bivouacs, the route being abandoned via Tiros de la Torca after the third night. On returning, Rabadá and Navarro solved the problem of the Gran Travesía, climbing the Gran Diedro and the NW Arête on the last day.

Early attempts at a winter ascent brought tragic results. The first pair to tackle the route in winter were Francisco Berrio and Ramón Ortiz. On February 2, 1969, after four days' climbing, the leader fell from the last hard move, taking the second with him. The following year Gervasio

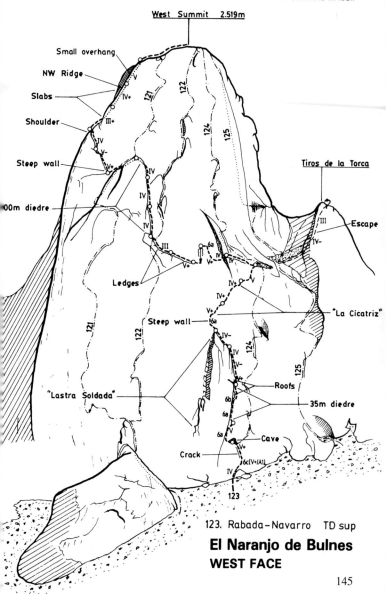

West Summit 2.519m

Small overhang
NW Ridge
Slabs
Shoulder
Steep wall
00m diedre

Tiros de la Torca
Escape
"La Cicatriz"

Ledges
Steep wall
"Lastra Soldada"
Roofs
35m diedre
Cave
Crack

123. Rabada-Navarro   TD sup

El Naranjo de Bulnes
WEST FACE

145

Lastra and Luis Arrabal also reached the final arête in four days. Suddenly, a terrible storm broke, trapping them for another four days and costing Arrabal his life. Three years later, in February 1973, Miguel Angel García Gallego and José Angel Lucas made the first winter ascent.

As with the Vía Murciana, the passing of time has seen a steady reduction in the amount of aid on the Rabadá-Navarro, and a number of parties have already climbed the route free. The main difficulties are concentrated in the lower half, particularly in the first 3 pitches if they are done free. The climbing is always good, and the Gran Traversía especially so. The rock, belays and protection do not create problems, and étriers and pegs are not really needed. First ascent: A. Rabadá and E. Navarro, August 1962 (summit on August 21). TD+, 700m, 8-12h. Diagram, p.145.

Start below and slightly R of the Lastra Soldada (memorial plaque). Climb polished rock, with one very hard move early on, to a cave stance. Climb the overhanging diedre to the L in four pitches, the first two being the hardest. From the top of the Lastra Soldada, a hard, steep wall gives access to a rising crack (La Cicatriz), which in turn leads to easy ground (Tiros de la Torca – escape possible R).

An easy traverse (difficult to find) goes L to an airy stance on the lip of the inclined roof. Descend easily then traverse L and up with increasing difficulty (poor in situ protection) to an exposed stance. Abseil 15m to continue the traverse to the foot of the Gran Diedro (escape possible down the Vía Murciana). Climb the diedre to the ledges of Rocasolano. A short wall and a ramp lead to the NW Arête, which is followed to the top, first on the edge and then further L, with one hard, final move over a shattered bulge.

124 West Face: Almirante

A fine climb - not done often, and underrated. Sustained free climbing throughout the lower half, and again in the upper section once the delights of the exit from the cave have been savoured. The poor rock is limited to the pitches before and after the second cave, the remainder being very good. The route has very little in-situ gear and almost all the belays need to be set up. Though in most cases this can be done with nuts, étriers and a selction of pegs will be needed. First ascent: J.L. and J.C. García Gallego, August 1982 over several days. ED/A3, 530m, 12-16h. Diagram, p. 147.

Pitch 1 of the Rabadá-Navarro. From the cave go R to a deep canalizo, which is entered with difficulty (poor protection) and leads to a small niche. Exit R (hard) and go up to a yellow roof. Pass this L, then go diag. R over easy slabs to below steep cracks. These give sustained climbing (PR) to below a niche. Cross R to a second niche, then exit L from this for the first of two hard, sustained pitches, the second taking a leaning corner to an easy traverse R below a large flake. Easy ground leads to

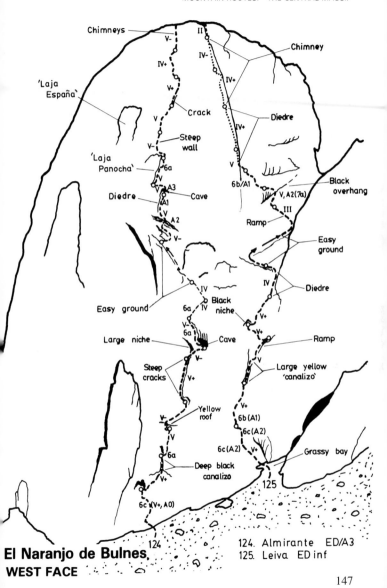

Chimneys

Chimney

'Laja España'

V−

II

IV−

IV+

IV+

V+

Diedre

V

Crack

V+

V

Steep wall

IV+

V−

'Laja Panocha'

6a

V

A3

Cave

V

6b/A1

Black overhang

Diedre

A1

A2

V

V, A2(7a)

III

V−

III

Ramp

Easy ground

IV

Easy ground

IV

IV

Diedre

6a

Black niche

IV

V−

V+

6a

Large niche

V−

Cave

V+

Ramp

Steep cracks

V

V+

Large yellow 'canalizo'

Yellow roof

V+

V+

V−

6b (A1)

V

6a

6c (A2)

6c (A2)

V+

Grassy bay

Deep black canalizo

V+

125

6c (V+, A0)

El Naranjo de Bulnes,
WEST FACE

124

124. Almirante ED/A3
125. Leiva ED inf

147

the Tiros de la Torca.

Scramble up an easy ramp to the L of a large roof. Go R to find a break in steep striated rock, then work back L to a diedre which finishes in a cave. Climb straight out of the cave on dubious aid then traverse L to an airy stance below a leaning diedre (La Panocha). Up the diedre (some poor rock) with one hard move just over halfway up. Five more pitches of steep, sustained climbing on good rock lead to the top.

125 West Face: Leiva

The third of the now classic trio of west face climbs. As with the Murciana and the Rabadá-Navarro, the Leiva has been subject to attempts at a free ascent from the mid-80s, a first free ascent being made in July, 1985 by members of a strong Czech party. Due to the poor protection at the start of the second half of the route, however, most parties are still making some use of the aid. The difficulties are concentrated in the first pitches of the two parts into which the route is clearly divided. The climbing is varied, and takes place on invariably good rock. FA: M. A. Díez Vives and F. Gómez de León, 7th to 13th July, 1979. ED inf., 500m, 7-10h. Diag. p.147.

Start some 50m R of the Rabadá-Navarro, at the L end of a grassy bay beneath overhangs. The first pitch climbs a grey slab to the L of the overhangs. The slab steepens to a wall, and the moves to the hanging stance prove very hard, as do the moves away from it. A sandy niche marks the end of the difficulties, and four pitches of rising traverses allows the Tiros de la Torca bay to be gained.

From the bay scramble up to a slab that rises diag. L beneath a black diagonal overhang. Climb this slab to a stance below the overhang, which is overcome by hard free climbing or delicate aid work (small 'Rocks' useful). A ledge is reached (bolt and peg belay on the L), from where a difficult rising traverse L ends at the foot of the final chimney. Four pitches of easy but enjoyable climbing (some loose rock on the first of them) lead directly to the summit.

PART II: THE WESTERN MASSIF

ARIO SECTOR

Despite the hut and the undeniable beauty of the area, the Vega de Ario is not a sector in which people stay for long, most passing through on their way to or from routes. There are no climbs of any note, and all the walks and scrambles given here can be successfully undertaken from the Vega de Enol in a single, though somewhat long day. Ario does have a special attraction for many people, however, and a short stay here would in no way be wasted, the recently improved 'Marqués de Villaviciosa' hut providing a comfortable base.

EL JULTAYU   1935m

Few summits in the Picos provide such memorable views as those from El Jultayu. The easy approach ends in sudden and quite surprising views of Caín, some 1,500m below in the Cares Gorge, the huge gullies of the Central Massif forming an intimidating backdrop.

126   Jultayu: Normal Route
A straightforward walk, but a classic outing which allows everyone to savour the heights. Grade B, 300m of ascent, 1-1½h from Ario. Map: GH Editores, 1:50,000.

Leave the hut on a track going WSW across the vega. When this dies out follow frequent yellow paint marks around a small rocky hillock (Spot ht. 1627m), then across broken rocky ground and W over a short stretch of grassy terrain. When the path turns sharp L (SE) towards the Trea, continue SW up an easy spur (cairns) to a junction with the spur that comes down from the summit, and which gives a view over the Jou Jultayu. Turn L here and climb the spur to the summit of the mountain and surprising views.

The descent is made down the same route. Alternatively, those adept at simple scrambling can go W along the ridge to the Juracado (a large, natural hole with views of Caín) then drop down to col between the Jultayu and Cuvicente. By following the ridge (odd moves of I+/II–), the summit of the Cuvicente is reached (20 min. from col), from where it is possible to descend further W to the Boca del Joón. Going N to the Pico Gustuteru (1812m), the path from Aliseda is met and followed back to Ario (1h from the Joón; 3½-4h for round trip).

LA ROBLIZA   2248m

A small, but not unattractive tower overlooking the very deep depression known as the Joón. Access to the tower is not easy, as a

149

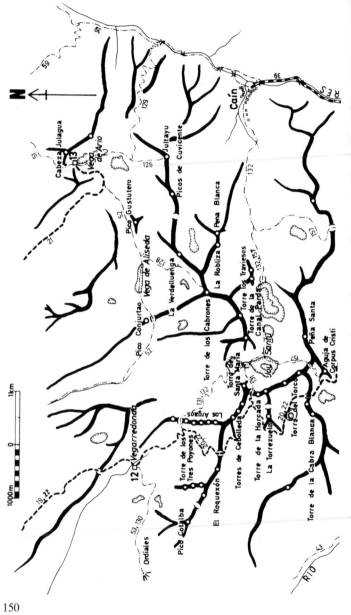

PICOS DE EUROPA Western Massif

151

result of which it is not often climbed, though those who return frequently to Ario seem to value its ascent.

127 Northeast Arête (Normal Route)
An exposed scramble up the narrow and exposed NE Arête. The rock needs care in places and a rope is recommended. FA: unknown. PD sup, 2h from Ario.

Go SW from Ario aiming for the Pico Gustuteru (1812m). Turn S and work up broken ground (no path) to reach the Boca del Joón, a col with good views of La Robliza and, to its L, Peña Blanca. Descend into the jou, then climb out to the col to the R (NW) of La Robliza. Follow the ridge with two rock steps which are avoided on the L.

TORRE DE LOS CABRONES   2290m

Despite its uninteresting appearance, the Torre de los Cabrones (Torre Blanca on some maps), provides unusual and remarkably good views of the Western and Central massifs.

128 Torre de los Cabrones: Normal Route
A good scramble to a summit which provides a good reason for going into an area which is very little visited. Grade B, 600m ascent, 2½h. Map: GH Editores, 1:50,000.

Follow Route 133 to the Pico Gustuteru, then continue W to the beginning of the long Vega de Aliseda. From here, work SW over slabs and broken ground, skirting round the W and SW flanks of the Verde-Iluenga to gain a col just SW of the summit (spot ht. 1970. 1½-2h from Ario. Excellent views into the Joón. The summit of the Verde-Iluenga is reached by a short, obvious scramble).

From the col avoid the first minor summit on the ridge going SW to the Torre de los Cabrones, but go over the others, and so reach the base of Pt. 2227. Pass below this to gain the spur running down NW from Pt 2268. This point was named the Punta Gregoriana by the Comte de Saint Saud in honour of El Cainejo – Gregorio Pérez. The summit of the Torre de los Cabrones lies a short distance away (2½h).

It is possible to continue this traverse SW to the Torre de los Traviesos (2396m) and then W to the Torre de la Canal Parda (2369m), though the return to Ario from the latter is complicated until the Vega de Aliseda is reached.

The final route based on the Vega de Ario is not to a peak, but down a gully. It is, however, a very large gully.

129 Canal de Trea
Roberto Frasinelli, a German gentleman who last century married and settled in the Picos, is reported as having declared "Ario by day. And by night the Canal de Trea, lit by the moon, is the most fantastic thing

man's imagination can dream of."

Certainly, the descent of the Canal de Trea stays in one's memory one way or the other, though to go down at night would seem to be taking things too far. This is a long descent in impressive, but unforgiving surroundings, one which can be combined with the ascent of the Cares gorge to Caín, or its descent to Poncebos. Occasionally, parties ascend Trea, but usually by mistake and never more than once. Grade B, 1,200m of descent, 3-4h. No current map marks the Canal de Trea with any accuracy at all.

Follow Route 132 until it begins to climb SW up a broad spur. Here cairns lead down SE. Follow these, ignoring the head of a large valley (the Valle Extremero) which appears on the L, until horizontal grassy ledges are reached, running L above a huge gully split into two by a large, isolated spur. The ledges are the Llanos de la Cruz, and lead to a long promontory which separates Trea from the Valle Extremero, and which provides excellent views of the Cares. A small path descends into the L of the Trea gullies from just before the promontory. The first section of descent ends in a huge cave in the L wall. Now go R, crossing a dry river just above a spring, and entering a wood. At a fork in the path go L, come out of the wood, and cross the river bed again to enter another wood. Do NOT follow the river bed directly down to the Cares. The path descends through the wood, coming out at the Puente Bolín above the River Cares.

VEGARREDONDA SECTOR

Vegarredonda is one of the most important bases for activities in the Picos de Europa, fulfilling a role similar to that of Fuente Dé in the Central Massif insomuch as it provides a wide range of routes from the simple and short, to the long and fairly hard. The area is attractive and access is relatively simple, though if vehicle access to the Pozo del Aleman is prohibited, as is planned, this will change. At the moment, however, the comfortable approach and the new hut make this a very popular target for many people.

Camping is possible near the old hut, but only for one night (see Mountain Bases notes on the Western Massif), whilst some people opt for a bivouac either in the Jou Santu or near La Mazada. It would also be possible to tackle most of the routes from a base in the Vega de Enol.

130 Mirador de Ordiales – Requexón Ridge
This pleasant outing, apart from visiting Ordiales and the tomb of the Marqués de Villaviciosa, provides enjoyable but reasonably simple scrambling over the chain of summits running E from Ordiales to La Mazada col. PD, 4-5h from Vegarredonda for the return trip. Map: GH Editores, 1:50,000.

Follow Route 53 to Ordiales (1h), then scramble easily up to the summit of the Pico Cotalba (2028m) (I–; 45 min). Descend SW and traverse over the summit of the Tiro de la Canal Vaquera (2044m) (I) and so reach the Hda del Poyo. Leave the col first slightly L, then diag. R beneath the walls of the 3rd of the Tres Poyones (2094m), which is climbed with a slight diversion L (I+), before scrambling down to the broad col (Hda Ancha) to the W of El Requexón (2170m). This is climbed going diag. R from the col to gully which leads to the summit in 90m (II). Descend the E Ridge to La Mazada to pick up the path back to Vegarredonda.

131   Tour of the Torre de Santa María group
A walking tour of the Torre de Santa María group which takes in some varied and impressive scenery. An ice axe may be necessary for the crossing of the Hda de Sta María which, even without snow, proves to be the most awkward part of the tour. Grade B, 850m of ascent, 4-5h. Map: GH Editores, 1:50,000.

From the hut follow a well-used path S past the old hut and up into a narrow valley. After 35-40 minutes the path divides, the R fork going up and R to pass below the monolithic Porru Bolu. Take the L fork and so gain the Cdo de la Fragua and views of the Torre de Sta María. Follow a comfortable path which rises SE, eventually passing below the Aguja de Enol and entering the Jou de los Asturianos, from where the Boca del Jou Santu is quickly gained, along with superb views of the N Face of Peña Santa de Castilla (1¾-2h).

The next section proves to be the trickiest, as an ascent is made diag. R over broken slabs to gain a large, flat platform below the E Ridge of the Torre de Sta María. From the platform continue to rise gently, until a vague path (small cairns) is picked up skirting round the very base of the slabs of the SE face of the mountain. The path leads to the foot of the final section of the gully which descends from the Hda de Sta María (snow), the col being reached in a further 15 mins. (1h).

The first 150 metres or so of descent are steep and trackless, but lead to a good path which is followed comfortably to La Mazada, passing first below the S and SW walls of Las Torres de Cabolleda. A spring (Fuente Prieta) lies just below the path level with the huge cave of the SW Face (45 min). The descent from La Mazada is straightforward and Vegarredonda is reached in a further 45 min.

132   Caín via the Canal de Mesones
A popular excursion which takes people past the most impressive peaks of the Western Massif, before making the descent of the Canal de Mesones, one of the longest of the many gullies that fall from the massif to the River Cares. Grade B, 600m of ascent and 1,600m of descent. 4-6h. Map: GH Editores, 1:50,000.

Follow the previous route to the Boca del Jou Santu, but stay on the path as it traverses round the E side of the jou to gain the broad col separating the two depressions which make up the Jou Santu (2h). A vague path contours E along the N slopes of the second depression (incorrectly marked on map), reaching the impressive gap between the walls of Peidras Lluengas on the L and the spur descending from Peña Sta de Castilla on the R (30 min). The gap, known as El Boquete, offers fine views of the Central Massif. Caín lies some 1500m below, 1-1¼h being usual to reach the cabins of the Majada de Mesones (1450m), and a further 1½-2h to reach Caín, the exact time being governed by one's ability to sustain the steep, unrelenting descent, during which care is needed so as not to be lead off the best route by the paths that the sheep and goats have created in moving from one area to another.

TORRE DE LOS TRES POYONES   2094m

Three attractive towers (especially when viewed from the E) which form a northerly offshoot of the ridge running from Ordiales to El Requexón, and which offer two good, short climbs and a difficult ridge.
   Descent: From the gap between the 2nd and 3rd towers scramble down L (E) to a peg. A 25m abseil and scrambling leads to the Jou del Requexón. For climbs ending on the 3rd tower, scramble down SW then return to the Jou del Requexón by traversing below the W and N walls. Alternatively, continue the traverse over El Requixón, which provides excellent views of the Tres Poyones.

133   Integral Traverse
A very enjoyable ridge climb, with one hard section starting the second tower. Good rock and good positions, escape being possible after each tower. First ascent: 6 October, 1973. D, 3-4h. Diagram, p.156.

   From Vegarredonda follow Route 20 to below the Porru Bolu. In a grassy hollow immediately after this leave the main path and continue W (vague path) to reach the NE edge of the Jou del Requexón.
   Scramble easily up the N Ridge to the summit of the 1st tower (I/II), then descend to the gap with the 2nd tower, keeping R at the end. Ascend a few feet, then traverse R to a short crack that leads to a shoulder. The slabby rock above is split by cracks. Take the one that descends to the shoulder for 30m (V–, PR) to gain a small niche. Leave L and gain a chimney which is climbed (IV+) to the end of the difficulties. From the gap with the 3rd tower climb a small pinnacle (IV) to a second gap and so on to the summit.

134   2nd Tower, East Face: "Les Cabres"
A short, but nonetheless interesting climb on excellent rock. The diminishing slab proves entertaining. First ascent: J. M. García and A. Menéndez, October 1977. D, 240m, 2-3h. Diagram, p.156.

   Approach as for the last route. Start below and R of the huge circular overhangs that dominate the face. Climb easily up to a grassy terrace. Step delicately L (V) and then up to a stance (pegs). Step L again then up

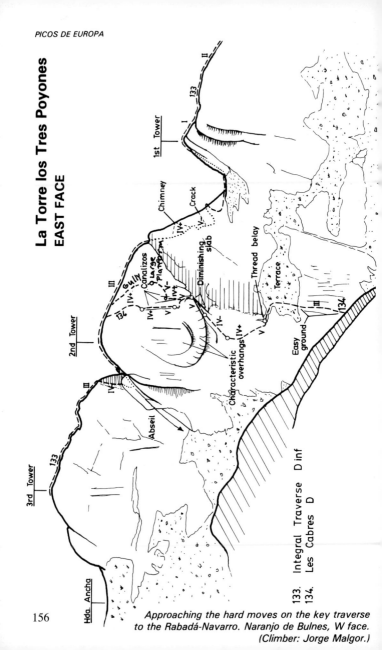

La Torre los Tres Poyones
EAST FACE

1st Tower

Chimney

Crack

Thread belay

Diminishing slab

2nd Tower

Candlizos

La 3ª
Plano

Characteristic overhangs

Terrace

Easy ground

3rd Tower

Abseil

Integral Traverse D inf
Les Cabres D

Hda. Ancha

156

Approaching the hard moves on the key traverse to the Rabadá-Navarro. Naranjo de Bulnes, W face. (Climber: Jorge Malgor.)

133. Integral Traverse D inf
134. Les Cabres D

to a right diagonal groove which leads to a stance below the R end of the roof. Follow an ever diminishing slab R (exposed - pegs) to a good stance when all roads seem to end. Climb the groove system above to a thread belay and then continue up a steep canalizo (poor protection) or escape off diag. R.

135 3rd Tower: W Gully
Another short climb, but a pleasant one at an easy standard and on good rock with good protection in the main. The face itself has a very remote feel about it. FA: J. M. Suárez, J. Marquínez and J. J. Iglesias, 2 July, 1973. AD, 130m, 1-1½h.

The west side of the 3rd tower is characterised by a tall detached tower and, to its R, a curving gully which narrows into a thin crack near the base of the wall. The climb starts some 70m down from the col, where a steepish slab gives access to the wall to the R of the gully (III+). A rising traverse L on easier ground (some loose rock) leads to the gully itself. This is followed throughout, the main difficulties being met in the middle section (III+ and III). When the gully ends a short section of slabs leads L to the summit.

EL REQUEXÓN 2170m

A satisfying summit offering fine views in all directions. Difficult from all sides except the east, El Requexón is especially hard from the north, the short but imposing wall providing one good climb, with scope for another up its blank central section. The unmistakable outline of the mountain is reminiscent in shape of a type of local cheese called requexón.

Descent: the Normal Route. For Route 137, return to the base of the North Face by scrambling down N from the obvious grassy col that marks the start of the scrambling on the E Ridge.

136 East Ridge (Normal Route)
A short and easy traverse along the ridge running W from La Mazada. Airy in places, with good scrambling up the final section. Grade B, 700m of ascent, 1½-2h from Vegarredonda. Map: GH Editores, 1:50,000.

From Vegarredonda follow Route 20 to La Mazada. Descend W over slabby ground, traverse a small tower and gain a grassy col. A short section of scree gives way to scrambling up broken rock which leads to the summit.

137 North Face: Direct Route
A good climb despite the vegetation that intrudes upon the start and finish. Sustained climbing, with some entertaining slab and chimney work. Mainly good rock and protection. First ascent: A. Zorzo, A. Menéndez and E. Sánchez, September 1972. TD-, 200m, 4-5h. Diagram, p.158.

Just below the 4th tower on the winter traverse of Los Argaos.

157

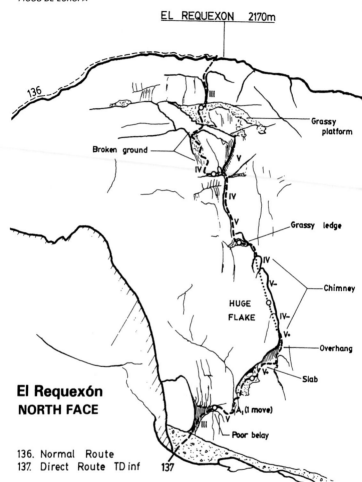

EL REQUEXON 2170m

136

Grassy platform

Broken ground

III

IV

V

Grassy ledge

IV

V–

Chimney

HUGE FLAKE

IV–

V+

Overhang

V+

Slab

El Requexón
NORTH FACE

A₁ (1 move)

V

III

Poor belay

136. Normal Route
137. Direct Route TD inf

137

Follow Route 20 from Vegarredonda. Break E (R) off this shortly after passing the Porru Bolu and gain a grassy spur. Climb this then cross SE to the W edge of the Jou del Requexón.

The climb starts on the L of the face, where an easy slab leads diag. R below a roof (possible stance – poor belays). Step down R to a hidden peg, then climb a steep, grassy groove before using a peg to overcome a short, blank section leading to easy ground and a small niche. Make a hard traverse R (PR) and climb a short hard groove (3PR) into the main chimney. Follow this with two hard sections, one early on. After the second, abandon the chimney L (hard – a direct finish would seem possible, thus avoiding this traverse), then climb broken ground to a grassy terrace. An easy gully leads to the summit.

PORRU BOLU   2025m

An elegant tower clearly visible from many points in the surrounding area despite its modest altitude. The path to the La Mazada col passes below the Porru Bolu, making access easy, whilst the two short routes given below provide pleasant training climbs, or routes which can be undertaken in doubtful weather.

Descent: From near the summit a short abseil leads to the SE gap, from where it is possible to scramble (or abseil) down the NE gully.

138   East Gully (Normal Route)
An easy climb, but one which leads to a satisfying summit. FA: E. Herreros and A. Tresaco, 12th Aug, 1934. AD inf., 90m, 1h. Diag, p.160.

When the path to La Mazada swings W below the Porru Bolu, continue S up the Llampa Cimera, then traverse R to gain the base of the deep gully to the S of the monolith. Scramble up this (III–) to the SE gap, from where a short section of climbing (IV– if taken direct, III+ on the L) leads to the summit.

139   Northeast Face
A short, but worthwhile training climb up the main face of the Porru Bolu. Rock good except at the top of the diedre. FA: C. Suárez and J. Alvarez, 19 May, 1964. Dsup, 100m, 1½h. Diag., p.160.

The lower section of the NE Face has a characteristic diedre. Gain this from below and to the L, and climb it exiting L up ramps. Traverse R to below a roof. Go up to this and avoid it on the L where cracks lead to the summit crest.

The chimney and diedre system to the L of Route 139 is reported to have been climbed at Dsup (V+, A1), whilst the crack system to the R has had at least one free ascent, which was thought to be at about 6b. Finally, the W Face sports one obvious line up to, and round triangular roof and up the wall above (V+, A2, V, V).

LOS ARGAOS   2130m

Los Argaos is the name given to the jagged ridge running S from the Cdo. de la Fragua to the Cuesta de Cebolleda. The five towers making up the crest are numbered beginning at the N end, and offer short climbs on their west side and an interesting traverse.

Descent: From the Cuesta de Cebolleda an easy descent is possible W to La Mazada. It is possible to abandon the ridge after the 2nd and 3rd

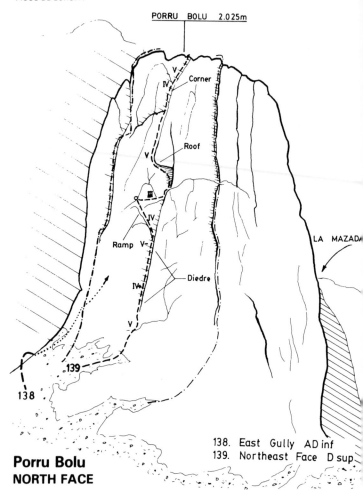

PORRU BOLU 2.025m

V
IV — Corner

V — Roof

III

IV

Ramp V

IV — Diedre

V

LA MAZADA

139
138

138. East Gully AD inf
139. Northeast Face D sup

Porru Bolu
NORTH FACE

towers using the gullies on the W side, and after the 4th tower by a gully
to the E.

140 Integral Traverse
*A classic ridge scramble which is never very hard, but which becomes
increasingly narrow and exposed. The main difficulties are concentrated on the 2nd and 3rd towers, though the knife-edge crest of the final*

*section can prove intimidating. A little grassy at first, with some loose
rock later on, though escape is possible W down the gullies between
each tower. AD, 4h.*

Follow Route 131 to the Cdo. de la Fragua. From the col a short pitch
up open grooves (IV) on the SE side of the 1st tower leads to easy slabs
and the summit. Follow the crest over the remaining towers, generally
avoiding any difficulties or poor rock (notably the 2nd tower) on the L.
From the gap after the 4th tower a very narrow ridge is followed to a
final step (IV–) which gives access to the 5th tower, from where the ridge
broadens out into Cuesta de Cebolleda.

The route is especially satisfying if continued over the Torres de
Cebolledo, and then on to the Torre de Santa María. (See below).

LAS TORRES DE CEBOLLEDA   2438m

These three towers form the SE continuation of Los Argaos. The
traverse of all three offers some airy scrambling, whilst the S and SW
walls of the 2nd tower provide several very good middle-grade climbs
on excellent rock and in the sun.

Descent: From the 2nd tower, either scramble down NW to La
Mazada, or follow the Integral Traverse to the Hda. de Sta. María (see
below).

141   Integral Traverse
*This fine ridge gives good scrambling in exposed positions. The rock, if
a little broken at first, improves as the difficulties increase. Combined
with the traverse of Los Argaos, finishing up the SW Ridge of the Torre
de Sta. María, the route provides a magnificant outing. ADsup, 2h.
Diagram, p.167.*

Follow Route 20 to La Mazada. Go W up the broad spur to gain the
Cuesta de Cebolleda, then swing SE to start the ridge. The 1st and 2nd
towers are climbed with little difficulty (II), but a hard move (IV) is
necessary to leave the gap between towers 2 and 3, with easier climbing
(III) leading to the summit. Exposed scrambling leads down to the base
of the Aguja GUA which is climbed or turned on poor rock to reach the
base of the SW Ridge of the Torre de Sta. María. Descend R to the Hda.
de Sta. María, or climb the ridge (see Route 153).

142   2nd Tower, SW Face: Gran Chimenea
*An entertaining climb on very good rock. Not sustained, the main
difficulties lie in the final pitches where both the deep canalizos and the
bomb-bay chimney require good technique. Pegs useful for some
belays. FA: J. Oscaby, C. Schneider and O. Beghinet, 1976. Dsup, 250m,
3-4h. Diag., p.162.*

Follow Route 20 over la Mazada and round a broken spur to above
Fuente Prieta. The route is now clearly visible.

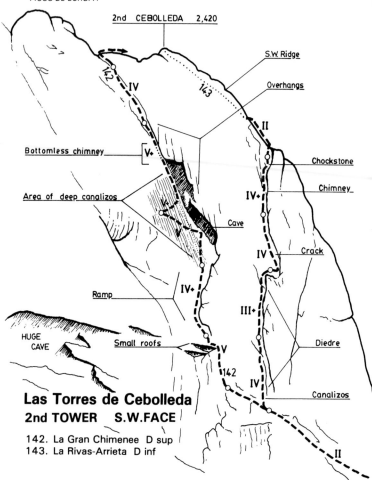

Las Torres de Cebolleda
2nd TOWER S.W. FACE

142. La Gran Chimenee D sup
143. La Rivas-Arrieta D inf

Start below the chimney of the Rivas-Arrieta line. An easy traverse L, steep cracks and a ramp finish in a cave at the base of the great chimney. The deeply grooved wall above can either be taken direct (poor protection), or by going out diag. L to an airy stance (poor peg belay), then traversing back R (hard) to the main line. Either way gain and climb the awkward, leaning chimney to reach the end of the difficulties.

162

143   2nd Tower, SW Face: Rivas-Arrieta

A fine route on very good rock. Nowhere difficult, the grade is maintained throughout, with one hard move in the upper chimney. FA: P. Rivas and J. Iglesias Arrieta, August 20, 1978. Dinf, 250m, 2½h. Diag., p.162.

Approach as for the last route. Start below the obvious diedre which is gained by climbing a steep, grooved wall. Move R along the platform at the end of this first diedre to gain a second. This opens into a chimney,

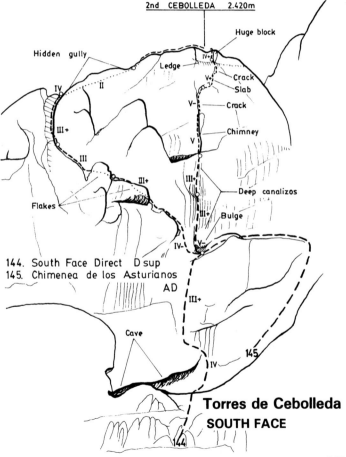

2nd CEBOLLEDA 2.420m

Huge block

Hidden gully

Ledge   IV+

V+   Crack

Slab

V-   Crack

Chimney

IV

II

III+

V

III

III+

III+

Flakes

III+   Bulge

IV-   V-

144. South Face Direct D sup
145. Chimenea de los Asturianos
AD

III+

Cave

IV

Torres de Cebolleda

SOUTH FACE

145

144

163

which finishes on the SW Ridge. Follow an easy gully and easy ground to the summit.

144   2nd Tower, S Face: Direct Route

A pleasant route offering increasingly difficult climbing up the centre of the face. Very good rock and good natural protection. FA: J. Oscaby, C. Schneider and O. Beghinet, 1976. D+, 200m, 2-3h. Diagram p. 163

Approach as for Route 142, staying on the path and climbing up E towards the Hda. de Sta. María.

Start directly below an obvious chimney-crack in the centre of the upper half of the wall. Go easily up canalizos to a platform below a steep bulge. Climb this and the easy grooved slab above to reach the chimney-crack. Ascend this with some difficulty, exiting R on to a smooth slab with a peg belay. Head diag. R with difficulty over steep slabs to gain a crack which finishes on a large, inclined platform. Climb up past an enormous block to reach the summit.

145   2nd Tower, South Face: Chimenea de los Asturianos

A logical climb making use of the large diedre which characterises the L side of the S Face. Straightforward but enjoyable climbing on very good rock. FA: B. Rodríguez, J. Bousoño and E. Lobeto, 13 June, 1976. AD, 240m, 1½-2h. Diag. p.163.

Start as for the last route, or up easier ground further R. Always following the easiest line, work diag. L to gain flakes which mark the entrance to the characteristic diedre. This is followed to the SW Ridge, which is climbed via a hidden gully.

TORRE DE SANTA MARÍA   2478m

The Torre de Santa María (still commonly called Peña Santa de Enol) is very much a mountaineer's summit, with no easy way up or off. The summit, despite being lower than the nearby Peña Santa de Castilla, can be seen from many places both in and beyond the range, the views from the Vega de Enol and from the Lago Ercina being particularly fine. More important still is the panorama from the summit itself, especially that of the mountains and coastal area to the north, and of the Jou Santu and North face of Peña Santa to the south.

The Torre de Santa María was first climbed in 1891 by the Comte de Saint Saud and Paul Labrouche in a mistaken attempt at a first ascent of Peña Santa de Castilla. Nowadays, the mountain boasts a number of climbs, though not on as good a rock as that of neighbouring peaks. In winter the roles are reversed, however, and the climbs of the Torre de Santa María become the centre of a great deal of attention.

Descent: Not an easy business. Either:

i) reverse the Normal Route. Exposed.

ii) reverse the Corredor del Marqués (Route 154 – care with the hard snow of the Cemba Vieya. Not really recommended).

iii) traverse W from the summit to a subsidiary top above the SW Ridge. A single 45m abseil (old slings mark the place) and scrambling lead back to the Hda. de Santa María. (The best winter descent, but also good for those with tight-fitting rock boots.)

146   South Face: Grieta Rubia (Normal Route)

The route used during the first ascent of the mountain and the most popular today. The rock requires care especially in the section known as the 'Grieta Rubia', a reddish vein that cuts across the face from bottom L to top R. Special care is needed if other parties are on the route at the same time, though an early start can usually avoid this eventuality. FA: P. Labrouche and A. d'Arlot de Saint Saud, Sept, 1891. PD, 150m, 45min from Hda. de Sta María. Diag. p.166.

From Vegarredonda follow Route 20 until it descends to go round the Torrezuela. Climb up E to the Hda. de Sta. María and drop down some 40m on the E side (2h). Climb a short, stepped wall below overhangs (II, 20m), then traverse R to a large, inclined terrace which is crossed R to the base of 'Grieta Rubia'. This is started by a short gully, and followed to a gap to the E of the summit (moves of I+ and II). From the gap descend a ramp on the N Face until a small gully climbs up L to the summit (3h from Vegarredonda).

147   SW Ridge

A short ridge of compact slabby rock which, whilst of limited interest as a climb in its own right, provides a very fitting continuation to the Integral Traverse of the Cebolledas (see Route 141). Poor protection. FA: F. Fernández, R. Alvarez, J. M. Suárez and E. González, 8 Sept, 1966. D–, 80m, 1h. Diags, p.166 & 167

Start from the Hda. de Sta. María (see last route) by scrambling up to the terrace between the Aguja GUA and the ridge proper. A short chimney ends at a ledge in the centre of the ridge (III+). Continue up to a small ledge to the L of the ridge (IV–), then follow the ridge itself to a step which is surmounted first by a crack on the L, then by moves on the R (IV+). From the W summit (abseil point) cross a small gap to reach the top.

148   N Face: Cemba Vieya

Used by some people as an alternative to the Normal Route despite the complication of the snowfield at the start of the route, which usually requires at least an ice axe. A classic winter climb, the Corredor del Marqués can be combined with the Normal Route (in descent) to make a very good traverse of the mountain. FA: Pedro Pidal (Marquis of Villaviciosa) in descent after the first ascent of the 'Espolón Norte', 4 Oct, 1907. PD, 300m + 100m of snowfield, 1½h. Diag, p.167.

Sta. Maria
SOUTH FACE

146. Grieta Rubia PD
147. Southwest Ridge D inf
151. East Gully AD inf
154. Normal Route
184. Right Gully Grade IV
185. Left Gully Grade III

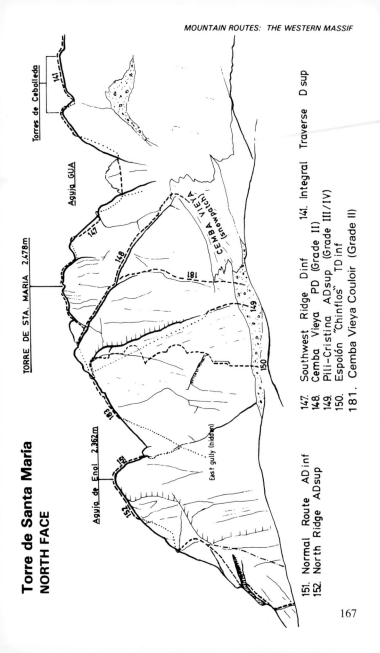

Torre de Santa María
NORTH FACE

Torres de Cebolleda

Aguja GUA

TORRE DE STA. MARIA 2.478m

Aguja de Enol 2.362m

East gully (hidden)

CEMBA VIEYA (snow patch)

151. Normal Route   AD inf
152. North Ridge   ADsup

147. Southwest Ridge D inf
148. Cemba Vieya   PD (Grade II)
149. Pili-Cristina   ADsup (Grade III/IV)
150. Espolón "Chinflos"   TD inf
181. Cemba Vieya Couloir (Grade II)

141. Integral Traverse   D sup

Follow Route 131 until below and N of the Aguja de Enol. Work up towards this, then traverse round below it to enter the cirque it forms with the Torre de Sta. María and the Cebolledas. Go up to the snowfield and climb it (40°) on the L to its highest point, from where a traverse horizontally L (I+) on poor rock leads to the base of a narrow gully. Climb this (II−) to the start of a great ramp rising L across the face, and leading to the last section of the Normal Route.

149 N Face: Pili-Cristina
The deep, square-cut chimney which characterises the L side of the N Face, and which provides a sombre route in the depths of the chimney. Very good rock, though with some looseness in the bed of the chimney, as might be expected. FA: J. J. Iglesias and L. Campo, 8th Oct, 1972. ADsup., 250m, 2h. Diags, p.167 & p.169.

The chimney as such narrows into a crack without actually reaching the ground. Start up this crack and so gain the chimney proper which is followed for some 150m to the Espolón Norte. Climb slabs diag. L to gain a shoulder overlooking the Grieta Rubia of the Normal Route which is now followed to the summit.

150 N Face: Espolón "Chinflos"
A relatively recent addition to the climbing on the Torre de Santa María, and one which uses the expanse of slabs to the L of the Pili-Cristina chimney. Good middle-grade climbing on sound rock, with one harder pitch early on. Good natural protection. FA: G. Meana and E. Oltra, 13th Aug, 1982. TD inf., 280m, 3-4h. Diags, p.167 & p.169.

Start at the lowest point of the wall L of the Pili-Cristina, directly below the R end of a long, characteristic roof. Gain and climb a small diedre, then avoid steep slabs by a hard pitch to their R, working back L to a stance below a small roof. Go up R below this, entering an easy gully which is followed to a large block. Break out R on to slabs leading up to a final overhang which is avoided on the L. A pitch up a ridge leads to a junction with the Pili-Cristina.

AGUJA DE ENOL 2362m

This attractive tower forms the continuation of the North Spur of the Torre de Sta. María, but, despite its appearance and the compact nature of its rock, it offers little climbing, the best routes being up its N Ridge.
  Descent: the Normal Route.

151 East Gully (Normal Route)
The first part of this route up to the gap between the Aguja and the Torre de Sta. María was climbed by Pedro Pidal during his first ascent of the N Spur of the latter. FA: unknown. AD inf, 200m, 30-40 min from the base of the tower. Diags, p.166, p.167 & p.201.

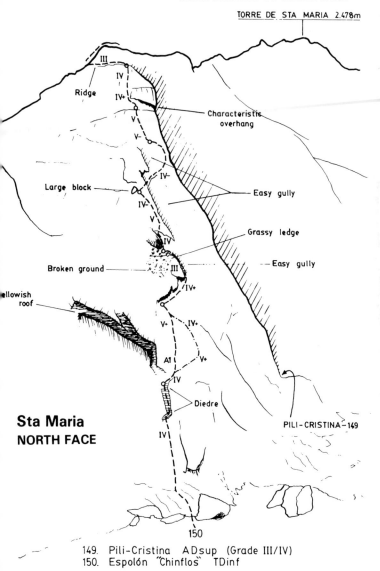

TORRE DE STA MARIA 2.478m

III

Ridge

IV

IV+

Characteristic overhang

V

V-

IV-

Large block

IV-

Easy gully

V-

IV

Grassy ledge

Broken ground

III

Easy gully

IV+

ellowish roof

V+

IV+

V+

A1

IV

Diedre

Sta Maria
NORTH FACE

PILI-CRISTINA-149

IV

150

149. Pili-Cristina ADsup (Grade III/IV)
150. Espolón "Chinflos" TDinf

Follow Route 131 as far as the N side of the Jou de los Asturianos (do not enter), from where the route can be studied. Cross slabs above the N edge of the jou and work up more slabs to gain the base of the gully (2h from Vegarredonda). Climb the gully (moves of (III), following the R branch to a gap. Scramble N up the final ridge.

152 North Ridge

A good route that avoids most of the difficulties of the ridge, yet provides interesting climbing. The rock is excellent, although its compact nature does make protection a little hard to find. FA: I. Cossent and J. Marquínez, 16 Sept, 1974. AD sup., 270m, 2-2½h. Diags p. 171 & p. 167.

Approach as for Route 131 until below and N of the Aguaja. Go straight up to a grassy col and so to the foot of the climb. Start climbing below the L end of the long roof that runs across the ridge some 25m above the ground. Climb an easy ramp diag. L, then work R to gain a break in the roof just to the R of its L end. Climb through the break to a stance. Work diag. R over slabs to the centre of the ridge, then go up to a large inclined slab below a triangular overhanging wall (belay in top L corner). Go L round the corner to cracks and a chimney which lead to the summit ridge in two pitches.

An alternative, direct start can be made up the slabs below and R of the huge roof which crosses the centre of the face. This provides harder climbing with little good protection.

TORRE DE LA CANAL PARDA 2369m

This is an insignificant looking summit, but it provides very good views of all of the summits surrounding the Jou Santu. An easy summit to climb, it is worth rising very early to watch the sunrise over the Central Massif.

153 North Ridge (Normal Route)

An easy ascent that can be combined with the traverse to the summit of the Torre de los Traviesos to provide an entertaining scramble in good situations. FA: unknown. PD–, 1h from the Jou de los Asturianos.

Follow Route 131 to the entrance to the Jou de los Asturianos (1¾h from Vegarredonda). Work E to gain the ridge that comes down N from the summit of the Torre de la Canal Parda, and follow it throughout (I+). A long, straightforward ridge runs E over a col then up to los Traviesos (I), from where a descent can be made NW into a large depression. Once in the depression work round its N side, and head E to pick up the path back to Vegarredonda.

TORRES DE ENMEDIO 2467m AND DE LA HORCADA 2450m

Lying just S of the Hda. de Sta. María as its name suggests, the Torre de

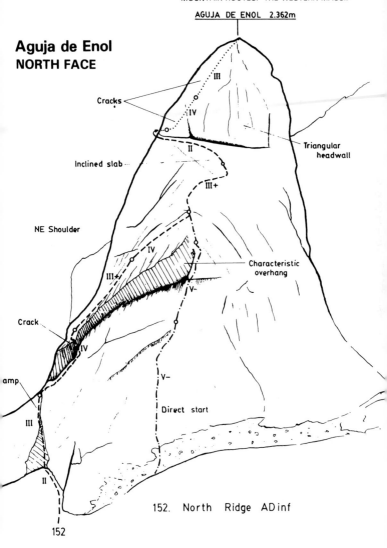

AGUJA DE ENOL 2.362m

**Aguja de Enol
NORTH FACE**

Cracks

III

IV

Triangular
headwall

II

Inclined slab

III+

NE Shoulder

IV

Characteristic
overhang

III+

V−

Crack

IV

amp

V−

III

Direct start

II

152. North Ridge AD inf

152

171

la Horcada, as with a number of peaks in this area, proves to be an excellent viewpoint. Its ascent is easily combined with any route crossing the col.

Descent: by the Normal Route, or N into the Hda de Sta María with one abseil.

154 Southwest gully (Normal Route)

A scramble over scree and rubble. FA: unknown. Grade C, 1,000m of ascent, 2½h from Vegarredonda. Map: GH Editores, 1:50,000.

Follow Route 20 past the SW Face of the Torres de Cebolleda and then strike off L (E) to gain the Hda. de Sta. María. Descend E from this until it is possible to skirt R round the base of the Torre de la Horcada. Scramble up the easy slabs of the East Face to the gap between the Horcada and Enmedio towers. Easy scrambling leads S to the summit of the latter, and true summit of the Horcada tower needing a short, but technical scramble (III+).

LA TORREZUELA   2302m

This attractive peak, especially when viewed from the North, is easily tackled by parties crossing between Vega Huerta and Vegarredonda. Offering little climbing of note in summer, it provides two excellent gullies in winter.

Descent: by the Normal Route.

155 East Ridge (Normal Route

A simple scramble up the narrow and airy East Ridge. FA: unknown. PDinf., 20 min. from the Hda del Alba to the E of the mountain.

Follow Route 20 until it begins its descent around the W side of the mountain (1h 40 min). Go S over slabs to the Hda del Alba (20 min). Climb the ridge throughout to the summit – exposed.

TORRE DEL TORCO   2450m

A solid mountain of excellent grey limestone, and another of the summits which provide good views of the Jou Santu peaks, and of Peña Santa de Castilla in particular.

Descent: by the Normal Route.

156 East Face (Normal Route)

A good mountaineering route, shorter but similar to the Canal Estrecha on Peña Santa de Castilla. An ice axe may be necessary, especially early in the season. FA: E. Ribera Pou and M. Pérez (nephew of 'El Cainejo'), 18 Aug 1933. PD sup, 300m. 1h from base of the main gully. Diag, p.180

Follow Route 132 to the broad col to the Jou Santu (2h from Vegarredonda) then descend R, passing the Fuente de las Balas, a diminutive and unreliable spring in rock which consists of numerous

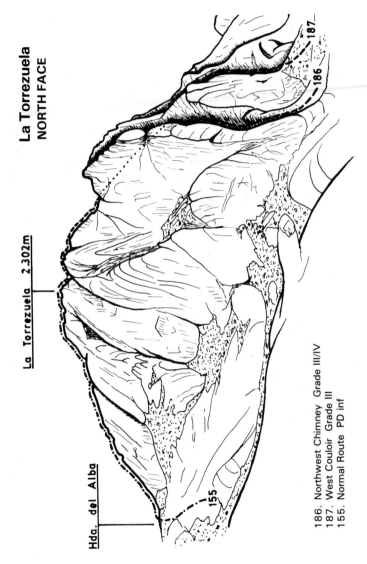

La Torrezuela
NORTH FACE

La Torrezuela 2,302m

Hda. del Alba

186. Northwest Chimney Grade III/IV
187. West Couloir Grade III
155. Normal Route PD inf

spherical stones (las balas). Rise SSW towards the snowfield of La Forcadona, until it is possible to work diag. R over slabs to gain the base of the gully descending from the gap to the R (N) of the peak. (30 min). Climb the gully with moves of II and III–, then go L at the gap over slabs (III–) leading to a short gully and the summit.

VEGA HUERTA SECTOR

Without any doubt, the main reason for staying in Vega Huerta is to climb on the South Face of Peña Santa de Castilla. However, in no way should this deter those of modest aims from visiting the area. The Estribos/Cabra Blanca ridge, the Aguja de Corpus Cristi and the R wing of the S Face all offer worthwhile activities. Vega Huerta is, of course, the ideal base for the circular tour of Peña Santa. Moreover, the beauty of the place is justification enough for a visit, were such justification necessary.

The old hut, as has been previously indicated, lies in ruins, and though ICONA has plans to rebuild it to provide accommodation for the park wardens, it seems unlikely that a climbers' hut will be built in the area. Camping, then, is obligatory, though a large cave in the N walls of the Torres de Cotalbín, will be of use as an emergency shelter for those who have had a bivouac interrupted by bad weather.

157 Circular Tour of Peña Santa
Few people seem to undertake this attractive tour, perhaps because of the difficulty presented by the crossing of La Forcadona, an ice axe being useful here until late in the season. The walk is one of sharp contrasts, as the relatively lushness of Vega Huerta is exchanged for the stark and sombre Jou Santu. The walk can be taken in either direction, but it would seem easier to ascend the Forcadona col as is given here. Grade B, 5-7h. Map: GH Editores, 1:50,000.

Start by picking up a small path which contours around the N side of the small, deep hoyo which lies immediately N of the ruins of the old hut. Once the Hoyo has been skirted head down NE over heavily grooved slabs which lead to the grassy slopes of the main part of Vega Huerta. Head E over trackless ground and so reach the Cerra del Frade, the broad grassy col that marks the E end of the main Peña Santa ridge.

The next section crosses to El Boquete and can be achieved by either a) descending N to the Majada de Mesones (500m of descent and 600m of re-ascent) and following the path from Caín, or b) by traversing over broken slabs without losing height (trackless and involving some scrambling). From El Boquete contour round the Jou Santu to the broad col that separates the two depressions making up the jou.

From the col head SW, descending slightly and passing the Fuente de las Balas before climbing up towards the obvious deep gap of La Forcadona. Much of the snow can be avoided by staying to the rocks on the R. At the head of the snowfield scramble off the snow and up to the

174

gap and the reward of views of Soto de Sajambre and Vegabaño. Descend screes to pick up a path (see Route 20) which leads S above a deep, circular depression (La Llerona), and then on to Vega Huerta.

TORRE DE LA CABRA BLANCA   2377m

The higher of the two towers which mark out the southern side of the Jou de las Pozas, and a summit which offers excellent views west along the Cordillera Cantábrica despite its modest height.

Descent: Follow the W Ridge (moves of II–) until a terrace is met descending diagonally across the N Face. Follow this into the Jou de las Pozas.

158   Los Estribos – Torre de la Cabra Blanca

The combination of these two summits provides a very good scramble along some exposed ridges. A rope and a few krabs and slings would be sensible to protect the scrambling which takes place on generally sound rock. FA: unknown. ADsup., 2-3h.

From Vega Huerta reverse Route 20 as far as the Hda de Pozas (1-1¼h). The approach allows the ridge to be studied in detail.

Ascend the first easy but broken section of the E Ridge of Los Estribos to reach a gap which is gained by scrambling R down slabs. From the gap climb slabs (moves up to III) to a superbly exposed ridge which

Torre de la Cabra Blanca
NORTH FACE

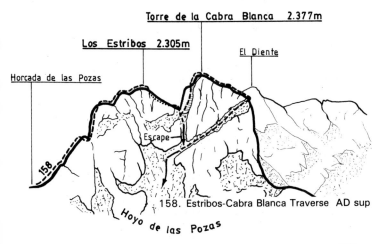

158. Estribos-Cabra Blanca Traverse AD sup

175

leads via an airy traverse to the main summit. Scramble down to the col between Los Estribos and the Cabra Blanca. Descend N a little, then cross W to reach a chimney via which the E Ridge of the Cabra Blanca is gained in good positions. Follow this until a difficult mantleshelf move (IV) ends suddenly on the summit.

AGUJA DE CORPUS CRISTI

This is the largest of the towers that make up the western end of the main ridge of Peña Santa, and as such attracts one's attention when viewed from Vega Huerta. The peak was first climbed in 1952 on the 'Dia del Corpus', a national holiday in Spain.

Descent: Go down the W Ridge to a gap to the S of which is a gully. Abseil or scramble down this (III+), then traverse W to above a second, grassy gully. Abseil or scramble down this, then go L to traverse back round the base of the mountain.

159   Southeast Face Direct
The attraction lies in the summit as much as in the climbing itself, which takes place on rock of uneven quality, though which is never bad for the harder moves. The route provides varied climbing, including a tunnel pitch. FA: L. Rubio and M. A. Rodríguez, 14th Aug, 1978. Dsup., 200m, 2-3h. Diag. p.182

Start at the foot of a huge diedre in the centre of the SE Face. Climb an easy gully (IV then III) to a chimney which leads with difficulty (V−) to a large chockstone. Climb the steep chimney above this (V), then a R-slanting diedre (IV+) which leads to easier ground and a stony platform. Go through a small tunnel to a broken gully which is later abandoned for the jagged ridge on the L. Follow the ridge (IV) to easier ground and the summit.

PEÑA SANTA DE CASTILLA (Torre Santa)   2,596m

Peña Santa de Castilla, or Torre Santa as it was once known, is the highest summit in the Western Massif, dominating the neighbouring peaks completely. It is not a simple mountain, and the intricacies of even its simplest route characterise perfectly a peak where both the climbs and the descents require more than just a minimum of mountaineering skill. Despite this, a visit to the Picos which does not include Peña Santa would be an incomplete affair, and nobody capable of doing so should return home without having reached the summit.

The mountain takes the form of an enormous east-west crest over 2km long from the Cerra del Frade to the Aguja del Corpus Cristi, the full traverse making an exhilarating day for anyone attracted by scrambling over long, exposed ridges. The outing can be seen perfectly from the normal base for activities on the mountain, Vega Huerta, from where the South Face, 600m high in its central section, can also be inspected.

At the moment, the most important rock climbs Peña Santa offers are found on this section, and there is every indication that climbing here still has much to offer. The North Face, smaller and less impressive in summer, offers a limited number of climbs at this time of year. In winter, however, the situation changes radically, and the North Face is the star attraction, its altitude and orientation bringing it into condition even in the leanest of years.

As already indicated, Vega Huerta provides the ideal base for activities on and around Peña Santa, and all the routes given below have been described with this in mind. It is also quite common to tackle routes on the North Face from a base in Vegarredonda, Route 131 being used as an approach to the Jou Santu, the starting point of these routes. It would, of course, be possible to tackle the South Face routes from Vegarredonda as well, but this has nothing at all to recommend it.

The attractions of Peña de Castilla are numerous. Despite this, relatively few people climb here. Perhaps the aproach to Vega Huerta, the lack of a hut, or the long descents from the summit, or several of these factors together explains this apparent lack of interest. It is to be hoped, however, that none of these elements change, as any such modification would only be to the detriment of what for many is the finest mountain in the range.

Descent: The descent from Peña Santa is governed by the base to which the climber is returning (Vega Huerta or Vegarredonda), the weather, and, to some extent, by the ability of the party. The first two descents given below could be considered 'normal', whilst the third, which involves abseiling down the lower section of the South Face Direct Route, is of interest to those climbing on the main section of the south wall.

For all three ascents follow paint marks a short way E from the summit, then scramble L (N) down a short gully. Follow yellow paint marks W across the N Face, cross the main ridge to the S side, and descend slabs in exposed positions above two large gullies. Step down to a ledge going R (NW) to a narrow gap (the Brecha Norte) where the paint marks descend into a gully (Canal Estrecha) on the N Face.

For the Jou Santu and Vegarredonda:

i) Descend the Canal Estrecha (2 abseils normal – care with stones) following the yellow paint marks then small cairns into the Jou Santu (1h) from where Route 132 leads back to Vegarredonda. (In bad weather, or to avoid the airy scrambling of Descent (ii), those based on Vega Huerta can combine the above descent with Route 157, going over La Forcadona to return to Vega Huerta. Long but relatively safe (2½h).)

For Vega Huerta:

ii) Follow Descent (i) to the Brecha Norte then climb out L and follow the main ridge W (narrow and exposed) with 3 or 4 abseils. Shortly after the last abseil cross to the S side and scramble down the R side of a long, broken ramp (cairns), swinging L at the end on a narrow ledge leading towards a small gully. Descend this then cross rocks R to a grassy col on the broad spur which leads SE to Vega Huerta. Avoid the intervening summit by slabs on the L (1½-2h). This reasonably fast descent is much used by local climbers, but is airy and, moreover, badly exposed to inclement weather.

For the more technically proficient the third descent may be of interest:

iii) Follow the common descent until above the two large gullies on the S side of the ridge. Do **NOT** go R towards the Brecha Norte. Instead scramble down into the top of the L-hand gully, looking for an abseil point high up on the R wall. After 1 abseil scramble down easy ground (huge cave off R), and then grooved slabs L of a deep hole. Enter the Nevero Central and descend as far as the R-hand side of the lip of the cirque. Scramble down easy terraces just L of a prominent chimney (locate carefully before descending) to gain the base of the chimney and a small slab with two old pegs. Six abseils, starting here and coinciding with the South Face Direct Route, lead to the foot of the wall.

Although some care is needed to locate the first abseil out of the Nevero Central, this descent should be borne in mind by those tackling Routes 162, 163 and 164, all of which pass through the great central cirque.

NORTH FACE

As has already been indicated above, the North Face of Peña Santa is at its best during the winter months. However, the Canal·Estrecha and the North Buttress route provide two attractive routes, the latter in very Alpine surroundings, with fine views east across the Jou Santu to the Central Massif.

If Vega Huerta is chosen as a base for either of these routes, the approach can be made by following Route 157 in reverse over the Forcadona gap, the descent being made as for the South Face routes. When approaching from Vegarredonda, the descent will be the Normal Route.

160 North Face. Canal Estrecha
The Canal Estrecha is generally considered to be the Normal Route for Peña Santa de Castilla, and is thought to be the route that was used during the first ascent of the mountain. It is a first class mountaineering route, and though the line taken in the second half is devious, it is easy to follow because of the abundant yellow paint marks. The rock is sound, but an early start is recommended because of the loose stones in the gully bed. FA: P. Labrouche, F. Sallés and V. Marcos, 4 Aug, 1892. ADinf, 500m, 1½-2h from the Jou Santu. Diag. p.180.

Follow Route 132 to the broad saddle that separates the two major depressions of the Jou Santu (2h from Vegarredonda – it is useful to spend some time at the Boca del Jou Santu trying to identify the start of the route). Make a rising traverse around the W side of the hillock due S

The entry to the Canal Estrecha (Peña Santa de Castilla)

of the saddle (exposed in places). Follow small cairns S, then SW through tortuous, honeycomb terrain, and next rising over slabs to the base of the climb.

An early section up the gully is stopped by a wall which is avoided by traversing L to gain a hidden niche. A hard move up and R to leave this is the crux (III+ – abseil peg in place), but finishes on an easy ledge which is followed R to regain the gully bed. Climb this with a number of entertaining chimney pitches (II and III) to gain the Brecha Norte, a narrow gap on the main E-W ridge. Traverse horizontally L on the S side of the ridge, then climb easy slabs L in exposed positions above two large, deep gullies to regain the ridge which is crossed onto the N Face. Go L (E) to a short, easy chimney and climb this (II+) until it is possible to continue traversing E across the face, passing below the summit line to reach an easy gully (I+) which finishes on the main ridge.

161 North Buttress

A classic climb in the traditional sense of the word, with some hard climbing and a lot of easy ground which can be climbed anywhere. The route, nevertheless, has a very alpine feel about it, and a certain degree of mountaineering skill is an undoubted asset. FA: J. Delgado and C. Acuña, 9 Aug, 1970. Direct finish by J. M. Ubieta and P. Udaondo, 22 Sept, 1974. Dsup, 500m, 3h. Diag.p.180.

From the saddle separating the two depressions of the Jou Santu, traverse around the hillock as for the last route, but breaking away SE as

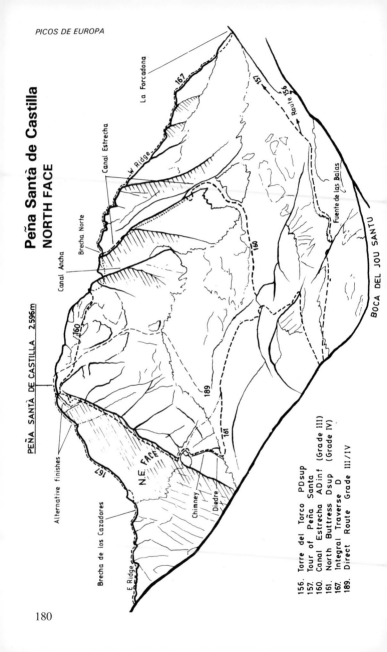

PICOS DE EUROPA

Peña Santà de Castilla
NORTH FACE

PEÑA SANTÀ DE CASTILLA 2.596m

La Forcadona

Canal Estrecha

Brecha Norte

Canal Andha

W Ridge

Route 156

Route 157

Fuente de las Balas

BOCA DEL JOU SANTU

Alternative finishes

Brecha de los Cazadores

E Ridge

N.E. FACE

Chimney

Diedre

156. Torre del Torco PDsup
157. Tour of Peña Santa
160. Canal Estrecha ADinf (Grade III)
161. North Buttress Dsup (Grade IV)
167. Integral Traverse D
189. Direct Route Grade III/IV

180

soon as possible to make a rising traverse L to reach the toe of the buttress and the start of the climb (15-20 mins from the saddle).

Climb an inclined diedre (IV–, V–) then a chimney (IV) before moving R to an obvious ledge. Follow this L over a shoulder to the foot of easy slabs to the L of the crest of the N Buttress. Follow the slabs throughout, always staying to the L of the line of the buttress. Just above half height a ledge rising L offers an easy escape to the main E-W ridge. Soon after a second ledge is reached with a large hole at its R end. From the L end of the ledge climb slabs, first up (IV+) then R to gain a steep fluted wall which is climbed with difficulty (V) to gain a sloping ledge below a diedre. A pitch up this (V–) ends on the summit slopes.

SOUTH FACE

The most important wall in the Picos de Europa after the West Face of El Naranjo de Bulnes, but a lot more complex. The majority of climbs tackle the central section of the face, though in the future interest could well turn to the large buttresses to the right. Early morning and late evening are the best times for viewing the face, as the midday sun tends to flatten its many features. Facing south, the wall is a suntrap, something worth bearing in mind when deciding how much water to take.

162   South Face: Manantial de la Noche
One of the two recent additions to the centre of the South Face, this route tackles the enormous diedre that splits the upper wall. With the variant given below, the rock is very good throughout, being excellent in the great diedre. Few belays are in place, and though nuts can be used on most occasions, two or three pegs would be a wise inclusion. Sustained climbing, but nowhere very hard, though exposed in the upper diedre. Little in-situ protection and belays. A small selection of pegs would be useful. FA: J. L. Rodríguez, E. Alvarez and M. Rodríguez, 8-12 Aug, 1982. TDsup, 600m, 7-9h. Diags, p.182 & p.183.

Start to the L of the South Face Direct, at slabs below and L of large block visible from Vega Huerta. Climb the slabs to a hard move R over a bulge to a scoop stance. Easier slabs lead L and up to a peg belay. Follow a faint crack to a second bulge (PR) and avoid this going L to gain easier ground, then go up R to a good ledge just R of an easy chimney. Climb this to a ledge with blocks, then go over a bulge to cracks which are abandoned L for a slab leading to broken ledges. Traverse easily R to a belay below a huge roof, then climb a vague grey groove leading to the long diedre just L of the roof. From L end of the terraces above the diedre a crack then slabs taken diag R lead to the Nevero Central.

Cross the cirque to an easy ramp which is followed diag. L, then work back R to a stance just L of a round yellow scar. Climb grooved slabs above (poor protection), finishing R to a large stance. Take the wall above, difficult cracks leading to a flake stance (2 bolts), from where a diedre is

182

Peña Santa de Castilla
SOUTH FACE

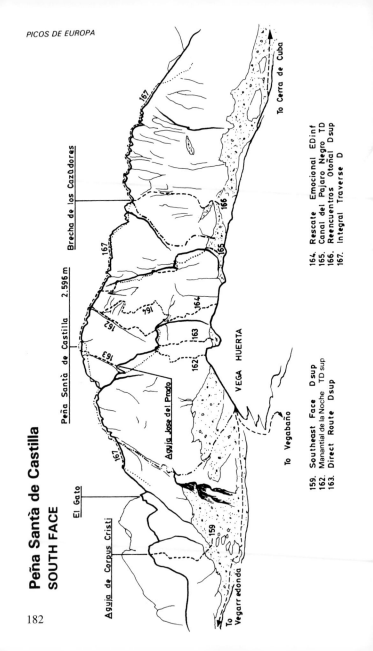

PICOS DE EUROPA

Peña Santa de Castilla   2.596 m

Brecha de los Cazadores

To Cerra de Cuba

El Gato

Aguja Jose del Prado

VEGA HUERTA

To Vegabaño

Aguja de Corpus Cristi

Aguja de Vegarredonda

To Vegarredonda

159. Southeast Face D sup
162. Manantial de la Noche TD sup
163. Direct Route D sup

164. Rescate Emocional ED inf
165. Canal del Pajaro Negro TD
166. Reencuentros Otoñal D sup
167. Integral Traverse D

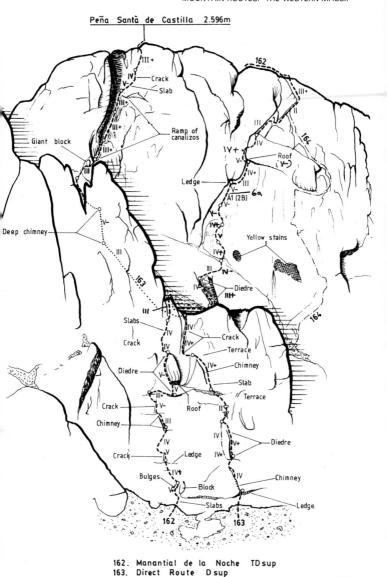

Peña Santà de Castilla 2.596m

III+
IV
V- — Crack
— Slab
III+
III+ — Ramp of canalizos
III+
Giant block
III

162
III+
II
III
IV
IV+ — Roof
V- (V)
IV+
Ledge — III
A1 (2B) 6a
IV+
V+
IV+
III — N
IV — Diedre
III+
Deep chimney
V-
III
163
III
Slabs
Crack
IV — IV
IV
IV — IV
V+ — Crack
— Terrace
Diedre
V- — IV+ — Chimney
V — Slab
— Terrace
III
Crack
V- — Roof — II
Chimney
III
IV — IV
Crack — IV+
V — Ledge — IV+ — Diedre
IV+
Bulges — IV+ — IV — Chimney
— Block
— Slabs — Ledge
162 — 163
Yellow stains
164

162. Manantial de la Noche TD sup
163. Direct Route D sup

183

followed to a roof. Avoid this R to a poor, exposed stance (2 bolts) which is left with difficulty and some aid from the bolts (crux) to gain a platform stance. Pass a hard bulge, then climb directly to a niche and stance which is abandoned going L with difficulty. A steep wall leads to a chimney then exposed but easy slabs which are crossed diag. R to the end of the difficulties. The whole of the upper diedre provides exposed climbing on excellent grey limestone, though good protection is not always easy to find.

163 South Face: Direct Route

The easiest of the big lines on Peña Santa and one of the classic routes of the range. Long and maintained, but only hard in two short sections. Quite exposed in places, but the rock is almost always very good. A must for middle-grade climbers. First ascent: J. G. Folliot, F. Fuentes and A.Rojas, 19 Aug., 1947. D+, 600m, 4½-6h. Diags, p.182 & p.183.

The climb starts on a good ledge (PB) just R of an open chimney and about 30m R of a large V-formation on the wall. The chimney leads to a steep diedre (easier variant to the L), which is climbed to easier ground. A pitch diag. R, then straight up easy slabs, leads to a terrace below a wall. Climb a slab then a chimney to a second terrace, from where cracks and finally a chimney go up to the huge central snowfield. Scramble up this to the foot of a deep chimney, which proves the hardest pitch on the climb if the easier lower variant has been taken. After more scrambling traverse round a large block in airy positions to gain the great ramp, which gives three pitches on superb, grooved rock, though with little protection. From a small terrace with a good stance climb up, then traverse R over a difficult slab before going up to the summit ridge.

164 South Face: Rescate Emocional

The first attempt at climbing the huge, blank wall above the R-hand end of the S Face snowfield, Rescate Emocional is generally considered to be a difficult, serious route. The first half of the climb provides straightforward, though poorly protected, slab climbing, whilst the second involves sustained, technical work following a vague line up the blank wall, before being forced off R by a band of overhangs. A reasonable amount of in-situ gear was left in place during the first ascent, but a selection of pegs should be carried. 'Friends' will prove invaluable for protecting the last difficult pitch of canalizos. When Peña Santa de Castilla finally receives the attention it deserves, Rescate Emocional will become a classic of its grade. FA: M. Rodríguez, J. A. Rodríguez & I. Orviz, Aug, 1981. EDinf, 600m, 8-10h. Diags p.182 & p.183

Start below the L end of a characteristic roof. Go up easy ground, passing the L-hand end of the roof to gain a diedre which is climbed to slabs. Two pitches up these (easy, but poorly protected) end in a diedre just below and R of twin roofs. Pass these on the R with difficulty, work diag. R to easy terraces, and go up these to a niche beneath a roof. Go over this then trend R to gain the central snowfield, which is crossed to a point below the R-hand end of the R of two yellow scars.

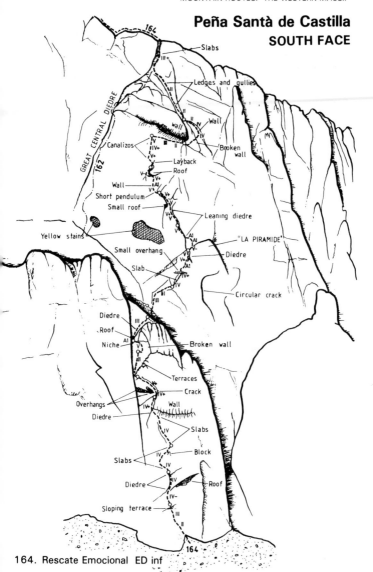

Peña Santà de Castilla
SOUTH FACE

164. Rescate Emocional ED inf

185

Climb easy slabs up and then diag R until a small roof indicates the start of the difficulties. Go over it and climb canalizos then a diedre. A poorly-defined diedre goes off diag L, entry to it proving hard and devious. A second pitch gives sustained climbing, first in the diedre, then past a small roof. A short pendulum gives access to a wall which is followed until forced off L by a roof. From a stance above the roof a layback is made until it is possible to work L to gain a wall of deep canalizos. These end below a band of overhangs, from where an easy traverse R, then two short walls, lead to easy climbing up ledges and small gullies.

165   South Face: Canal del Pájaro Negro
Historically an important route, being the object of much attention during the late 40s and early 50s. For many years this was the hardest route on the face, though the hard climbing is limited to the entry to the Losa (a slab of perfect grey rock) and the upper chimney-crack. The climbing and positions are varied, whilst the rock is good in general, though care is needed when leaving the gully, first to gain the Pilar, and later the upper chimneys. All pegs in place. First ascent: P. Udaondo and A.Landa, 19 Sept. 1958. TD, 600m, 5-7h. Diags., p.182 & p.187

The climb starts up the obvious huge gully to the R of the centre of the face. The difficulty here depends on the amount of snow, but there is usually one chockstone pitch. When the gully steepens move out L over delicate rock to gain a shoulder. From the L end of a ledge climb a bulge ((A1-2/3 moves) and go up the Pilar to gain the Losa. Climb this (good positions) until a short rope manoeuvre allows the gully bed to be reached. Scramble up this for 20m, then climb out L. Poor rock leads steeply up to a deep chimney on the L wall of the gully. The chimney proves strenuous and ends below a steep crack system, above which easier ground leads to a huge sloping ledge. This is crossed L to gain a large, open gully which leads to the main ridge without difficulty. Scramble to the summit.

166   S Face: Reencuentros Otoñal
This is the first of two routes which explore the enormous R-wing of the S Face of Peña Santa. The climb tackles slabs and a wide gully to the L of the obvious, large buttress which comes down from the Brecha de los Cazadores. The climbing is nowhere difficult, but the rock is excellent throughout and the route provides a pleasant outing for an easy day, as well as an alternative start to what in effect is a shortened version of the Integral Traverse. A couple of medium channel pegs and slings for threads allow good belays to be taken. No gear was left during the first ascent. FA: A. Alvarez and M. A. Adrados, 22 Sept, 1983. Dsup, 300m, 2½-3h. Diag. p.182.

Start at a white slab at the foot of the wall directly below the Brecha de los Cazadores. Scramble up diag. L to a large scree from where it is possible to climb easily back R (II) to gain the L end of a terrace at the foot

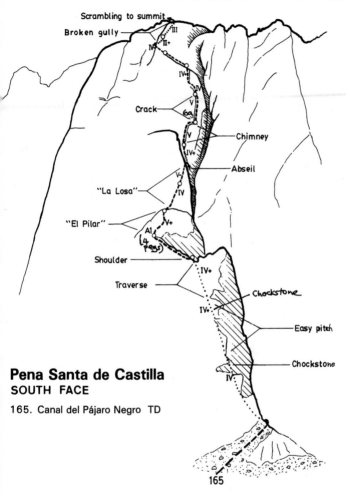

Scrambling to summit
Broken gully
III
III+
IV
IV+
IV
V
6A
V
IV+
V-
V
IV
V+
A1
(4 Pegs)
Shoulder
Traverse
IV+
IV+
IV
Chockstone
Easy pitch
Chockstone
"La Losa"
"El Pilar"
Crack
Chimney
Abseil

Pena Santa de Castilla
SOUTH FACE

165. Canal del Pájaro Negro TD

165

of a slab with canalizos. Tackle the slab in two pitches, the first going up a black streak from the L end of the ledge (V), the second following a crack slightly R (IV+). A wide gully is gained by moving diag. R (IV). Follow this easily for 80m, and when it steepens continue with two more pitches (III+, IV) to reach the summit slopes.

Descent: As has already been suggested, an attractive complement to this route is the section of the Integral Traverse remaining to the summit of the mountain. However, it is possible to descend directly to Vega Huerta by following the ramp which goes down diag R (facing S) from the Brecha de los Cazadores. Scrambling (moves of III) and a couple of abseils.

167   Integral Traverse

The full traverse of Peña Santa de Castilla, starting from Los Basares, is a major ridge route, and one which is far longer than the map distance would suggest. A rope and a selection of nuts, krabs and slings will be necessary, whilst some spare slings for abseil loops would seem wise. The rock is good for such an exposed ridge, and the situations excellent, which makes it all the more surprising that the ridge is done so little. FA: J. Bousoño and G. Suárez, 26/27th July, 1974. D, approx 2km, 8h from the start of the climbing to the summit. Diags, p.180 & p.182.

From Vega Huerta follow Route 157 to the Cerra del Frade, then descend diag. L towards the area known as Los Basares, the ground below the north-east end of the mountain. At the base of the central of three well-defined spurs is a minor col which separates the spur from two small pinnacles. Climb the col and then the spur (moves of IV+) to gain the main ridge, which is now followed west over five small towers (moves of IV). (The first full traverse saw this section done without a single abseil).

Climbing down from the last tower a flat, circular col (the Brecha de las Cazadores) is reached (descent possible to Vega Huerta – see last route). Avoid the towers beyond the col on their R and so gain the next horizontal section of the ridge, this section providing airy scrambling on a narrow crest (IV).

Eventually, the ridge broadens out and climbs up the final slopes to the summit. From here double back a little to continue, then descend a short gully down on to the North Face. Yellow paint-marks lead west across the face, then down a short, awkward chimney (II+) before swinging across the ridge itself to the south side of the mountain. An exposed descent is made down slabs (II+) until perched above the depths of two huge gullies, at which point the route doubles back R and crosses to the second of two notches in the main ridge. This is the Brecha Norte and it offers an emergency exit N down to the Jou Santu (scrambling with two abseils).

To continue, climb left out of the gap and get back on to the ridge where more good scrambling, exposed throughout, leads west with 3 or 4 abseils, to easier ground at a broad shoulder. To the left (S) a broken ramp goes down to Vega Huerta (see standard descents). Ahead (but only for the purist) lie the summits of El Gato and the Aguja de Corpus Cristi, the hardest way of finishing the traverse. A third alternative (the best) is to continue NW down the main ridge to reach La Forcadona, from where Route 157 leads back to Vega Huerta.

6: MULTI-DAY WALKING TOURS

Nothing is more rewarding than to spend a few days walking across or around a major mountain range, and the Picos de Europa, as should be clear by now, offer numerous possibilities for extended trips. In my contacts with visiting parties, however, I have found that most people do not fully exploit this potential. In some cases they are put off by the poor mapping, whilst other teams come to grief through overestimating what can realistically be done in a day over such rugged terrain. As was suggested in the geology notes, Naismith is not as firm a guide in the Picos as in Britain.

With this problem in mind, there follows a handful of extended walks ranging from four to eight days. As must be obvious, this small selection is by no means a definitive guide to this type of activity. Indeed, if the tours given here spur people on to put together their own outings, they will have served their purpose handsomely.

The walks have been put together firstly in order to cover as much as possible of the range, and secondly, on a purely practical note, because they should be perfectly possible for fit people used to such terrain. The first two are the shortest and attempt to cover the most significant parts of the Central and Western massifs, respectively. The third route is a traverse, though one with a long history, as it is the route held to have been used by the defeated Arab soldiers in their flight from Covadonga (see General History notes). The last two tours are also traverses, one crossing the range from west to east, in search of the best it has to offer, whilst the other takes the ascent of the highest point in each massif as its *raison d'étre*.

With certain exceptions, all the stopovers provide accommodation, either in the form of a hut or of a *hostal*. Camping has a lot to recommend it, nevertheless, as all accommodation tends to be full in the summer months. Food, in the form of full meals, is available in all the villages, as well as in the major huts. However, only a handful of villages have food shops, a point to be borne in mind when calculating supplies. Information on the above, and on the stages of each walk, can be found in the relevant section of the guide.

168   Tour of the Central Massif   (4 days)
This is a straightforward walk over well-marked terrain, but one which combines the south-north traverse of the massif with the walking of the Cares Gorge. By dropping down from Liordes to Fuente Dé, the tour can be reduced to 3 days, though the night at Cdo Jermoso is worth the extra time.

Day 1   El Cable – Horcados Rojos – Vega Urriello – Bulnes
       Time: 6-7h   Details: Routes 10 and 12.

A classic day which allows El Naranjo to be seen from a number of good vantage points, the light changing for the photographer's benefit as the walk progresses. The descent to Bulnes is steep, but the exit from the Balcosín gorge highlights the remarkable setting of the village's twin hamlets.

Day 2   Bulnes – Poncebos – Cares Gorge – Cordiñanes
            Time: 5-6h   Details: Routes 12 and 39.

Longer than it looks on paper, especially the final haul up to Cordiñanes from Caín. An early start avoids the heat (and the crowds) in the Cares Gorge. There is no official campsite at Cordiñanes, so those with tents may prefer to spend the night at Puente Capozo, 3km north of the village.

Day 3   Cordiñanes – Asotín – Liordes – Cdo Jermoso
            Time: 5-6h   Details: Routes 6 and 4.

An uphill day, but one which bestows ample rewards on us for our efforts, with a night being spent at Cdo Jermoso. Those with excess energy on arrival at the hut can make a quick ascent of the Torre del Llambrión.

Day 4   Cdo Jermoso – Cdna de las Nieves – El Cable – Fuente Dé
            Time: 4½-5½h   Details: Routes 5 and 1.

The return to Fuente Dé via the Cdna de las Nieves allows an ascent of La Padiorna to be included before plunging down into the confines of the La Jenduda gully. (Going down in the cable car would seem like cheating!).

169   Tour of the Western Massif   (4 days)

A parallel outing to the last one, insomuch as it visits most of the important areas of the massif. The terrain covered is more varied, however, and, with the exception of the Canal de Trea, there are no really hard ascents or descents.

Day 1   Lago Ercine – Vega de Ario – Ascent of Jultayu
            Time: 5h   Details: Routes 21 and 126.

An easy day to start the tour. The afternoon ascent of the Jultayu offers superb views of Caín and the Cares, whilst also allowing a preliminary exploration of the Canal de Trea.

Day 2   Vega de Ario – Canal de Trea – Caín – Soto de Valdeón
            Time: 5-6h   Details: Routes 129 and 39.

It is worth getting up early so as to reach the head of the Canal de Trea with the sun still low in the sky. The descent is steep but satisfying. Just before the bridge at Cordiñanes, a footpath along the true L bank of the Cares gives an alternative to the road.

Day 3   Soto – Cdo del Frade – Vega Huerta – Vegarredonda
            Time: 7-8h   Details: Routes 24 and 20.

A long day which begins with the haul up to Vega Huerta, an excellent spot for a well-deserved lunch break. The traverse to Vegarredonda can be made following Route 20 throughout, or by reversing Route 157 into the Jou Santu, then taking Route 131 down to Vegarredonda. The latter s longer but more complete.

Day 4 Vegarredonda – Ordiales – Vegarredonda – Lago Enol
　　　　Time: 4-5h Details: Routes 53 and 19.

A short day to finish, with the visit to Ordiales being an optional extra. Those without transport at the Vega de Enol may like to reverse Route 49 to Fana, from where Route 44 can be taken down to Covadonga via Orandi.

170 The flight of the Arabs (4 days)

The more one studies this tour, especially the crossing of the Cares Gorge, the more one wonders if it were possible for 8th century soldiers to undertake such a traverse. Eminent historians seem to believe so, however, one having gone so far as to follow the supposed route in 1930 in search of evidence. Fact or fantasy, this is an interesting and original way of crossing the range. Camping obligatory due to the absence of a hut in Vega Maor, and the uncertain condition of those at Amuesa and the Vega de Sotres. There is nowhere along the route where food can be bought.

Day 1 Covadonga – Vega de Comeya – Mda de Arnaedo – Vega Maor
　　　　Time: 5-6h Details: See below.

From Covadonga go up the road to the lakes for 5km then take the old mine track off E and so enter the Vega de Comeya (2-2½h). Reverse Route 49 almost to Belbín, then Route 51 to Vega Maor. A steady uphill walk where each step takes us further away from the crowds of the National Shrine.

Day 2 Vega Maor – Ostón – Culiembro – Canal de la Raiz – Amuesa
　　　　Time: 5-6h Details: Routes 59 and 57.

A hard day involving the loss and subsequent regaining of a lot of height. The second half of the ascent is made over difficult terrain. It would be wise to carry sufficient water from the spring at the small majada in the Canal de la Raíz as the spring at Amuesa is often dry by mid-summer.

Day 3 Amuesa – Bulnes – Pandébano – Vegas de Sotres
　　　　Time: 4½-5h Details: Routes 56, 11 and 17.

Another down and up day, though over far better terrain and with less height change. The head of the Canal de Amuesa provides an attractive view of the route ahead. Cheese and a very small selection of tinned goods can usually be purchased in Bulnes.

Day 4 Vegas de Sotres – Aliva – Portillas del Boquerón – Pembes
　　　　Time: 3-4h Details: see below.

An easy day to finish. From the Vegas de Sotres follow the jeep track to Aliva. Cross the meadows and descend towards Espinama. After some 20 mins a track goes off L (SE). Take this to a fork, the L branch descending to Pembes. Legend has it that the fleeing Arab soldiers got this far only to be buried by a giant landslide, no doubt of Divine origin. A far more attractive way to end this traverse would be to dine in the

191

excellent restaurant of the Hotel del Oso in Cosgaya, where the local *pote* will compensate amply for the privations of the last few days.

171 Tour of the Three Tops (6 days)

This is another tour with a sense of history, imitating as it does the summer of 1892 when Saint-Saud and Labrouche climbed the Pico Cortés before making first ascents of the Torre de Cerredo and Peña Santa de Castilla. Here the Morra de Lechugales is substituted for the Pico Cortés in order to give the outing a more logical start.

As became obvious in Route 170, crossing the Picos in an east-west direction involves a great deal of gain and loss of height. This is especially true in this traverse, which, as an added complication, involves occasional scrambling of up to III+ in difficulty. The descent of Peña Santa involves at least one abseil for most people, for which a length of light rope will be needed. Camping is once again obligatory, and food can only be bought in Sotres and Caín, though in both cases this is limited to very basic items.

Day 1 Argüébanes – Cdo de San Carlos – Pozo de Andara
  Time: 5-6h Details: Routes 28 and 66.
  The first big ascent, the section up the Canal de San Carlos seeming endless, though finding the way to the foot of the canal from the village may well prove the day's hardest task. Camping is possible near the crossroads by Casetón de Andara (spring), or just beyond the Pozo de Andara tarn (natural spring).

Day 2 Pozo Andara – Lechugales – Vegas de Sotres – Pandébano
  Time: 7-8h Details: Routes 66, 17 and 11.
  This is a long day although thankfully a large part of it is in descent. The sacks can be left at the Cdo Valdominguero during the climbing of the Morra de Lechugales, as the descent to the Duje valley will be made down the Canal de Jidiello. Water is not always available at Pandébano so either camp just before this near the Bar los Picos, or carry water up from here.

Day 3 Pandébano – Vega de Urriello – Jou de los Cabrones
  Time: 7-8h Details: Routes 11 and 13.
  Another long day starting easily enough but finishing over some fairly wild terrain. The crossing of the Corona del Raso will allow the West Face of El Naranjo to be seen under favourable lighting conditions.

Day 4 Cabrones – Torre de Cerredo – Dobresengos – Caín
  Time: 6-8h Details: Routes 96, 7 and 38
  The pace begins to tell on this, the third full day. The exact time taken depends heavily on the speed of the ascent of the Torre de Cerredo, though for some people the long descent of the Canal de Dobresengos will prove to be the crux. No water is available after leaving the hut in the morning.

Day 5 Caín – Jou Santu – Peña Santa – Vega Huerta
  Time: 8-9h Details: Routes 132, 160 and 157.
  With over 2,000m of ascent to be made, most of it up the gruelling

Canal de Mesones, this fifth day proves to be a real test of stamina and determination. From the summit of Peña Santa the end is in sight, however, whilst a good part of the previous two days' toil lies beyond us to the east.

Day 6 Vega Huerta – Vegabaño – Oseja de Sajambre
Time: 4-5h Details: see below.

It is all downhill now, and all the hard work lies behind us. After a leisurely start watching the dawn light play on the South Face of Peña Santa, reverse Route 23 to Vegabaño. Follow the jeep track away from the hut and, some 200m after leaving the vega and entering the woods, pick up a good path which goes off R to Soto de Sajambre, avoiding the monotony of the track. Tired travellers will be made very welcome in the Hostal Peña Santa in Soto, Oseja de Sajambre being an hour or so away by road.

172 Traverse of the Three Massifs (8 days)

This is a long tour which tries to visit the places of most interest in each of the three massifs, avoiding at the same time the technical ground of Route 171. With the exception of the Canal de Trea, none of the steep Picos gullies is tackled, whilst the most difficult section is in the crossing of the Tiro Callejo (short section of I+) at the start of the sixth day. Food and supplies are available at the halfway point in Posada de Valdeón.

Day 1 Soto de Sajambre – Vegabaño – Vega Huerta
Time: 4-5h Details: see below.

Go up through Soto de Sajambre as far as the bridge over the stream which runs through the village. A track goes off left just after the bridge, goes up gently through fields into a wood then climbs R more steeply through the woods to come out at a track. Turn L and reach Vegabaño in 500m. Cross the meadow to the hut and then follow Route 23 to Vega Huerta.

Day 2 Vega Huerta – Jou de las Pozas – Vegarredonda – Ordiales
Time: 6-7h Details: Routes 20 and 53.

The Vega Huerta-Vegarredonda traverse covers a variety of terrain which is highly representative of the Picos de Europa. The visit to Ordiales is almost obligatory because of its historical significance. A classic Picos day.

Day 3 Vegarredonda – Vega de Enol – Vega de Ario
Time: 4½-5h Details: Routes 19, 49 and 21.

This is an easier day to give us a chance to draw breath. Once in the Vega de Enol, pick up Route 49 and follow it past the Vega del Bricial to join up with Route 21 at the W side of the Lago de la Ercina. Those with sufficient energy to spare on reaching Ario can climb the Jultayu in the afternoon (see Route 126).

Day 4 Ario – Canal de Trea – Caín – Soto de Valdeón
Time: 5-6h Details: Routes 129 and 39.

This stage coincides with Day 2 of the Tour of the Western Massif (Route 169), a rest day in Valdeón being an option worth considering.

Day 5   Soto – Santa Marina – Caben de Remoña – Liordes – Jermoso
   Time: 5-6h   Details: See below.

From Posada de Valdeón take the road through Santa Marina. At the first major hairpin bend R after the village (approx 1h from Posada) strike E up the hillside using paths high up on the true R bank of the small stream which crosses the road just after the bend. From the Caben de Remoña (Cdo de Valdeón on some maps: 1-1½h from road) go up the Canal de Pedabejo to enter the Vega de Liordes (1h) and cross above the W side of the vega to join Route 4 at the Cdo de la Padiorna (30mins). Cdo Jermoso is reached in a further 1½h.

Day 6   Cdo Jermoso – Hoyo Grande – Hoyo de Cerredo – Urriello
   Time: 7-8h   Details: Routes 7 and 13.

Without doubt this is the hardest day of the tour, not only for the time needed to reach Urriello, but also for the nature of the terrain. The paths followed are vague in places and pass through the remotest parts of the massif. However, the arrival at Vega Urriello in the early evening will reveal the West Face of El Naranjo at its best as we descend from our vantage point at the Corona del Raso.

Day 7   Urriello – Cda Bonita – Las Moñetas – Vegas de Sotres
   Time: 4h   Details: Routes 104 and 65.

A shorter stage after the efforts of the previous day. Until the hut at the Vegas de Sotres comes into use, camping is obligatory, although by extending the day by an hour or so accommodation can be sought in one of the two pensions in Sotres. An earlyish start is recommended for photographers, who will want to follow the sun as it works round first the east and then the south faces of El Naranjo.

Day 8   Vegas de Sotres – Sotres – Tresviso – Urdón
   Time: 5-6h   Details: see below.

From the Vegas de Sotres follow the track N along the Duje valley, then go up the road to Sotres (1¼-1½h). Leave Sotres heading east on a jeep track and so reach the junction at the Jito de Escarandi (1h). Bear L (N) here and follow the jeep track comfortably as it contours around the head of the Valle de Sobra then descends east to the tiny village of Tresviso (1½-2h), famous for its strong blue cheese. A quite remarkable path now descends the most improbable terrain in a seemingly endless series of hairpins, coming out at Urdón in the Hermida Gorge (1½h). This spectacular finish to the final stage was, until the building of the track from Sotres, the only means of contact the villagers had with the outside world.

7: WINTER MOUNTAINEERING

For the modern technician in search of easily reached ribbons of vertical ice, the Picos de Europa have little or nothing to offer. Given their latitude and their proximity to the relatively warm waters of the Bay of Biscay, the range does not enjoy the right conditions for formation of such frozen delights. Nevertheless, a number of mountains do regularly come into condition, either due to their orientation, as is the case with Peña Santa de Castilla, or due to the avalanches which sweep down their gullies after heavy snowfall, as happens with the Central Gully of the Torre del Friero.

What is on offer in the Picos, then, particularly in the months of March and April when the snow has consolidated sufficiently, are a number of first-class mountaineering routes, sometimes over mixed terrain, though generally characterised by short steep sections of hard ice between easier snow-ice slopes of variable consistency. The majority of the climbs follow gullies or chimneys, with a small number tackling buttresses or open faces, the complications of approach and descent add another dimension to the outing.

The best conditions for climbing are usually brought about by anticyclones centred over the peninsula, producing east or north-easterly air streams whose clear blue skies signal warm days and sub-zero nights, minimum temperatures sometimes dropping as low as –20°C. Such high pressure weather is slow to move off and the good conditions invariably last for several days at a time.

With pressure low, winds from the southwest to north bring precipitation, rain or snow depending on the wind's direction. Of these winds, the frontal troughs which charge in off the N Atlantic covering everything with large quantities of fresh snow, provide good conditions for visiting the countless cafés and bars in order to try the wines, cider and other miscellaneous attractions of the region.

The equipment needed for winter mountaineering in the Picos is much the same as that required by the Scottish winter, both in terms of clothing and hardwear. Thus, for the winter ascent of most Normal Routes an alpine axe and a single 9mm rope will prove sufficient, whilst many of the climbs detailed below will require a full complement of winter gear: technical axes, ice-screws, pegs and dead-men. A tent able to withstand the rigours of winter is another useful item as the huts are generally too far away to be of much use as bases. With good weather camping or a bivouac adds to the pleasure of any route. If in addition the approaches coincide with a full moon, the whole experience becomes quite memorable.

Apart from the Normal Routes already mentioned, the long ridges described in the guide provide excellent sport and are obviously less effected by conditions. However, as neither these nor the Normal

Routes are radically altered by the snow cover in terms of route-finding, they will not be detailed further below.

There is but a small band of activists at work each winter in the Picos at the moment, but the number is growing as is the number and quality of the routes, for the area still has a lot to offer, especially for anyone willing to accept the conditions, and looking to tackle mixed climbing on remote faces. Finally, it should be noted that effective mountain rescue is almost non-existent in winter.

PART A – THE CENTRAL MASSIF

EL CABLE/ALIVA

The Normal Routes to Peña Vieja, the Torre de Horcados Rojos, the Tesorero and the Pico de la Padiorna provide straightforward mountaineering days, but special attention in this sector is centred on two routes on Peña Vieja. The cable car opens late in winter, so camping in Aliva or at El Cable would seem obligatory.

173   Peña Vieja, SE Face: Espolón de los Franceses. 800m, Grade IV/V.

The winter ascent of the Espolón de los Franceses has a certain prestige amongst Spanish climbers, and is one of the few Picos climbs that regularly attracts climbers from other regions. Sadly, the climb has been the scene of a number of accidents, some fatal.

The climb follows the summer route throughout, conditions on the long upper ridge often creating more problems than the lower buttress, which seldom retains much snow.

Few parties complete the route in a day. Diag. as for Route 71. Descent by the Normal Route. Straightforward. *Diag, p.95.*

174   Peña Vieja, SE Face: Classic Route. 700m, Grade III/IV.

The climb takes the long gully going off R from the S cirque. The gully presents few difficulties, though care is necessary with avalanches due to the orientation of the route. The last section is common with Route 173 and will normally create most problems.

There is an obvious cirque to the L of the last route in the lower half of the broken face below the Olvidada-Vieja ridge. Gain the cirque and enter the gully going off R. Follow this throughout to join the final ridge of the last route at the first deep gap.

Allow 6-9h. *Diag. p.95.* Descent as for the last route.

LIORDES/JERMOSO SECTOR

With a base in the Vega de Asotín, which is easy of access and is often free from snow by late March, the Liordes/Jermoso sector offers a variety of climbs in a relatively small area, from the short gullies on the

Torre del Hoyo de Liordes

176. Northwest Gullies Grade II

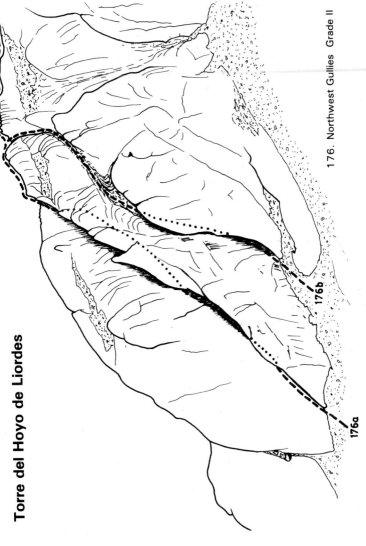

176b

176a

197

Torre del Hoyo de Liordes to the far longer ones of the Torre del Friero.

175 Torre de Salinas: N Gully. 200m, Grade III/IV

The route follows the deep gully/chimney to the R of 'Casiopea' on the Torre de Salinas. The gully narrows in a number of places, presenting moves of certain difficulty, one of which was overcome using a bolt on the first ascent.

Allow 2-3h. *Diag. p.110.* Descent via the Normal Route. Easy.

176 Torre del Hoyo de Liordes, NW Gullies. 200m, Grade II

Two clearly defined gullies split the NW face of the mountain, coming out at gaps either side of the NE summit. The climbs take these gullies, which are similar in grade and style, with any difficulties that may be encountered being limited to the first half.

Allow 2h. *Diag. p.197.* Descent via the Normal Route. Care needed with route-finding.

177 Torre del Friero, N Face: Central Couloir. 1,100m, Grade III

Whilst far from being the most difficult, this is the longest and one of the most attractive winter climbs in the Picos. The route is best tackled late in the season, when the danger from avalanche is at its lowest. On no account should the climb be attempted after fresh, heavy snowfall.

The gully is the L-hand and the narrowest of the two which descend the N face of the mountain to Asotín. A jammed block some 150m from the avalanche cone at the start of the gully provides the first obstacle, the difficulty depending heavily on the build-up and quality of the snow. Above the block, after one or two short steps, the gully opens out (45°) before swinging L and narrowing again. Two or three steeper sections (50/60°) lead to a huge jammed block which is taken on the R or, in lean conditions, by-passed via a tunnel to the L. A final ice-filled chimney ends just below the NE shoulder, from where the small gullies on the R lead to the summit.

Allow 4-7h. *Diag. p.113.* Descent by the Normal Route. Easy.

178 Torre del Friero, N Ridge. 1,200m, Grade IV

This long, complex ridge provides a summer route of alpine proportions, which in winter, the season in which the first ascent was made, turns into a fine line not exempt of difficulty. The summer route is followed throughout, with the major difficulties coinciding with this.

Allow 7-9h. Diag. as for Route 92. Descent as for last route.

Hoyo de Cerredo sector

Being the highest sector of the Picos, one of the main problems the climbs here present is that of access. This should be made from Poncebos via Amuesa (see Route 9 – allow anything from 7-10h), and will usually prove long and arduous, the feeling of remoteness and commitment being essential ingredients in the climbing in this sector. Ample food should be carried in case bad weather makes the path down impassable. The hut in the Jou de los Cabrones is an ideal base.

179 Torre de Cerredo, N Face: Casal-Martínez. 500m, Grade III

The climb tackles the gully to the R of the N buttress of the mountain. Start by climbing the slopes of the Jou Negro (40°) to the base of the gully which comes down from the amphitheatre to the R of the N buttress. The remaining 250m of the climb follow this gully to a small gap on the Cabrones-Cerredo ridge, from where a final rock step (IV) gives access to the summit.

Allow 3h. Descent by Normal Route sometimes awkward.

180 Picos de los Cabrones: N Chimney. 350m, Grade III/IV

The north face of the peak is cut by a deep chimney which goes first diagonally L then back R up the wall. The route follows this chimney with a difficult step at the very beginning, and several others in the chimney itself, which steepens to near vertical in places. The final section can be tackled either by going off R to the NE Arête, or by breaking out onto the NE Arête and so to the top.

Allow 4-6h. *Diag, p.124.* Descent from the Pico de los Cabrones is as problematical in winter as in summer, if not more so. The normal descent is often not in good conditions because of its southerly orientation, and it is often wiser to abseil back down the route.

Anybody operating in the Cerredo sector might also like to tackle the Cabrones-Cerredo ridge (see Route 101) or the gully between the Agujas and the Pico de los Cabrones, finishing up the NE ridge of the latter.

PART B – The Central Massif

Vegarredonda sector

Without a doubt this is the most important sector of the Picos de Europa for the practice of winter mountaineering. Over half of the winter climbs in the range are concentrated here, and most of these are found either on the Torre de Santa María or on Peña Santa de Castilla.

For anything but a very short stay, the best base is camping in the Jou de los Asturianos, thus avoiding the demoralising trudge back and forth from the Vegarredonda hut. The jou is approached from the Vega de Enol along Routes 19 and 131, for which anything between 5-9h should be allowed, depending on conditions. All but the two Torrezuela routes can be reached with ease from this base, the former being tackled equally well from Vegarredonda (approach along Route 20) or, for those already established in the Jou de los Asturianos, via the Hda de Santa María (see Route 131).

181 Torre de Santa María, N Face: Cemba Vieya Couloir. 300m, Grade II

This couloir is in fact the obvious ramp that rises diagonally L across the North Face of the Torre de Santa María. The difficulties lie in the entry to the ramp, which itself is easy. A classic winter route.

Go up the snowfield until it is possible to traverse L to gain the foot of a narrow gully. Climb this to reach the main ramp which is abandoned just before the top for a smaller ramp going off R to the summit.

Allow 1-3h. *Diag, as for Route 148, p.167.* Descent via the same route or by abseiling down the SW Ridge to the Hda de Santa María (see summer notes).

In a good winter a narrow but important curtain of ice falls from the middle of the Cemba Vieya ramp to the base of the N face, providing almost 100m of near vertical climbing. Normally done in three pitches, this direct variation on the last route is one of the most interesting ice-climbs in the range. Grade IV. Allow 3h.

182 Torre de Santa María, N Face: Pili-Cristina. 250m, Grade III/IV

A deep, left-slanting chimney characterises the L side of the N Face. The climb takes this chimney to the slabs of the N spur, which are followed to the summit.

Start slightly L of the natural base of the chimney, where a narrow curtain of steep ice (one short vertical section) gives access to the chimney proper some 40m from the ground. This first pitch is the crux and, depending on conditions, may involve rock-climbing. The chimney is climbed in 4 pitches, the second of which climbs a steep, icy bulge (75°). The N spur is followed easily to a shoulder connecting the S Face Grieta Rubia to the last route.

Allow 3-4h. *Diag, see Route 149, p.169.* Descent as for last route.

183 Torre de Santa María, N Spur. 400m, Grade II

A straightforward route with few if any difficulties, but one which is often in condition.

Start above the Jou de los Asturianos, at the base of the gully descending from a ridge between the Torre de Sta María and the Aguja de Enol. 4 pitches of increasing steepness (max. 60°) lead to a gap on the ridge, from where the broad N spur is followed easily to the shoulder of the last route.

Allow 3-4h. *Diag. p.201.* Descent as for Route 181.

184 Torre de Santa María, E Face: R Gully. 350m, Grade IV

Two parallel gullies run the height of the centre of the E Face of the mountain, both of them coming out on the N spur. This climb tackles the R-hand gully, normally being at its best early in the season. The main difficulties are concentrated in the first pitch.

Start above the Jou de los Asturianos where a 40m wall of ice gives access to the gully proper. The wall is continually steep (75-90°), and the

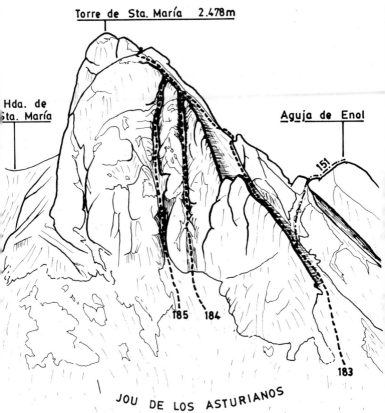

Torre de Sta. María 2.478m

Hda. de Sta. María

Aguja de Enol

151

185 184

183

JOU DE LOS ASTURIANOS

Torre de Santa María
EAST FACE

183. North Spur Grade II
184. Right Gully Grade IV
185. left Gully Grade III
151. Normal Route AD inf

ice is often mediocre, both in quantity and quality. In lean years, or late in the season, this pitch may not form at all.

Two easy pitches (50°) lead to a narrowing in the gully, the next two pitches to the N spur having occasional short steps (75°).

Allow 3-5h. *Diag, above and p.166.* Descent as for Route 181.

185 Torre de Santa María, E Face: L Gully. 350m, Grade III
The second gully provides an easier route, but one which is in condition

Approaching the N face of Peña Santa, the Jou Snatu and the S and E faces of the Torre de Santa María in the background.

longer than last climb.

Start up a narrow gully (50°) which leads to ice-covered bulges. Climb past these with difficulty (2 short vertical steps) to gain the upper half of the gully, which proves to be similar to the second half of the last route.

Allow 3-4h. *Diag. p.201 and p.166.* Descent as for Route 181.

186 La Torrezuela: NW chimney. 250m, Grade III/IV

The west end of this isolated, but attractive mountain is cut by two chimneys, the R-hand (most westerly) of which is only partially visible from the first sighting of the mountain from La Mazada. This climb, the more difficult of the two, takes the L-hand chimney.

Climb the chimney in 4 pitches, the second of which is the most difficult, with several steep sections. The chimney comes out on to an attractive ridge which leads E to the summit, although not without occasional problems.

Allow 3-5h. *Diag, p.173.* Descent E to the Hda del Alba as for the Normal Route, or, from the top of the chimney, by abseiling down Route 186.

187 La Torrezuela: W Couloir. 250m, Grade II

The R-hand chimney, easier but more often in good conditions than the last route. A classic winter climb.

Start a short distance to the R of the last route. The main difficulties lie in the entry to the couloir, where a short step usually creates problems. After this the couloir is followed to a junction with the last route.

Allow 2-4h. *Diag, p.173.* Descent as for the last route, the traverse of the mountain to the Hda del Alba making a superb day.

188 Peña Santa de Castilla, N Face: Narrow Gully. 500m, Grade III

This is one of the most popular winter routes in the Picos, and rightly so. The climb is typical of the range, insomuch as the difficulties are in no way limited to the gully itself. Getting from the Brecha Norte to the summit is not exempt of problems, whilst the descent also requires more than a minimum of mountaineering skill and experience. As in summer, Peña Santa shows itself to be very much a mountaineer's summit.

Approach and start as for Route 160, the start of which is converted into a 15m ice-fall. Take this direct (IV), or avoid it to the L (III), and enter the main gully. This is followed (40-50°) to a second step (60-70°) some 70m below the Brecha Norte. From here follow the summer route as it wanders across first the south, then the north face to the summit.

Allow 4-6h. Diag. as for Route 160. Descend by the same route. The section down to and across the S Face can be largely avoided by abseiling directly to the gap to the E of the Brecha Norte. From here descend to the upper step. A small rock usually protrudes from the ice, providing a dubious abseil point. The gully is then descended to the entry, which is abseiled using pegs in place on the L wall. 2h.

A wider, parallel gully (the Canal Ancha) lies to the L of the last route, providing a shorter climb, but one which depends heavily on a good build-up of ice at the crux section, a difficult step to enter the gully proper.

189   Peña Santa de Castilla, N Face: Direct Route. 300m, Grade III
One of the best winter climbs in the range, providing continually interesting climbing up the centre of the attractive N face of the mountain.

Start at the highest point of the huge snowfield between the last route and the N Buttress. A steep entry (70-80°) leads to an easier section, after which a second ice-wall (70° – sometimes banked over) ends on easier slopes which lead to a rock belay at a point where an easy ramp goes off R.

Ignore the ramp and climb an awkward corner to the L (70-80°). A pitch up an open corner (75° to finish) signals the end of the difficulties, the top being reached after two more pitches (45-55°), the second finishing up a small gully below and R of the summit.

Allow 3-4h. *Diag, p.180.* Descent as for the last route.

190   Peña Santa de Castilla: N Buttress. 500m, Grade IV
The line taken is that of the summer route (Route 161), the hardest moves coming at the beginning unless the direct summer exit is taken. Either one of the two alternative finishes would be more in keeping with the nature of the route in winter, however. The atmosphere on the climb is superb, with superb views across the Jou Santu and the West Ridge to the Central Massif.

Allow 3-6h. Diag. as for Route 161. Descent as for Route 188.

The NE Face of Peña Santa de Castilla, and the numerous chimneys and gullies which descend from the section of the West Ridge to the east of Brecha de los Cazadores, offer a number of possibilities for new routes. Also of great interest in winter is the Integral Traverse of the mountain, for a bivouac will probably be needed, possibly at the Brecha de los Cazadores, the only really flat point along the whole ridge with the exception of the summit. The continuation of the Peña Santa ridge around the Jou Santu to the Torre de Santa María and on to Los Traviesos would provide a major winter ridge, with 2 or 3 bivouacs.

APPENDIX A: GLOSSARY

MAP NAMES AND TERMS

Names in the Picos, as everywhere, invariably tell us a great deal about the place concerned if we can interpret them correctly. The following names and terms are common, and in some cases exclusive, to the Picos de Europa.

Aguja	pinnacle, aiguille.
Boca	see 'collado'.
Cabezo/a	a rounded summit between 1500m and 2000m in height, and often suitable for grazing.
Camino	a footpath, often fit for use by mules, etc.
Canal	a gully, though behind this innocent word can lie some difficult terrain as in the 'canales' descending to the Cares gorge.
Collado(a)	a col or pass, generally easy to cross with a good path (also 'colláu' and 'pan').
Cueto(u)	a well-defined summit of no great height, with easy access on at least one side.
Cueva	cave.
Cuevona	large cave.
Fuente	a spring or drinking trough.
Horcado(a)	a col, but with access difficult on at least one side where scrambling may be involved (see also 'jorcáu').
Hoyo/Jou	a circular depression produced by karstification and giving the Picos landscape a lunar feel.
Invernales	huts and pens used as low-lying winter shelter.
Majada	small, high mountain pastures, invariably containing a number of simple cabins.
Mirador	a lookout or viewing platform.
Neverón	a summit covered by snow for most of the year, and whose slopes are prone to avalanche.
Peña	a term peculiar to the picos, implying a sizeable, often elongated, mass of rock in the high mountains.
Pico(u)	an isolated, tower-like summit. The original (and correct) name for El Naranjo is the 'Picu Urriellu'.
Playa	steeply sloping, band of grassy terrain with outcrops of rock interspersed.
Porro(u)	a small, isolated tower-like summit on the lower slopes of the mountain, the Porru Bolu above Vegarredonda being an exception in this sense.
Puerto	a pass between two valleys, often transitable by car.
Senda	a footpath, though often smaller or more precarious than a 'camino'.

Hoyo de los Boches (Central Massif - El Naranjo just visible)

Sedo	the high mountain paths often cross ridges or traverse round gully bed. The short, obligatory moves of scrambling made whilst effecting such crossing are known as 'sedos' (also 'seu').
Tiro(u)	the term originally referred to a place favoured by hunters waiting for game, usually a col or breche. Nowadays the word is used to refer to the nearest summit to the col.
Vega	a large area of upland pasture, often circular and crossed by a stream.

CLIMBING TERMS

The following, brief glossary should make it possible to follow the route diagrams often available in the huts for routes not included in this guide.

General Mountain Features

arista – arête
canalizo – water-worn groove
cara – face
cima – summit
cornisa – ledge, gangway
desplome – bulge
extraplomo – overhang
fisura – crack on face
grieta – crack in horizontal terrain
hombro – shoulder
horquilla – narrow col
laja – flake
lastra – detached flake
llambria – smooth, friction slab
mancha – mark, stain
muro – wall
ojal – huge thread
placa – featureless area of rock,
    possibly steep
repisa – ledge
techo – roof
vira – shelf, ledge

Climbing Hardwear

buril – bolt
chapa – bolt hanger
clavo – peg
cuerda – rope
driza – tape
empotrador – nut
estribo – étrier
fisurero – nut
gatos – rock boots
gancho – skyhook
maza – hammer
mosquetón – krab
piolet – ice-axe
uña – skyhook

Features On Climbs

agarre – hold
bavaresa – layback
desnivel – vertical height difference
largo – pitch
longitud – length
paso – move
puente – thread
reunión – belay, stance
rapel – abseil
recorrido – actual distance climbed
seguro – runner
tramo – section of a climb
tirada – pitch

APPENDIX B: PICOS DE EUROPA: EXPLOITATION OR CONSERVATION?

Tourism in the Picos de Europa, as has been suggested earlier, has been developing slowly in the hands of private developers since the beginning of this century, and, with such limited growth, the only serious incursion on the sanctity of the range was that of the télèpherique at Fuente Dé. In 1985 this situation changed radically.

With their newly-won autonomous powers, the regional governments with jurisdiction over the Picos began to look to them with a view to large-scale tourism. The Asturian government was most active in this initial period, with plans to equip their part of the range with new 150- or 80-bed huts, a network of graded footpaths, and a triple télèpherique based on the Bulnes. A year later the Cantabrian government entered the arena by re-opening the hut in the Puertos de Aliva, raised now to hotel status. They also seriously considered extending the télèpherique from El Cable to Horcados Rojos, whilst entrepreneurs from León vied with the idea of a ski-station in Vega Liordes and a cable car to Collado Jermoso from Cordiñanes.

Amidst such gloomy news, the suggestion by Cantabria that the Central and Eastern massifs be granted the protection of *Parque Natural* status, brought a glimmer of hope, but this was quickly extinguished early in 1988 when the Asturian government revived its original scheme for Bulnes and the three regional powers returned to the race for the biggest share of the tourist potential of the range.

In the light of such threats to the integrity of this unique range, mountaineers and ecologists from the regions involved have been campaigning since early in 1986 in defence of the mountains, and in favour of the rational development of certain types of tourism. The first of these groups to take a stance was the *Colectivo Montañero por la Defensa de los Picos de Europa (CMDPE),* which in June 1986 handed the Asturian government a petition backed by over 21,000 signatures, including several hundred from Great Britain. The petition and pressures from other areas were never acknowledged, but the new hut in Vegarredonda saw its capacity halved, the graded path to Vega Urriellu was finished in better style than it had been started, and the Bulnes télèpherique was temporarily shelved, the fierce opposition of the villagers playing a fundamental part here.

Also in 1986, Central Government in Madrid completed a very full study of tourist development in the Picos, the report rejecting any form of tourism which might damage the high mountains, and showing in detail how and why future tourist development had to be confined to the surrounding valleys. Later, in spring of 1988, a visit on behalf of *Mountain Wilderness* by Kurt Diemberger, brought home once again the need for protection for these areas, whilst working to improve the standard of living of the local people. An indefatigable campaigner. Diemberger visited the region on several occasions over the next three years, and accepted the Honorary Presidency of the *Colectivo,* whose members were themselves active in 1989, first in Biella in Italy, where they put the Picos problem to *Mountain Wilderness,* and then in Barcelona, where they briefed the *Mountain Protection Commission* of the *UIAA.*

The situation became a lot more positive in the summer of 1990 when the Asturian Regional Government totally abandoned the idea of téléferiques in their sector of the range. Not everything was roses, of course, and Cantabria went ahead in July 1990 with the amplification of the Fuente Dé cable car from 2,000 to 6,000 people a day. The battle, however, was basically moving away from ideas of exploitation at this point, and towards concepts of conservation, with the various figures of **National, Natural** and **Regional Park** being considered. Naturally, conservationists and mountaineers defended the former as the only way of guaranteeing a homogeneous, coordinated treatment of the Picos, which would, at the same time, provide adequate levels of protection and funding. The regional authorities, on the other hand, preferred the idea of a Natural Park, a figure which allows them to maintain a far fuller control of the Picos mountains.

In the spring of 1991 a campaign under the slogan "Picos de Europa: National Park NOW!" was launched by conservationists through a series of abseil descent down city-centre buildings in Santander and Oviedo. The first of these was timed to coincide with the presence in Oviedo of Reinhold Messner, who offered a firm defence of the idea of a future Picos de Europa National Park during his visit. The campaigners efforts were rewarded in September 1991, when the then newly-elected Asturian president announced his intention to push forward the legislation needed to turn the whole of the range into a single National Park. Given the Asturian government's previously stern opposition to this idea, conservation groups were as surprised by the announcement as they were suspicious of it. Nevertheless, the steps towards the declaration of the Picos as a National Park are slowly being completed.

Of course, the road towards the Picos de Europa National Park is still a difficult one, for although the European Community has been placing greater emphasis on the protection of the continent's wild places, many of them are in the poorer European nations or regions. It is to be hoped, then, that when the moment arrives Europe will be coherent with its own philosophies and help to protect them, since in the case of the Picos de Europa at least, the overriding fear of those locals affected by the park project is for their livelihood. The September '91 proposal, for example, came precisely at a time when EEC dairy policies are decimating herds in Spain. Once again, we discover that so much of effective long-terms conservation is a question of economics, and to an uncomfortable extent is in the hands of our representatives in our regional and national parliaments, in the Mountain Intergroup of Euro MPs and, of course, in the European Commission. *Oviedo, October 1992*

LIST OF ROUTES

APPROACHES TO MOUNTAIN BASES

Macizo Central

Macizo Occidental

VALLEY BASED ACTIVITIES

Liebana Valley

MOUNTAIN ACTIVITIES

Central Massif

Aliva/El Cable Sector

068 El Jiso: S Ridge (TDinf)
069 Pico Valdecoro: S Face (TDinf)
070 Peña Vieja: Normal Route (Grade B)
071 Peña Vieja, SE Face: Espolón de los Franceses (TDinf)
072 Peña Olvidada, Aguja de Ostaicoechea: S Face (D)
073 Peña Olvidada, SW Face: Las Placas (ED inf)
074 Aguja de la Canalona: Normal Route (ADsup)
075 Aguja de la Canalona, SW Face; Capricho (TDinf)
076 Aguja de Bustamante, E Face: East Ridge (D)
077 Aguja de Bustamante, E Face: El Diedro (Dsup)
078 Picos de Santa Ana: Normal Route (Grade A)
079 Picos de Santa Ana, West Face: Espolón Rojizo (ADsup)
080 Torre de Horc Rojos: Normal Route (Grade A)
081 Torre de Horc Rojos, S Face: Direct Route (Dsup)
082 Pico Tesorero: Normal Route (PD)
083 Torre del Llambrión: Normal Route (PD)
084 Madejuno-Llambrión Traverse (ADsup)
085 Pico de la Padiorna: Normal Route (Grade A)

Liordes/Jermoso Sector

086 Peña Remoña: Normal Route (Grade B)
087 Pena la Regaliz, NW Face: Divertimento (Dsup)
088 Torre de Salinas: Normal Route (PDinf)
089 Torre de Salinas, N Face: Casiopea (TDinf)
090 Torre del Hoyo de Liordes: NE ridge and traverse to summit (AD)
091 Torre del Friero: Normal Route (Grade B)
092 Torre del Friero: North Ridge (Dsup)
093 Torre de Peñalba, S Face: Gran Diedro (D sup)
094 Peñalba-Palanca Traverse (ADinf)

Jou Cerredo/Cabrones Sector

095 Torre del Coello: SW Face (TDinf)
096 Torre de Cerredo, SE Face: Normal Route (PDinf)
097 Torre de Cerredo, E Ridge (PDsup)
098 Torre de Cerredo: North Buttress (TDinf)
099 Pico de los Cabrones: SE Face (Dinf)
100 Pico de los Cabrones: NW Ridge (ADinf)
101 Cabrones-Cerredo Traverse (Dinf)
102 Agujas de los Cabrones: South Face (Normal Route) (PDsup)
103 Pico del Albo: W Gully (Normal Route) (PDinf)

Vega Urriellu Sector

WESTERN MASSIF

Ario Sector

Vegarredonda Sector

Vega Huerta Sector

MULTI-DAY TOURS

WINTER CLIMBS

Central Massif

180   Pico de los Cabrones: N Chimney (Grade III)

Western Massif
181   Torre de Santa María, N Face: Cemba Vieya (Grade II)
182   Torre de Santa María, N Face: Pili-Cristina (Grade III/IV)
183   Torre de Santa María: N Spur (Grade II)
184   Torre de Santa María, E Face: R Gully (Grade IV)
185   Torre de Santa María, E Face: L Gully (Grade III)
186   Torrezuela: NW Chimney (Grade III/IV)
187   Torrezuela: W Couloir (Grade III)
188   Peña Santa de Castilla, N Face: Narrow Gully (Grade III)
189   Peña Santa de Castilla, N Face: Direct Route (Grade III/IV)
190   Peña Santa de Castilla, N Buttress (Grade IV)

CICERONE INTERNATIONAL GUIDES

INTERNATIONAL CHALLENGES, COLLECTIONS AND ACTIVITIES

Canyoning
Canyoning in the Alps
Europe's High Points
The Via Francigena: 1&2

EUROPEAN CYCLING

Cycle Touring in France
Cycle Touring in Ireland
Cycle Touring in Spain
Cycle Touring in Switzerland
Cycling in the French Alps
Cycling the Canal du Midi
Cycling the River Loire
The Danube Cycleway Vol 1
The Grand Traverse of the Massif Central
The Moselle Cycle Route
The Rhine Cycle Route
The Way of St James

AFRICA

Climbing in the Moroccan Anti-Atlas
Kilimanjaro
Mountaineering in the Moroccan High Atlas
The High Atlas
Trekking in the Atlas Mountains
Walking in the Drakensberg

ALPS – CROSS-BORDER ROUTES

100 Hut Walks in the Alps
Across the Eastern Alps: E5
Alpine Points of View
Alpine Ski Mountaineering
1 Western Alps
2 Central and Eastern Alps
Chamonix to Zermatt
Snowshoeing
Tour of Mont Blanc
Tour of the Matterhorn
Trekking in the Alps

Trekking in the Silvretta and Rätikon Alps
Walking in the Alps
Walks and Treks in the Maritime Alps

PYRENEES AND FRANCE/ SPAIN CROSS-BORDER ROUTES

The GR10 Trail
The GR11 Trail – La Senda
The Mountains of Andorra
The Pyrenean Haute Route
The Pyrenees
The Way of St James: France & Spain
Walks and Climbs in the Pyrenees

AUSTRIA

The Adlerweg
Trekking in Austria's Hohe Tauern
Trekking in the Stubai Alps
Trekking in the Zillertal Alps
Walking in Austria

BELGIUM AND LUXEMBOURG

Walking in the Ardennes

EASTERN EUROPE

The High Tatras
The Mountains of Romania
Walking in Bulgaria's National Parks
Walking in Hungary

FRANCE

Chamonix Mountain Adventures
Ecrins National Park
Mont Blanc Walks
Mountain Adventures in the Maurienne
The Cathar Way
The GR20 Corsica
The GR5 Trail

The Robert Louis Stevenson Trail
Tour of the Oisans: The GR54
Tour of the Queyras
Tour of the Vanoise
Trekking in the Vosges and Jura
Vanoise Ski Touring
Via Ferratas of the French Alps
Walking in Corsica
Walking in Provence – East
Walking in Provence – West
Walking in the Auvergne
Walking in the Cevennes
Walking in the Dordogne
Walking in the Haute Savoie –North & South
Walking in the Languedoc
Walking in the Tarentaise and Beaufortain Alps
Walks in the Cathar Region

GERMANY

Germany's Romantic Road
Hiking and Biking in the Black Forest
Walking in the Bavarian Alps

HIMALAYA

Annapurna
Bhutan
Everest
Garhwal and Kumaon
Langtang with Gosainkund and Helambu
Manaslu
The Mount Kailash Trek
Trekking in Ladakh
Trekking in the Himalaya

ICELAND & GREENLAND

Trekking in Greenland
Walking and Trekking in Iceland

For a full listing of Cicerone's
British climbing, cycling,
walking and backpacking
guides, and more information
on all our guides, books and
eBooks, visit our website:
www.cicerone.co.uk.

PICOS DE EUROPA Eastern Massif

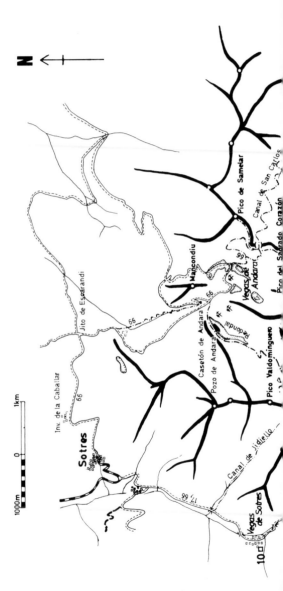

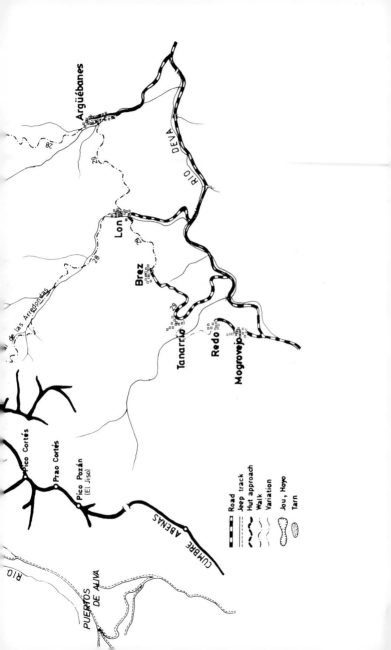

Argüébanes

RIO DEVA

28

29

Lon

28

29

de las Arredondas

Brez

Tanarrio

Redo

Mogrovejo

Pico Cortés

Prao Cortés

Pico Pozán
(El Jiso)

CUMBRE ABENAS

PUERTOS
DE ALIVA

RIO

Road
Jeep track
Hut approach
Walk
Variation
Jou, Hoyo
Tarn

Walking – Trekking – Mountaineering – Climbing – Cycling

Over 40 years, Cicerone have built up an outstanding collection of over 300 guides, inspiring all sorts of amazing adventures.

Every guide comes from extensive exploration and research by our expert authors, all with a passion for their subjects. They are frequently praised, endorsed and used by clubs, instructors and outdoor organisations.

All our titles can now be bought as **e-books**, **ePubs** and **Kindle** files and we also have an online magazine – **Cicerone Extra** – with features to help cyclists, climbers, walkers and trekkers choose their next adventure, at home or abroad.

Our website shows any **new information** we've had in since a book was published. Please do let us know if you find anything has changed, so that we can publish the latest details. On our **website** you'll also find great ideas and lots of detailed information about what's inside every guide and you can buy **individual routes** from many of them online.

It's easy to keep in touch with what's going on at Cicerone by getting our monthly **free e-newsletter**, which is full of offers, competitions, up-to-date information and topical articles. You can subscribe on our home page and also follow us on **Facebook** and **Twitter** or dip into our **blog**.

Cicerone – the very best guides for exploring the world.

CICERONE

2 Police Square Milnthorpe Cumbria LA7 7PY
Tel: 015395 62069 info@cicerone.co.uk
www.cicerone.co.uk and **www.cicerone-extra.com**